New Masses was at the vortex of the cultural upheaval of the 1930s. Most of the leading writers and artists of that decade found a ready forum in the weekly magazine. Joseph North, one of its founders and editors, has selected from its pages the short stories, poetry, reportage, essays, criticism and columns which express the revolutionary spirit and literary quality of that dynamic periodical. In a Prologue, the editor tells of the inside history of the weekly *New Masses* and of its meaning for then and now. He has also made a liberal selection from the cartoons and drawings which helped make the weekly famous. An introductory essay on the place of that cultural revival in American literature by the American critic Maxwell Geismar is also included in this exciting anthology.

INTERNATIONAL PUBLISHERS
381 Park Avenue South NEW YORK, N.Y. 10016

New Masses
An Anthology of the Rebel Thirties

Robert Minor—Artist and Crusader

No Men Are Strangers

Cuba—Hope of a Hemisphere

New Masses

An Anthology of the Rebel Thirties

Edited and with a Prologue
by Joseph North

Introduction
by Maxwell Geismar

International Publishers New York

First published by International Publishers, New York, 1969.
This edition is published simultaneously by
International Publishers, New York and
Seven Seas Publishers, Berlin, 1972
ISBN 0-7178-0355-4

To Augusta
and to Nora and her Generation

INTRODUCTION
Maxwell Geismar

I welcome this anthology for several reasons, but mainly because it is part of something which I have begun to think of
as our "buried history" in the Cold War period. Recently a
group of American historians have been digging into, one
might say "excavating," the true facts of this Cold War Culture–the curious period from the mid-forties to the mid-
sixties–and the results are very interesting. We have had almost a quarter of a century of conformity, comfort, com-
placency and mediocrity in American literature–this epoch
of "instant masterpieces"–and only now can we begin to put
the pieces together and find a consistent pattern.

True enough, as early as 1958, in my *American Moderns,*
I sensed there was something very wrong in contemporary
history and literature. "It was not a fresh period," I wrote
then about what I now consider to be the Fatal Fifties, "but
then, how could it be? The social atmosphere was so heavy,
dense, oppressive. The aesthetic air was so thin, pure and abstract. There was indeed a state of general inertia in the
arts. . . ." But I thought then that this was mainly due to a
kind of *self-induced* immobility on the part of our artists and
intellectuals; a self-repression, a type of do-it-yourself censorship. As a historian of American literature I wondered
why all the major figures whom I admired – from Howells
and Mark Twain to Dreiser, Sherwood Anderson, Ellen
Glasgow and Thomas Wolfe–were in such eclipse. I wondered why Melville, a great American radical and social re-
former, was being made into such a conservative. I wondered
why Faulkner, a social analyst of the southern racial sickness,
was being made into a religious fanatic. I wondered why
Scott Fitzgerald, an attractive novelist of manners at best,
was being revived so heavily, while the American Twenties
were being glorified all over again. I wondered why Henry

James, a master of literary entertainment on the baroque side, was considered as America's greatest writer. I still wonder.

As a literary critic emerging from the 1930s (though one who came to respect the earlier periods of our literature, and who came to see the modern American literary revival as one movement from the 1890s to the 1940s) I wondered particularly why I had so misunderstood the epoch of my own youth. I had always thought of the Thirties as a brilliant, lively, exciting and hopeful period; in my later thinking I saw it as the last true outburst of our social and literary creativity before the somnolence of the 1940s, the silence of the 1950s. But I was wrong, it seemed. I had been deceived. The Thirties had been a period of deceit and disenchantment, of failure and frustration, of political conspiracy and agit-prop. The period itself was barely to be spoken of, and then only in terms of suspicion and disdain. It was a bad time, a hard time, a nasty time; and everything connected with it was to be avoided. It was then I suddenly realized why Sherwood Anderson, Dreiser, Tom Wolfe, who had all been radical figures of the period, were being read out of American literature; and why perhaps John Dos Passos and John Steinbeck had completely reversed their early literary direction in favor of—what?

I remembered the particular excitement which had surrounded the early plays of Clifford Odets. I remembered the nostalgic charm of the first union-made musical comedy, Harold Rome's *Pins and Needles*. I remembered the *New Masses*. . . . But it was the *New Masses* in particular which was at the center of all this revisionist history of the 1940s and '50s. It was the *New Masses* which was the object of abuse, attack, invective, and of ponderous accusations. If the Thirties were to be blocked out completely from the national consciousness—as dangerous a thing for a nation as for an individual—then the *New Masses* was at the center of what appeared to be a cultural and literary trauma; and what we have recently discovered to be a cultural and literary "fix." But first, let us look at the record, and check the anthology itself.

For there is no question the *New Masses* was *the* magazine of the period. Just take a look at the contributors. Among the poets, Kenneth Fearing, Maxwell Bodenheim, Kenneth Patchen, Muriel Rukeyser, Edwin Rolfe (paying ironic homage to T. S. Eliot), James Agee, Ruth Lechlitner, Gene-vieve Taggard, and Federico Garcia Lorca translated by Langston Hughes. Here is also the first published work of a "young Negro poet" named Richard Wright. It was a nice editorial intuition that used the section of poetry to open this anthology. For these beautiful selections repudiate once and for all the charges of inferior writing in the *New Masses*, of topical writing, of mere reportage, of political propaganda, and the rest. This opening section of verse is varied in con-tent and technique alike, it is all crafted to a high degree, it is still pertinent and relevant to our own day, it shows a great range of temperament and poetic mood from the lyrical, the nostalgic, the sentimental, to the ironic, the angry, the wrath-ful, the prophetic. It is informative, and elegant.

It is, in a word, very good stuff, and with Lorca, of course, we reach the highest levels of contemporary poetry. In the short story section there are Albert Halper, William Saroyan, Albert Maltz, Millen Brand, Alvah Bessie—but I should say at once that the short fiction section of this anthology seems to me the weakest part of it. The major figures of the period who lent their names to the *New Masses*, from Hemingway to Dreiser, did not give their fiction to it. There is inciden-tally a poorish and heavy contribution by Thomas Wolfe which seems to me must have been an early draft of an epi-sode in *You Can't Go Home Again*. Or perhaps it was a final draft, for in that uneven but valuable novel, there are some very fine things indeed, and some that must be skipped.

The section of reportage *is* reportage, of a high order, and perhaps no decade since the Thirties has given rise to so much good writing in that genre—and raised the genre itself, at its best, to an art form. Even Edmund Wilson, in those days, used this literary form to high advantage, though he is not listed here; and in these pages I miss also the work of Sher-wood Anderson, whose *Puzzled America*, in 1935, was one of the best documentaries of the depression years. But here is Erskine Caldwell, the early Caldwell, full of hope and promise and anger and eloquence, writing about the countless murders—unreported, unrecorded, unlisted murders—of Negroes in the South at that time; and still going on today.

Here is John L. Spivak of the *Daily Graphic*, no less, writing an extraordinary letter to President Roosevelt from a fifteen-year-old Mexican girl among the California migratory farm workers. (That problem has not been solved yet, even if you stop buying grapes.) Here is Joseph North on the great taxi strike of that epoch, when taxi drivers who worked for wages revolted against the fleet-owners; and when the unions were militant and independent of the Establishment. Here is Josephine Herbst speaking most prophetically of the Cuban revolution, already then stirring in Realengo 18. Here is Richard Wright again, talking of Joe Louis' knock-out of Max Baer, the Nordic Menace, in terms directly anticipating Eldridge Cleaver's essay, twenty years later, on Muhammed Ali, also known as Cassius Clay.

The list of these notable essays continues. If the verse section of this anthology shows the upper limits of its art, the documentaries are at the core of the volume and are equally of historical importance and permanent literary value. They bring the period back directly and immediately; the poverty, the suffering, the pain, the social misery of, then as now, the richest and most powerful nation in the world; and yes, the heroism, the gallantry, the heroic stance, never again to be repeated perhaps, in any historical epoch that I can now envisage, of the ordinary American people. Jack Conroy's "A Groundhog's Death" is another example: a wise, ironical, hard-bitten and bittersweet episode of the coal-mining country.

Albert Maltz, better in this area than in fiction, and a famous member of the Hollywood Ten Case (one of the most disgraceful hoaxes ever perpetuated against artists by governmental agencies and show biz working together in ecstatic harmony of paranoid patriotism), has a brilliant scenario of a General Motors strike at the Fisher Body plant in Flint, Michigan. It is another nostalgic moment in history to recall Walter Reuther's voice directing the strikers in person. America was promises then. Dorothy Parker, talking about her visit to Madrid during the Spanish Civil War, is not wisecracking any more. This is one of her most eloquent, appealing and touching pieces of writing; and while the central focus of the anthology is on the U.S.A. of the depression years, the Spanish War (the first act of or the tragic prelude to World War II, which has been again misinterpreted during the Cold War decades) is an underlying theme, or counter-theme in these pages.

Ernest Hemingway comes back with a notable contribution called "Who Murdered the Vets? A First-hand Report on the Florida Hurricane," and I only wish I could quote some passages that remind me of nothing so much as his "vignettes" of World War I in his first famous book, *In Our Time,* in 1925. He has another celebrated piece, an ode to "The Americans Dead in Spain" which has been translated into many different foreign languages. Now I only wish I could mention a few more of these contributions to the *New Masses* anthology by such names as Henri Barbusse, Alfred Kerr (on Gerhart Hauptmann's shameful acquiescence to the Nazis), Robert Forsythe (a brilliantly sophisticated wit, unusual in this group), Edward Dahlberg on Waldo Frank, William Carlos Williams, Romain Rolland, Mike Gold on John Reed.

There are more; but enough is enough. We must stop the analysis of this anthology, and get on with the larger story.

3

The final sketch by Ruth McKenney, "New Masses is Home," is a somewhat sentimental and tear-jerking account of a meeting to raise money for the magazine during the critical time of the Nazi-Soviet non-aggression pact. A series of outward historical events–like the Stalin purge trials of the 1930s and the suppression of the anarcho-syndicalists in the closing trauma of the Spanish Civil War–had disheartened some contributors to the magazine. And then the Hitler-Stalin pact, although viewed today in a different light, disillusioned and disenchanted many American Communists and fellow travelers and sympathizers among the leading intellectuals and artists. Coming out of the New Deal myself, I was astonished to find some of these radicals earlier in the Thirties linking the New Deal with "social fascism." It was the New Deal which accomplished the sweeping social reforms of the period; while it was sparked and prodded and pushed and perhaps even harried along, by the exultant radical energy of the Left, as this anthology testifies.

Fortunately, the *New Masses* weathered the crisis on the eve of the war and in the 1940s it thrived and prospered again; important new writers such as Marc Blitzstein, John La Touche, Earl Robinson, Christina Stead, joined the ranks of the contributors. And the artists remained among its staunchest supporters; an art auction for the benefit of the magazine in 1945, included: Alexander Brook, David Burliuk, Nikolai Cikovski, Philip Evergood, Hugo Gellert, William Gropper, Chaim Gross, Rockwell Kent, Anton Refregier, John Sloan, Raphael Soyer, Max Weber. And their drawings for *New Masses* continued through all the years.

There was some squabbling about the nature and content of such things as "proletarian fiction" and "truly revolutionary literature" versus bourgeois decadence. It may seem merely quaint today; some of it never had relevance to the American scene. Jack London who did indeed write proletarian and revolutionary literature ended up as a Nietzschean Superman, with fascist and racist inclinations. Dreiser, from a proletarian background, flirted with wealth and fame and power to become equally mystical and radical, at the end joining the Communist Party. Mark Twain, perhaps the richest of all American writers, and the court jester of the robber barons and tycoons, was the sharpest critic of American imperialism, and of the oligarchy which he saw as transforming the older democracy into a "monarchy," or dictatorship. Before the contemporary period, nearly all American writers were proletarian writers, without knowing it.

Yet in these pages we have the curious correspondence between Mike Gold and John Howard Lawson about the lack of revolutionary fervor in Lawson's plays. We also have Matthew Josephson's acute essay about this narrow political dogmatism; and we have the opposite example of it in Edwin Berry Burgum's study of Hemingway.

And it was the Cold War that brought about the downfall, in 1949, of one of the most brilliant journalistic enterprises in our literary history. At the war's end, a new epoch of repression was about to start. Another great achievement of the Depression years was the WPA Federal Theater Project; and Halle Flanagan's history of this, in her book *Arena*, ends with the congressional investigation and foreclosure of the

Federal Theater by political figures who are, by Divine Grace or special dispensation, still active in Washington today. Even though World War II held up the process a little, by war's end the shadows were falling on American democracy, and the "Communist conspiracy" was looming upon the national consciousness. What was the real truth, the true historical dimension, of the Cold War? As I said in opening this Introduction, a new group of Cold War historians have been giving us a whole new set of impressions, which, alas, most of those who lived through the period, and are so certain of their convictions, will not even bother to read and to think about.*

For if they did–and I am thinking of our Cold War Liberals in politics and in the arts alike–the Schlesingers, the Galbraiths, the Kristols, the Max Lerners, the Trillings, the Bells, the Rahvs, the Kazins, the Irving Howes: all these outstanding, upstanding figures of our political-cultural scene today–they would have to admit both their own illusions for the last twenty years, and the fact that they have deliberately deluded their readers about the historical facts of our period. Since it was they who fastened the Cold War noose around all our necks, how can we expect them to remove it?–even though, as in the cases of Mary McCarthy and Dwight Mac-Donald, and the estimable *New York Review of Books*, they have bowed a little to the changing winds of fashion today. Due to student protests at base, and student confrontations on Cold War issues, Professors Bell and Trilling have indeed moved on from Columbia to Harvard University–but after Harvard what?

Mr. Trilling has even "resigned" from contemporary literature, saying at long last that he does not understand it–but only after he led the attack for twenty years on such figures as the historian Vernon Parrington, the novelist Dreiser, the short-story writer Sherwood Anderson, and other such figures

*Among the older historians of American Cold War culture, are notably Professors D. F. Fleming, William A. Williams and Herbert Aptheker, along with such well known figures as the British historian A. P. J. Taylor, and the China expert, Edgar Snow. Among a whole new group of younger historians, I can only mention a few at random: Gar Alperowitz (*Atomic Diplomacy*); John Lukacs (*A History of the Cold War*); and in particular David Horowitz (*The Free World Colossus, Containment and Revolution, editor*).

of our literary history. And only after the Columbia University English Department had taken the lead in setting up Henry James as "Receiver" in what amounted to the bankruptcy of our national literature. The Cold War Liberals, historians, critics and so-called sociologists, also clustered around a set of prestigious literary magazines like *Partisan Review, The New Leader, Encounter* of London, *Der Monat* of Berlin, which had in effect set the tone and the values of the "Free World" culture. When it was revealed, about two years ago, that these leading cultural publications and organizations (the various Congresses and Committees for "Cultural Freedom"), as well as some student organizations and big unions of the AFL-CIO, were in fact being financed and controlled by Central Intelligence Agency—the game was up.

The game had really ended, and the Cold War Curtain had been penetrated when, in the early 1960s, white and black students both had made the great pilgrimage South for the start of the Civil Rights movement. Whatever we may think now of that earlier crusade, it was the seedbed for the passive resistance movement which centered around Martin Luther King, and *then* the radical militancy of both younger generation whites and black nationalists: separate but *more* equal in the case of the blacks today. When the books of Frantz Fanon, for example, when in the United States *The Autobiography of Malcolm X* and Eldridge Cleaver's *Soul on Ice* became bestsellers, the Cold War epoch was perhaps coming to an end in our literature and our politics and our culture alike—and we could once more see our own history in its totality and truthfulness.

That totality and that truth must include the epoch of the 1930s once more (history, phoenix-wise, always rises again; history absolves itself!), and in the whole social-historical context of the Thirties it is simply impossible to omit the brilliant span of the *New Masses* which this anthology conveys so well. How long will our present period of new radicalism and historical revisionism really exist? Has the Cold War *really* ended, or is it just a deceptive lull between wars? Will the United States in any case ever return to the full freedom of the older democracy, and the old republic; or are we to retain the trappings of democracy and "freedom" under the benevolent, or perhaps not so benevolent rule of the military-scientific industrial complex which has been in effect running the country for the last quarter of a century? Well, who *does* run the country? Like Mark Twain, who witnessed the beginnings of all this—after the exploitation of our internal empire—I have a ready answer: "I don't know."

But meanwhile, in the few years of grace which may be left to us—and one can only hope that these years of grace may extend to a better future than our recent past—let us at least try to know the facts about ourselves and our historical period. This pertinent and brilliant anthology (it could be double the size, and perhaps will be, in the future) of *New Masses* writing and art is an attempt to fill a vacuum which has existed in our whole concept of the 1930s, to break an official silence about this magazine. As such, I welcome it in the interests of truth, accuracy and reason. I am glad to accord to it the rightful place which it deserves in the annals of our literary history; I recommend it to all those who still have living memories or who want to emerge as whole souls from repression, silence and shame.

Harrison, New York
July 4, 1969

"Peace in Our Time"   SORIANO

"In their excavations of the radical past, the historians have dug up little but fragments and ruins. Yet surely a movement which involved so many intelligent and generous men and women cannot be barren of significance.... The strong impact of Communism's program even upon those writers who opposed it must be reckoned with. So must the vitalizing influence of the left-wing intellectuals who stirred up controversies, discovered new novelists and playwrights, opened up hitherto neglected areas of American life, and broke down the barriers that had isolated many writers from the great issues of our times.... We who precariously survive in the sixties can regret their inadequacies and failures, their romanticism, their capacity for self-deception, their shrillness, their self-righteousness. It is less easy to scorn their efforts, however blundering and ineffective, to change the world."

Jack Conroy, *The Carleton Miscellany* (Winter 1965)

"In the light of later recantation and 'revelation' by some of the persons involved in the left-wing activities here described, and their later claim that it was part of a vast underground 'conspiracy' to use writers and scholars as 'dupes' who would deliver the people into the hands of the Bolshevist, I should like to deny all such allegations with all my heart. I cannot for the life of me recall anything partaking of the nature of a conspiracy."

Matthew Josephson, *Infidel in the Temple*

America free Tom Mooney
America save the Spanish loyalists
America Sacco & Vanzetti must not die
America I am the Scottsboro boys

Allen Ginsberg, *America*

CONTENTS

2 SHORT STORIES AND SKETCHES

3 REPORTAGE

4 THE WRITER AND SOCIETY

5 ESSAYS AND COMMENT

APPENDIX

"There's the trouble."   JOHN GROTH

PROLOGUE

Joseph North

In the Forties they began to rewrite the Thirties, and as so often happens in amending history, since the time, say, the Roman historians described Spartacus–heroes were reduced; good was transformed into its opposite; a veneer of acceptability and respectability was laid over all that could not be brooked during the time in question. So a new generation was given an image of reality very different from the one we had who lived through it. I still blink when I read Granville Hicks on the Thirties, or any one of the others who were my contemporaries in the days of the *New Masses*, and who subsequently decided to follow a different but more orthodox drummer.

Maybe the strongest parallel would be the history of the Reconstruction. Enough has been written in recent decades since the pioneering work of Dr. W.E.B. Du Bois, and others, like James S. Allen, who first brought the truth to me, which demonstrated that that dozen years was one of the most fertile times in American history. But the versions of that day, which I first encountered at the University of Pennsylvania in the Twenties, painted it as one of horror–worse than the Confederate treason. That version persists to this day, for–to my dismay–recently I picked up the Columbia-Viking Desk Encyclopedia, "compiled and edited at Columbia University," and found the following in its third printing, dated September 1964, purporting to define the Reconstruction:

"South was reduced to degradation, with state governments falling to Carpetbaggers and scalawags. Aided by Freedman's Bureau and Union League Clubs, they shamelessly manipulated Negro votes, terrorized communities with Negro troops. In some districts anarchy and crime ruled; Ku Klux Klan appeared. Its own corruption broke down the carpetbagger governmental structure. . . ."

This version of reality corresponds to a Kluxist mentality

and it comes from the august halls of Columbia, regarded by many as the first university of the land.

At my elbow is a heavy shelf of books dealing with the literature of the Thirties and the role of the weekly magazine, the *New Masses,* within that time. As a founder and one of the editors of the weekly *New Masses* for most of its history–from 1934 to 1949–naturally, I am interested. I have read Granville Hicks' *A Part of the Truth,* Howard Fast's *The Naked God,* Ralph Ellison's *The Invisible Man,* Robert Bendiner's *Just Around the Corner*–to name a few. These are far from all. But all these have something in common. The authors feel they must justify themselves, put their version of history on the record, tell why they crossed the lines to join armies they opposed at one stage of their lives. The path of renegacy is hard and never fully succeeds. If the back-slider convinces his audience, he can scarcely ever convince himself. Evidence of that is in these books; for to the discerning reader the impression prevails that the author doth protest too much.

It is an old and sad story–to me at least, and I know to many others like me who played our part in those times. Herein is *my* version of the Thirties, of the *New Masses,* which was, I submit, the conscience of the literary world in that time. And I want to tell my story my way: that is, to produce as witnesses, the writers, the writings of that time. And you be the judge.

The bill of particulars the prosecutor presents charges us –the men of the Left, the Marxists, the Communists of that time, the rebels who stood with us and with whom we stood– as laying hairy hands on the literature, the culture of that day, and reviling it. We were the despoilers. The indictment says we cared nothing for literature, for truth, for beauty; we were guided by a bleakly fanatic loyalty to an alien philosophy: Marxism, Communism. We believed that the ends justified the means. Our ends were to capture–no less–the parapets of American culture and preach our foreign philosophy from those ramparts. We were infiltrators. We were the unamericans. The indictment says we put a premium on any work that carried "our line," our thesis, no matter how crude the writing, no matter how threadbare the quality–we called it good and we passed it on to the public, counterfeit goods. I have listened to this detraction for a long time. It has galled me. And finally I was compelled to compile this collection of writings and drawings from the *New Masses* to argue my position.

So let me tell my own story. I came into the Thirties a shiny-eyed admirer of Mike Gold. The monthly *New Masses* arrived at my mailbox in a Pennsylvania city and I could not wait until I tore the wrapper off. Mike's page I loved most. It breathed the truth of that day. I was then a young newspaperman—scarcely out of my teens—on a Pennsylvania journal. In the course of my journalistic duties I had encountered the Left (as I tell in some detail in my own personal history, *No Men Are Strangers*). I was taken by the sense of purpose, the dedication, the commitment to the common man. That appealed to all my own instincts, my attitudes toward life. I came from that class Mike Gold extolled. My father was a blacksmith who had never mastered the reading or writing of English; my mother a seamstress who taught herself to read and write; I, myself, a rivet-passer in the shipyard when I wasn't in the books. Mike Gold was Isaiah to me. I remember the thick, yellowish pages, even the heavy lines that separated the poetry from the prose, the bold, thick lines of the cartoons, Bill Gropper, Lozowick, Ellis, the rough-hewn poetry that dealt with turbines, looms, trucks, cranes, the paraphernalia of the industrial age. I had come up through all that, and it seemed to tell it truly. And it spoke of the soul of those who worked the machinery, their simple aspiration for freedom.

I can understand why those who come from a different environment cannot see these truths, or be moved by them. This reality was strange to the heroes—say, of Henry James' experience or imagination, and later of, say, Sinclair Lewis, or of F. Scott Fitzgerald, or even Ernest Hemingway, or Theodore Dreiser, who became a Communist. Jack London, the young longshoreman in his earlier years could understand: but really, very few did, until the Thirties. For then it was during that decade that we of the working class were flushed out of our garrets by Mike Gold and his people. We thrilled to his "Go Left, Young Man," perhaps as multitudes did several generations before to Horace Greeley when he advised the young to "Go West."

I saw what many of the writers in *New Masses* were doing, or at least, were trying to do: describe the life of the workingmen. Nobody before had succeeded, not truly. Upton Sinclair, perhaps, in his Jurgis of *The Jungle*. To a degree. But there was no full literature on this phase, this *essence* of American life. And perhaps not even yet has there been an adequate portrayal of the life of the industrial proletarian, his relationship to his work as well as to his contemporaries. I felt that, for I had been through something in my own life, the day of a workingman, its fierce disciplines; like that of the miner lying on cold damp soil under seams of coal that might collapse on him any moment; or the locomotive engineer with a thousand lives in his train dependent on his consciousness; or the weaver with the clattering machine repeating its infinite rhythm all the hours of the day. I could never forget my time when I was fifteen in the smoky hold of a ship in hot July with a dozen riveting guns hammering at hard steel, the rust particles flying about like burning snowflakes, a torrent of fire, rendering everything a choky crimson that blocked the breath, filled the lung, mingled with the sweat; all this with an awareness of the God-given daylight visible through the holes in the steel the reamer had drilled, affording a telescopic-sized glimpse of the serene river, the wheeling gulls, all of which became mockery of reality, a reality that became a daily nightmare that swallowed men up until the close of the working day when the siren blew. I can never forget the roar of a sudden silence when the day ended. Nobody caught that. It was a private mystery to the workingman. But the *New Masses* did try. Its men, its writers and artists understood this kind of a life existed. I found none of that in the *New Republic*, the *Nation*, or any other contemporary journal.

I enlisted in the *New Masses*.

I wrote my first pieces for it, and when Mike Gold responded to a piece on the life in the jungle of the ghetto in my industrial town, it changed my life. He wrote: "As sure as God made big red apples, you can write." I walked on air.

Later I was invited to come to New York to a conference to help save the *New Masses*. I was one of those who thought that the way to save it was to bring it out four times as often—weekly—(when it had languished in the time of the deepest depression as a monthly). Needless to say, many older heads than mine then regarded our formula as lunatic. But we persisted, and we prevailed.

It lasted for fifteen years as a weekly, after it had died as a monthly. Primarily because we captured the spirit of the time, because we triumphed over alienation, the bleak sense of human wastefulness, of universal desolation, of primal aloneness. We took those who felt an apartheid from life by the hand and brought them to a haven of purpose. We had purpose. We portrayed a reality and we pursued a goal—the Marxist, the socialist objective. We did so in prose, poetry, criticism, art, that did *not* violate the judgement, the perception, the aesthetic, of the existent generation. (It took another day to dare to argue that. You couldn't during that time and make sense.) That has not been adequately portrayed yet; it requires the perception of Dante to tell it. The hunger. The wrecked home. The family on the city pavement. The grandmother in her rocking chair, dry-eyed, on the sidewalk. In rain. Hopelessness. The crying child. The staring, anguished mother. The shamed, bitter father. The cold Hooverville. The jots of life on the outskirt of every city. Waste, refuse; humankind on the dump. I repeat: the hunger. A continent in starvation. 17,000,000 jobless. Milk dumped into rivers, obscene, like a social onanism. Oranges burned, wheat burned . . . to keep the prices up. How can you describe it so that a generation who did not live through it can understand? It is like war; only the soldier who went through the hailstorm of fire can know the frontline. Nobody else.

The Thirties began with the cold hell of hunger, the unparalleled assault of starvation. Then it passed into a time of unparalleled counterattack. It is this latter aspect that troubled the authorities in the following decades—the Forties, and especially the Fifties, the era of incipient domestic Hitlerism, Senator Joe McCarthy. Something stamped the Thirties as historically different from the other times of mass hunger in America that came with tragic regularity in economic depressions called the "Panic"—1837, 1857, 1877, 1893, 1907, and now 1929: the greatest of them all. This was different in the scope and depth of the counterattack, the movement against hunger, that had a sweep, a daring, an imaginativeness, a gallantry and a program—and yes, a leadership that transcended that of any other time. It was the time of the

Reds. The Marxists, the Communists' idea had produced that revolution in October of 1917 that shook the world.

I was a fairly typical case history of the day. I was very young then, a lad from the sticks, the provinces, but I was moved by a sense of commitment based on Marxism that seemed to surpass that of most of my contemporaries on the left literary front. I was reading everything in English that dealt with Marxism. All Marx and Engels wrote; Lenin and Stalin. They fascinated me. Then Gorky ... Sholokhov ... Whitman ... Dreiser ... Jack London ... the earlier Upton Sinclair–these were my gods. I read the *Daily Worker*. Then I wrote for it. If it had weaknesses, they were mine too. Its strength I knew and I had a serene confidence it would prevail in the short or the long run. That sense of the inevitable triumph of humanity's cause sustained me, come what came, then, as well as now. It sustained many more then, who later became disillusioned, fell away, for reasons I deplore, some out of honest difference, others out of concern for immediate safety, for self gain, still others, because they had not the strength to stand with a minority, to hold ground alone, but needed the herd safety of the majority, the strength in numbers.

I became an editor of the weekly *New Masses*. Our offices seemed always to look over the roofs of New York, the lower East Side generally, an honest place of work. Part of the time we were in the ancient Bible House across from Cooper Union where Abe Lincoln had spoken. Ours was nothing like the old English gentility of the *New Republic* offices; a few battered yellow desks, large, uncurtained windows, bare floors, but all was lit by the paste-ups of the bravest cartoons of the time: the glorious Minors, Ellises, Groppers, Art Youngs, Gellerts, Redfields, the early Burcks, Richters, the youthful Ad Reinhardts, Ned Hiltons, Gardner Reas–the constellation of the times' best cartoonists, touched with fire and genius, men who could laugh uproariously.

They came, the new writers, some shyly, others blustery, through the door, with the open or concealed air of the newcomer, not ever certain whether he was welcome, whether his work would be read, and if read, whether it would be praised or scorned out of hand. So they always had the artist's uncertainty which provoked in some an air of cocky bellicosity–youth's defense–a sort of know-it-all superiority.

And some of the best of the time had that unpleasant air. One of these was Edwin Rolfe, not yet twenty-two, lean-faced, his bony elbows protruding like a sparrow's wings, his cheeks high and thin giving him the look of an eager, hungering hawk. I loved them all, sensing, somehow, that their flaring defensiveness derived from ignorance, their lack of confidence. Rolfe, I felt then, wrote the most consistently good poetry of the day—a blend of militant but precise dedication, a sense of the classic in verse and sometimes a hint of the dry didactic, tending toward what I defined as the editorial-in-verse, a kind of poetry that was common in that time of threadbare reality, a day of hunger as palpable as a white skeleton on a taut wire in a laboratory. I did not recoil from such poetry, for I felt that much of Whitman was in it; and Milton of the *Areopagiticus*, or Blake. I thought, having already read much of Greek and Roman literature (my favorite), that if Lucretius could make didactic poetry of the seasons, of the life that he understood, the science of his time, why couldn't the militant poets of my day? A poet is a bugle too.

So I was in the office when Rolfe brought his poem "These Men Are Revolution," sometime in the late summer of 1934, which we printed in the September 9 issue of that year. Its credo moved him and many others abided by it, for two years later he was in the International Brigades and fighting in Spain—this gentle, wide-eyed poet who probably jumped when he encountered his shadow. I met him at headquarters in Madrid, a skinny soldier in a khaki-colored beret plastered above a long skinny face, his pants baggy over a skinny rump, a tiny pistol like a quatrain at his side, and his air of quiet militancy unveiled here in the country of Quixote. His poem, the first *New Masses* printed, said:

> *Come brother, come millhand, come miner, come friend—*
> *we're off! and we'll see the thing through to the end.*
> *There's nothing that can stop us, not cannon not dungeon*
> *nor blustering bosses, their foremen and gunmen.*
>
> *We will return to our books some day,*
> *to sweetheart and friend, new kinship and love,*
> *to our tool, to the lathe and tractor and plow*
> *when the battle is over—but there's fighting on now!*

There was prescience (and a bit of doggerel) in this verse, a forecast of his generation, some 3,500 of whom left this country–illegally, our government said–climbed the snow-tipped Pyrenees to come down on the other, sunny side of Spain, to carry arms (poor, outdated, flimsy arms) for the Republic. And some 1,200 never returned. This poet came back, but he did not stay long among the living–the wear and tear of the war had cut through to his heart, and he was soon dead, his generous gifts unrealized; we had only seen the first glimpses of them in the years he wrote before he became the poet-soldier in that war that was, as Camus said, an ache in the heart of his generation.

I had not seen much of the work of Mayakovsky in that time, one or two poems; but there was an echo of the Soviet poet in much that we received and printed; a sense of the gigantic in life, a flaunting of youth's passion to live, within the context of a total acceptance–nay, fiery dedication–to the Revolution: to fellow man. I could see in Rolfe's poetry, though he had read T. S. Eliot, as most of the young had, and been influenced (consciously) by the mystic's verse-mechanics, and by his tone and mood (unconsciously). One felt Whitman, too, in their work–Whitman our patron saint–but there was little of the tautness of Emerson, the music of Longfellow or the colloquialism of Whittier, the giants of the Abolitionist era. Whitman came through, something of Eliot, more of Mayakovsky.

Sol Funaroff was one of those who flared and burned with the Revolution. He was American kin to the Russian Maya-kovsky. The sockets of his eyes were deep and his glance burned; he moved his tall, thin frame perpendicularly into our shabby office; he was angular, physically, and he seemed always to want to fight, this poet of love and hope and dedi-cation. I cottoned to him, perhaps more than to any other of his generation, withal his sharp corners; for honesty was printed on his forehead like a postage stamp on a letter. He, like Rolfe, could take a "unit assignment," the task allotted them by their Communist Party branch, and find poetry in it; lyrics in distributing the *Daily Worker*, in bidding people to attend the meetings of the Unemployed Councils, or the mass meetings to demand lifting the embargo on Republican Spain. You should understand, for the time today is reminis-cent of the time then, the resolve, the commitment, the unyielding dedication. Believe me, there was no money in it, nor kudos—a snatch of fame, perhaps, when their work appeared in *New Masses* and their contemporaries eyed them with new respect, as most people in the ranks the world over eye the writer, the poet, the man of literature.

The magazine, an oracle of the time, I felt then and feel today, attracted the daring, the sensitive, the rebellious. Through our doors came that tall, pale-eyed enigma, Maxwell Bodenheim, who had achieved considerable fame, if not notoriety, with his verse and his novel (*Replenishing Jessica*), who had been invited to Hollywood. He could not take the artificiality he felt there, unlike his best friend Ben Hecht who made it big. Bodenheim came through that doorway, his blond hair up, unruly, a cowlick in the back, a smell of alcohol like an aura about him, and was converted to the cause of the proletariat. He compared the two worlds: the affluent where he had been; and the disinherited where he now was. And so, he wrote his ode to a working-class girl as he saw her, and we printed his poem in the April 3 issue of 1934, despite the fact that he was—like no few of his day—what I regarded as "super-revolutionary"—a man who saw life in black-and-white, or rather, as it might be today, in a garish technicolor. So he wrote of the Revolutionary Girl he envisaged:

> *We do not like romance*
> *In our present time—to us*
> *It reeks of flowered screens*
> *Over garbage-cans, of pretty words*
> *Bringing hollowness, not flesh,*
> *To every skeleton . . .*

He looked forward, he told his Revolutionary Girl, "To your time of violets . . ." and so on, despairing despite his glimpse of hope, he went down and down, ending his tragic and unfulfilled life as a Bowery bum, dying in a drunken brawl, not unlike a predecessor, a poet in a turbulent time also—François Villon.

So they came through that door at the Bible House, or on Fourth Avenue, immigrant son or son of Yankee, blacks beginning to come—among the first was Richard Wright—women beginning to come—Josephine Herbst who rode a horse over the Cuban mountains for us to do Realengo 18, the first Communist farm as we saw it in the Western Hemisphere. Some came, stayed a while and departed—and it is no use naming them, they have advertised themselves aplenty, their redemptive wail could be heard across the Rockies and back. They stayed so long as the climate for radicalism was suitable. When it became less the fashion in their circles, when the dollar grew back into its strength, they retreated—some decorously, some pell-mell—back safely again into the tents of their fathers, wondering aloud in millions of words, why they had ever come out of Egypt into the Holy Land!

They came, the young and the old, the novitiates and the famous, through the door and into our pages: poets, novelists, essayists, critics, artists, devil-may-care journalists—like John L. Spivak, who strolled into the den of the home-grown fascists and came out with their scalp, journalistically speaking (though the Brahmins of our literary fold virtually regarded him as infiltrator in our ranks from the *Daily Graphic*, his revelations helped put the magazine into many new homes). Our crusade against fascism, here and abroad, brought many newcomers to our pages; Dorothy Parker who saw the face of the era under the bombs of Madrid and called upon all writers to come down out of the ivory tower; for the only window in it, she wrote, opens out on fascism. From abroad—J. B. S. Haldane, the scientist, Sean O'Casey, Bertolt Brecht, Heinrich Mann, Maxim Gorky, Ilya Ehrenburg—so many more, the roster of the most gifted and bravest of the time appeared here.

Then came the illustrious of our own land, the men of renown whose names were in lights: Hemingway, Thomas Wolfe, Theodore Dreiser, Langston Hughes. Hemingway, rebel from way back, had encountered a magazine named *New Masses* on a dark night and gone home with it—he said to me with that grin of the strong boy who is head of the gang. His first writing was for the monthly *New Masses,* Joseph Freeman told me, a prose poem which, for some reason, Hemingway had never made public. Joe's memory may have been wrong. I believe Hemingway would have mentioned it to me somewhere along the line of our friendship which began, actually, in Madrid, in 1937. There, I suspect, he kept an eye on Falange spies who would get through the lines that were a jig saw around University City. We walked through the streets late one inky night, with Martha Gellhorn, and he said there were two kinds of men: one kind carried the parts of the machine guns and set them up; the other fired the gun and got the glory. The carriers, he said, had the right to share glory, should get more than fifty per cent because they did the work that made the firing possible. Without them, the firer might as well stick his finger through the crook of a jug of Scotch. Regardless of many an apocryphal story about him and his egotism, his high-handed treatment of his peers, he was a simple man with a big heart. As simple as that. It is best illustrated in that unforgettable photograph where he is in earnest conversation with the chief of an African Pigmy tribe, who must have been waist-high to Ernest, and the two chat away like two old cronies at the bar. I found him that way with all ordinary people. As I saw in Spain, and as they told me in Cuba where he wrote *The Old Man and the Sea,* in the fishing village of Cardenas. There, every fisherman to whom I talked told me in confidence that he was Juan, the hero of the book.

Well, I had enlisted Hemingway to write for *New Masses* by investing the cost of a Western Union telegram after the 1934 hurricane. It drowned some 400 World War I veterans working on a federal project for the jobless in Florida. The news of the calamity was in the *New York Times* and I had read that Hemingway was living near the scene. We did not have the cost of a telegram in the *New Masses* till, at the time. I remember the managing editor asking what made me think there was money to throw away! Why should Hemingway write for us when he could get a grand or more doing it for *Colliers?* I believed in the long-chance then, as I do now, and I panhandled every member of the staff until we made it. Three days later, just before press time, I jubilated when we got the long, thick envelope date-marked Key West, Florida. And that began our relationship. Hemingway read the magazine and told me in an offhand way that he liked it. I asked him in 1939 to do a piece on the anniversary of the Lincoln Brigade in Spain. He wrote an elegy, a moving piece—"The dead sleep cold in Spain tonight," it began—which we published in our February 14, 1939 issue. He wrote me that he spent five days working on it. It is now on a disk and played in all parts of the world where Spain's name is sacred.

Hemingway told me with an embarrassed laugh that he

could never become a Marxist, it was not his style of thought and life; he was too much the individualist. He said he respected the Marxist as a fighting man, having seen his bravery in battle. But he could never take Marx. He said facetiously that he could not read the old Moor (I do not know where he learned that that was the soubriquet Marx's family endowed Marx with because he was swarthy). "I can't read the Moor," Hemingway said, "he could only spoil my style. Pretty soon I'd be saying things like 'surplus value,' 'absolute and relative impoverishment of the proletariat,' 'alienation,' 'dictatorship of the proletariat.'" He said every writer fashions the reader in his own image, that is the price one pays for buying a book. He feared that the mighty Moor would color his vocabulary, and he would prefer to keep his own, thank you. He admitted to an inheritance from Mark Twain's *Huckleberry Finn*, and a few things from Gertrude Stein. Years later I visited his home in Cuba—deeded by him in his will to its people, after the revolution. I went through his private library, the biggest in the land. In a place of honor on the shelves, were the earmarked works of Flaubert and Stendhal. The crystal style of these Frenchmen, the idiomatic, earthy and unparalleled colloquialism of Mark Twain, which conveyed his humanism seemed to be the seedbed of Hemingway's "lean" style.

Memory sometimes comes back like a high wave. How clear Hemingway is in my mind; and Dreiser—perhaps the most impressive of all writers I met: tall, hefty, wall-eyed, big-headed and pig-headed. He was a ponderous man, resembling his prose, yet sensitive to every current of his time and finding it in every man and woman he encountered and, in his lumbering way, studied. I have told in *No Men Are Strangers* how he came to *New Masses'* office to defend himself against charges of anti-Semitism. We convinced him that he erred in his description of two cheating publishers, by mentioning they were Jews. Would he have accented their origin if they were Catholics, or Methodists, Swedes or French? One of us offered him a volume of Lenin's writings containing an essay on anti-Semitism. He took it home, read it that night, and wrote an apology, an admission of error, which we received the next day. There was grandeur in the man, his simplicity and honesty armored him, and he was ultimately invulnerable to the many shafts that flew his way.

I cannot close this incomplete and sketchy list of those who came to *New Masses* without remembering that martyr who carried himself like a "Mediterranean prince," as Louis Aragon said of the French journalist, Gabriel Peri. Captured by the Nazis during the war while he worked in the Resistance, this Communist who had become a deputy in the government, a member of the Foreign Affairs Commission, wrote his last testament on the eve of his execution. Among the prideful facts of his life he put down on paper in that dungeon before they took him out to the firing squad was that he had also contributed to "the American weekly, the *New Masses*."

Some say we lay claim to being a magazine of high literary quality because we adhered to Marxism. I never said that. I have seen better writing in other American magazines—say, the old *Atlantic Monthly* when William Dean Howells edited it. *Atlantic Monthly* was the leading magazine of the time. It could command the most skilled writers and it traveled on a high plain of quality. (Incidentally, Howells went on to become the first American writer who threw his lot in with socialism, this old, best friend of Mark Twain's.) We never put in a voucher for that much kudos. But I submit that in our time, in the Thirties especially, ours was the purest voice in the chorus of American literary journalism. I believe that history will come to us, more than to our contemporaries, to see America as it was then. We had a bead on the time that went to its heart. Most of our readers felt that. I know most of our writers did. That was why we were able to continue publication—sans foundation, sans big-time angels, sans subsidies of any sort (how we could have spent that Moscow gold the headlines saw!). I know that our readers loved us—blemishes, gaucheries, errors and all. We made our mistakes, yes, but they were of a different nature than those of our contemporaries, our opponents. *New Masses* erred frequently. We published some "inferior" stuff because we were searching for new talent, especially among working people, among the under-educated. If writing had truth and touched the heart, we favored publication. I confess, *mea culpa, mea culpa*. We cut corners on excellence. It was not easy to ask someone who lived on the margins of hunger, who worked many hours a day for bread, to rewrite until he met our aesthetic satisfaction. Especially when he never got a penny's reward. There were some writers with whom we would argue. Others were guided by their aesthetic or political responsibility.

I admit it: I did not think the first poem of an unknown, young Negro writer we published was, say, the equal of Langston Hughes' work or Carl Sandburg's or Robert Frost's. The poem's title was "I Have Seen Black Hands" and the author's name was Richard Wright. But we published it hoping to encourage whoever he was. I believe I could argue that our editorial laxness had its wisdom.

I do not see how it is possible for a just critic of *New Masses* to judge it adequately by reading the page cold. It seems to me he must know the time, the purpose, the circumstances.

Did we catch the essence of the time? Yes, I think we did. It is in our pages, brighter than it is on the paper of any other journal of that time. This is my contention.

I had another guideline, Tolstoyan. The Master said, "Belief in the triumph of good vitalizes a race; enlightened optimism fosters in man a constructive purpose and frees him from fears that fetter his thoughts." I lived by that, edited the *New Masses* with that as my goal. That was true of my associates who lasted. These pages are evidence that I was not wrong.

This book is no indulgence in nostalgia. Its purpose is to set the record straight, to show how much in common the Sixties had with the Thirties. But most vital, the aim of this anthology is to help get a bead on the Seventies by revealing the power inherent in our people throughout our most embattled times. The people's movements of the Thirties reached their apex when they shattered the effort of the Establishment to divide them. As ever, in our time, the instrument of division, like a hacksaw, is Red-baiting. Hitler got away with it for a dozen years and fifty million people died. The cumulative coalition of Marxist and non-Marxist, Communist and non-Communist, finally did him in. This book offers you the creative work of non-Marxist and Marxist, black and white, whose union constituted a power that fascism failed to break. This moral holds today.

The Masses was born in 1911. A magazine of politics and arts, it reflected the rebellious America of its day. The government closed it down for its vigorous opposition to the entry of our country into World War I. Two trials were held under the Sedition Act of 1917, on the charge of "conspiring to promote insubordination and mutiny in the military and naval forces of the United States and to obstruct the recruiting and enlistment to the injury of the service." The prosecutors failed to hang the editors.

It reopened as *The Liberator,* and after a series of vicissitudes, it became the *New Masses* as a monthly in 1926. Through the years from 1911 national and world renowned writers and artists appeared in it: like John Reed, Floyd Dell, Claude McKay, Edna St. Vincent Millay, Carl Sandburg, Bertolt Brecht, Robert Minor, Art Young, William Gropper, Hugo Gellert, Orozco, Siqueiros and Rivera. The monthly *New Masses* lasted until the summer of 1933. It reappeared in a new reincarnation as the weekly *New Masses* in January 1934. I was a principal founder of the weekly and became its chief editor when I returned from covering the war in Spain in 1938.

My principal collaborators when the weekly magazine was founded were Herman Michelson, Joshua Kunitz and Stanley Burnshaw. A number of other writers and artists were listed on the editorial board at the time, some remaining for a brief stay, others longer, and some weathered the political and economic storms.

The selections in this anthology come from the *New Masses* of the Thirties, the time of vast economic crisis and questing turbulence in the country when the magazine had its strongest impact. Some day we hope to continue this anthology throughout the wartime Forties to its final issue in the weekly format in 1949, when the periodical was badly hurt by the outbreak of the Cold War.

It became *Masses and Mainstream,* a quarterly, and later in the Fifties, changed to a monthly. There is a direct lineage to its present incarnation, *American Dialog.*

It was hard to make the selections. There were so many candidates that a number of volumes would have been required to include all pieces that merited selection. Since the laws of life, and printing, are such that space is a premium, only a limited number were chosen, this bookful. These had to meet the specifications of quality and typicality. They represent not only the best of the time, but also the kinds of work printed.

We thank those whose pieces are included: we beg the forbearance of those whose works were omitted. We hope the appearance of this book will induce many interested scholars and students to go to the New York Public Library where the issues, in totality, are available in microfilm.

Thanks are also due to Nora North for her valuable research into the period, to Hugo Gellert, Michael Myerson, Anca Vrbovska and Jacqueline Frieder for their editorial help.

New York
March 1969

"It's a scorching denunciation of the Communist Party's shameful capitulation to the bourgeoisie. I've sold it to Hearst."   JOHN HELIKER

East Tenth Street Jungle

An etching by REGINALD MARSH

1
Poetry

ROBERT MINOR

"And he's the most *radical* thing you ever heard of. Why he's already talking of a *Fourth* International." GARDNER REA

Kenneth Fearing

[1]

The Program

ACT ONE, *Barcelona, Time, the present*
  ACT TWO, *Paris in springtime, during the siege*
    ACT THREE, *London, Bank Holiday, after an air raid*
      ACT FOUR, *a short time later in the U.S.A.*
EAT ZEPHYR BONBONS
  (*do not run for the exit in case of fire*
    the Rome-Berlin Theater has no exits)
      SUZANNE BRASSIERES FOR PERFECT FORM
CAST, IN THE ORDER OF DISAPPEARANCE
  Infants
    women and children
      soldiers, sailors, miscellaneous crowds
With 2,000 wounded and 1,000 dead
  12,000 wounded and 6,000 dead
    100,000 wounded and 50,000 dead
      10,000,000 wounded and 5,000,000 dead
(*Scenes by Neville Chamberlain*
  costumes, courtesy of Daladier
    Spanish embargo by the U.S. Congress
      music and lighting by Pius XI)
SMOKE EL DEMOCRACIES
  TRY THE NEW GOLGOTHA FOR COCKTAILS
    AFTER THE SHOW

September 6, 1934

[2]

Dirge

1-2-3 was the number he played but today the number came
  3-2-1; bought his Carbide at 30 and it went to 29; had
    the favorite at Havana but the track was slow—

40

O, executive type, would you like to drive a floating-power,
    knee-action, silk-upholstered six? Wed a Hollywood
    star? Shoot the course in 58? Draw to the ace, king,
    jack?
O, fellow with a will who won't take no, watch out
    for three cigarettes on the same single match; O,
    democratic voter born in August under Mars, beware
    of liquidated rails—
Denouement to denouement, he took a personal pride in the
    certain, certain way he lived his own personal life,
    but nevertheless, they shut off his gas; nevertheless,
    the bank foreclosed; nevertheless, the landlord called;
    nevertheless, the radio broke,
And twelve o'clock arrived just once too often,
    just the same he wore one grey tweed suit, bought one
    straw hat, drank one straight Scotch, walked one
    short step, took one long look, drew one deep breath,
    just one too many,
And wow he died as wow he lived,
    going whop to the office and blooie home to sleep and
    biff got married and bam had children and oof got
    fired,
    zowie did he live and zowie did he die,
With who the hell are you at the corner of his casket, and
    where the hell are we going on the right-hand silver
    knob, and who the hell cares walking second from
    the end with an American Beauty wreath from why
    the hell not,
Very much missed by the circulation staff of the New York
    Evening Post; deeply, deeply mourned by the B.
    M. T.,
Wham, Mr. Roosevelt; pow, Sears Roebuck, awk, big dipper;
    bop, summer rain;
    bong, Mr., bong, Mr., bong, Mr., bong.

December 18, 1934

[3]

Mr. Jesse James Will Some Day Die

*Where will we ever again find food to eat, clothes to wear,
    a roof and a bed, now that the Wall Street plunger
    has gone to his hushed, exclusive, paid-up tomb?*

How can we get downtown today, with the traction
    king stretched flat on his back in the sand at Miami
    Beach?
And now that the mayor has denounced the bankers,
    now that the D.A. denies all charges of graft, now
    that the clergy have spoken in defense of the home,
O, dauntless khaki soldier, O, steadfast pauper,
    O, experienced vagrant, O picturesque mechanic, O,
    happy hired man,
    O, still unopened skeleton, O, tall and handsome target,
    O, neat, thrifty, strong, ambitious, brave prospective
    ghost, is there anything left for the people to do, is there
    anything at all that remains unsaid?
But who shot down the man in the blue overalls? Who
    stopped the mill?
    Who took the mattress, the table, the birdcage, and piled
    them in the street? Who drove teargas in the picket's
    face?
    Who burned the crops? Who killed the herd? Who
    leveled the walls of the packing box city? Who held the
    torch to the
    Negro pyre? Who stuffed the windows and turned on
    the gas for the family of three?
No more breadlines. No more blackjacks. No more Roose-
velts.
    No more Hearsts.
    No more vag tanks, Winchells, True Stories, deputies,
    no more scabs.
    No more trueblue, patriotic, doublecross leagues. No more
    Ku Klux Klan. No more heart-to-heart shakedowns. No
    more D.A.R.
No more gentlemen of the old guard commissioned to
    safeguard, as chief commanding blackguard in the
    rearguard of the homeguard, the 1 inch, 3 inch, 6 inch,
    10 inch, 12 inch.
No more 14, 16, 18 inch shells.

                                           December 18, 1934

Maxwell Bodenheim

To a Revolutionary Girl

Violets peer out in streaks
On the covered ribs
Of hills, and meet the air
In a million trembling
Lips on fields throughout the world:
Stretch along the highways,
Small and mighty in the drip of rain:
Dot the base of mountains,
Equal purpose in disguise:
Signal friendship
To the rocks,
Take the darkness
From cave-outlets
And ravines—

You are a girl,
A revolutionist, a worker
Sworn to give the last, undaunted jerk
Of your body and every atom
Of your mind and heart
To every other worker
In the slow, hard fight
That leads to barricade, to victory
Against the ruling swine.
Yet, in the softer regions of your heart,
The shut-off, personal, illogical
Disturbance of your mind,
You long for crumpled 'kerchiefs, notes
Of nonsense understood
Only by a lover:
Long for colors on your dresses,
Ribboned sleeves, unnecessary buttons:
Bits of laughter chased and never

Dying: *challenge of a hat*
Buoyant over hair.
Youth and sex, distinctions
Still unmarred by centuries of pain,
Will not be downed, survive
In spite of hunger, strikes, and riot-guns,
Sternness in the ranks.
We frown upon your sensitive demands:

We do not like romance
In our present time—to us
It reeks of flowered screens
Over garbage-cans, of pretty words
Bringing hollowness, not flesh,
To every skeleton.
It stamps the living death of Hollywood,
The tactics of a factory
Shipped in boxes round, price-marked
With lying sweetness, trivial
Melodrama doping eyes and ears.
And yet romance, expelled from actual life,
Sneaks back in middle age,
Impossible in groan and taunt.
Their gilt on top, mould underneath,
Revolt us—

But you are a girl.
Your problem cannot be denied.
In the Russia of the past
Women once pinned flowers
To their shoulders, chained to lovers,
Flogged by snarling guards
In the exile to Siberia,
And in the Russia of today
Men and women, proud of working-hours,
Sturdy, far from blood-steeped tinsel,
Take their summer vacations
On the steppes, in cleaner games,
In flowers, pledges, loyalties,
Clear-growing, inevitable,
Deepening in their youth.
Steal, for an hour, now and then,

To your time of violets, the hope
Of less impeded tenderness
In a freedom yet to come,
Then fold it in your heart for unapparent,
Secretly unyielding strength
On every picket-line throughout the world,
Revolutionary girl.

April 3, 1934

Kenneth Patchen

American Heritage

How now return to lecture halls:
O we who thought to cultivate this land
Have crouched like cattle in a freight;
Have scented death and lived too late;
Have whimpered as we fell between the cars;
And chance we live, our sight is dull without the scars.

How now return to faith:
For some of us the measure of our love is hate.
What softness, woman lips and arms
Can ease the sting of lice, can slow the swaying steel.
As runaway the freights slosh through the pools of sleep
(Their whistles, bells, and wheels that thud too deep.)
This is our history: quivering laurels, unsown . . .
We plumb a rattling grave
And follow rain into the hungry drift . . . unknown.

Your Sophocles and Spengler please, we must rehearse
Perhaps an orchestra of words will soar the brakeman's curse.

What softness (warm and tender)
woman lips and arms can reach us now.

Then let us praise this heritage, this humble lot
Revere this God, this flag, this tommyrot.

April 10, 1934

Joe Hill Listens to the Praying

Look at the steady rifles, Joe.
It's all over now—"Murder, first degree,"
The jury said. It's too late now
To go back. Listen Joe, the chaplain is reading:

Lord Jesus Christ who didst
so mercifully promise heaven
To the thief that humbly confessed
His injustice
    throw back your head

Joe; remember that song of yours
We used to sing in jails all over
These United States—tell it to him:
"I'll introduce to you
A man that is a credit to our Red, White
and Blue,
His head is made of lumber and solid as
a rock;
He is a Christian Father and his name is
Mr. Block."

        Remember, Joe—
"You take the cake,
You make me ache,
Tie a rock on your block and jump
in the lake,
Kindly do that for Liberty's sake."

Behold me, I beseech Thee, with
The same eyes of mercy that

                on the other
Hand we're driftin' into Jungles
From Kansas to the coast, wrapped
    round brake beams on a thousand
    freights; San Joaquin and Omaha
    brush under the wheels—"God made the summer
    for the hobo and the bummer"—we've been
    everywhere, seen everything.
Winning the West for the good citizens;
Driving golden spikes into the U.P.;
Harvest hands, lumbermen drifting—
    now Iowa, now Oregon—
God, how clean the sky; the lovely wine
Of coffee in a can. This land
    is our lover. How greenly beautiful
Her hair; her great pure breasts
    that are
The Rockies on a day of mist and rain.

We love this land of corn and cotton,
Virginia and Ohio, sleeping on
With our love, with our love—
O burst of Alabama loveliness, sleeping on
In the strength of our love; O Mississippi flowing
Through our nights, a giant mother.

Pardon, and in the end
How green is her hair,
how pure are her breasts; the little farms
nuzzling into her flanks
drawing forth life, big rich life
Under the deep chant of her skies
And rivers—but we, we're driftin'
Into trouble from Kansas to the coast, clapped
into the stink and rot of country jails
and clubbed by dicks and cops
Because we didn't give a damn—
remember Joe
How little we cared, how we sang
the nights away in their filthy jails;
and how, when
We got wind of a guy called Marx
we sang less, just talked
And talked. "Blanket-stiffs" we were
But we could talk, they couldn't jail us
For that—but they did—
remember Joe
Of my life be strengthened
One Big Union:
our convention in Chi; the Red Cards,
leaflets; sleeping in the parks,
the Boul Mich; "wobblies" now, cheering
the guys that spoke our lingo, singing
down the others. "Hear that train blow,
Boys, hear that train blow."

Now confessing my crimes, I may obtain
Millions of stars, Joe—millions of miles.

Remember Vincent St. John
In the Goldfield strike; the timid little squirt
with the funny voice, getting onto the platform

and slinging words at us that rolled
down our chins and into our hearts,
like boulders hell-bent down a mountain side.
And Orchard, angel of peace
    —with a stick of dynamite in either hand.
    Pettibone and Moyer: "The strike
Is your weapon, to hell with politics."
        Big Bill—remember him—
At Boise—great red eye rolling like a lame bull
    through the furniture and men
    of the courtroom—"This bastard,
His Honor."

    Hobo Convention:
(Millions of stars, Joe—millions of miles.)
"Hallelujah, I'm a bum,
Hallelujah, I'm a bum." His Honor,
    the sonofabitch!
One Big Strike, Lawrence, Mass—
    23,000 strong, from every neck
    of every woods in America, 23,000,
Joe, remember. "We don't need
    a leader. We'll fix things up
    among ourselves."
"Blackie" Ford and "Double-nose" Suhr in
Wheatland—"I.W.W.'s don't destroy
    property"—and they got life. "I've counted
The stars, boys, counted a million of these prison bars."

    San Diego, soap boxes,
Hundreds of them! And always
    their jail shutting out the sky,
    the clean rhythm of the wheels
    on a fast freight; disinfectant getting
    into the lung-pits, spitting blood
But singing—Christ, how we sang,
        remember the singing
Joe, One Big Union,
    One Big
        hope to be
What do they matter, Joe, these rifles,
They can't reach the towns, the skies, the songs,

that now are part of more
than any of us—we were
The homeless, the drifters, but, our songs
had hair and blood on them.
There are no soap boxes in the sky.
We won't eat pie, now, or ever
when we die,
but Joe
We had something they didn't have;
our love for these States
was real and deep;
to be with Thee
In heaven. Amen.
(How steady are
the rifles.) We had slept
naked on this earth on the coldest nights
listening to the words of a guy named Marx.
Let them burn us, hang us, shoot us,

Joe Hill,

For at the last we had what it takes
to make songs with.

November 20, 1934

Muriel Rukeyser

[1]

Movie

Spotlight her face   her face has no light in it
touch the cheek with light   inform the eyes
press meanings on those lips
                See cities from the air,
fix a cloud in the sky, one bird in the bright air,
one perfect mechanical flower in her hair,

Make your young men ride over the mesquite plains;
produce our country on film: here are the flaming shrubs,
the Negroes put up their hands in Hallelujahs,
the young men balance at the penthouse door.
We goggle at the screen: look   they tell us
you are a nation of similar whores   remember the Maine
remember you have a democracy of champagne—

And slowly the female face kisses the young man,
over his face the twelve-foot female head
the yard-long mouth enlarges and yawns
                          The End
Here is a city   here the village grows
here are the rich men standing rows on rows,
but the crowd seeps behind the cowboy the lover the king,
past the constructed sets America rises
the bevelled classic doorways   the alleys of trees are witness
America rises in a wave a mass
pushing away the rot.

                The Director cries Cut!
hoarsely CUT   and the people send pistons of force
crashing against the CUT! CUT! of the straw men.

Light is superfluous upon these eyes,
across our minds push new portents of strength
destroying the sets, the flat faces, the mock skies.

June 12, 1934

[2]

The Cornfield

Error, disease, snow, sudden weather.
For those given to contemplation: this house,
wading in snow, its cracks are sealed with clay,
walls papered with print, newsprint repeating,
in-focus gray across the room, and squared
ads for a book: Heaven's My Destination,
Heaven's My ... Heaven ... *Thornton Wilder.*
The long-faced man rises long-handed jams the door
tight against snow, long-boned, he shivers.
Contemplate.

Swear by the corn,
the found-land corn, those who like ritual. He
rides in a good car, they say blind corpses rode
with him in front, knees broken into angles,
head clamped ahead. Overalls. Affidavits.
He signs all papers. His office: where he sits,
feet on the stove, loaded trestles through door,
satin-lined, silk-lined, unlined, cheap.
The papers in the drawer. On the desk, photograph
H.C. White, Funeral Services (new car and eldest son);
tells about Negroes who got wet at work,
shot craps, drank and took cold, pneumonia, died.
Shows the sworn papers. Swear by the corn.
Pneumonia, pneumonia, pleurisy, t.b.

For those given to voyages: these roads
discover gullies, invade. Where does it go now?
Now turn upstream twenty-five yards. Now road again.
Ask the man on the road. Saying, That cornfield?
Over the second hill, through the gate,
watch for the dogs. Buried, five at a time,

pine boxes, Rinehart & Dennis paid him fifty-five dollars
a head for burying those men in plain pine boxes.
George Robinson: I knew a man
who died at four in the morning at the camp.
At seven his wife took clothes to dress her dead
husband, and at the undertaker's
they told her the husband was already buried.
—Tell me this, the men with whom you are acquainted,
the men who have this disease
have been told that sooner or later they are going to die?
—Yes, sir.
—How does that seem to affect the majority of the people?
—It don't work on anything but their wind.
—Do they seem to be living in fear
or do they wish to die?
—They are getting to breathe a little faster.
For those given to keeping their own garden:
Here is the cornfield, white and wired by thorns,
old cornstalks, snow, the planted home.
Stands bare against a line of farther field,
unmarked except for wood stakes, charred at tip,
few scratched and named (pencil or nail).
Washed-off. Under the mounds,
all the anonymous.
Abel America, calling from under the corn,
Earth, uncover my blood!
Did the undertaker know the man was married?
Uncover.
Do they seem to fear death?
Contemplate.
Does Mellon's ghost walk, povertied at last
walking in furrows of corn, still sowing,
do apparitions come?
Voyage.
Think of your gardens. But here is corn to keep.
Marked pointed sticks to name the crop beneath.
Sowing is over, harvest is coming ripe.
—No, sir; they want to go on.
They want to live as long as they can.

December 7, 1937

53

Richard Wright

I Have Seen Black Hands

I

*I am black and I have seen black hands, millions and millions
        of them—*
*Out of millions of bundles of wool and flannel tiny black
        fingers have reached restlessly and hungrily for life.*
*Reached out for the black nipples at the black breasts of black
        mothers,*
*And they've held red, green, blue, yellow, orange, white, and
        purple toys in the childish grips of possession,*
*And chocolate drops, peppermint sticks, lollypops, wineballs,
        ice cream cones, and sugared cookies in fingers
        sticky and gummy,*
*And they've held balls and bats and gloves and marbles and
        jack-knives and sling-shots and spinning tops in the
        thrill of sport and play,*
*And pennies and nickels and dimes and quarters and some-
        times on New Year's, Easter, Lincoln's Birthday,
        May Day, a brand new green dollar bill,*
*They've held pens and rulers and maps and tablets and books
        in palms spotted and smeared with ink,*
*And they've held dice and cards and half-pint flasks and cue
        sticks and cigars and cigarettes in the pride of new
        maturity. . . .*

II

*I am black and I have seen black hands, millions and millions
        of them—*
*They were tired and awkward and calloused and grimy and
        covered with hangnails,*
*And they were caught in the fast-moving belts of machines
        and snagged and smashed and crushed,*

And they jerked up and down at the throbbing machines
   massing taller and taller the heaps of gold in the
   banks of bosses,
And they piled higher and higher the steel, iron, the lumber,
   wheat, rye, the oats, corn, the cotton, the wool, the
   oil, the coal, the meat, the fruit, the glass, and the
   stone until there was too much to be used,
And they grabbed guns and slung them on their shoulders
   and marched and groped in trenches and fought
   and killed and conquered nations who were cus-
   tomers for what the good black hands had made,
And again black hands stacked goods higher and higher until
   there was too much to be used,
And then the black hands held trembling at the factory gates
   the dreaded lay-off slip,
And the black hands hung idle and swung empty and grew
   soft and got weak and bony from unemployment
   and starvation,
And they grew nervous and sweaty, and opened and shut in
   anguish and doubt and hesitation and
   irresolution. . . .

III

I am black and I have seen black hands, millions and millions
   of them—
Reaching hesitantly out of days of slow death for the goods
   they had made, but the bosses warned that the
   goods were private and did not belong to them,
And the black hands struck desperately out in defense of life
   and there was blood, but the enraged bosses de-
   creed that this too was wrong,
And the black hands felt the cold steel bars of the prison they
   had made, in despair tested their strength and found
   that they could neither bend nor break them,
And the black hands fought and scratched and held back but
   a thousand white hands took them and tied them,
And the black hands, lifted palms in mute and futile
   supplication to the sodden faces of mobs wild in
   the revelries of sadism,
And the black hands strained and clawed and struggled in

  vain at the noose that tightened about the black
    throat,
And the black hands waved and beat fearfully at the tall
    flames that cooked and charred the black flesh . . .

IV

I am black and I have seen black hands
Raised in fists of revolt, side by side with the white fists of
    white workers,
And some day—and it is only this which sustains me—
Some day there shall be millions and millions of them,
On some red day in a burst of fists on a new horizon!

           June 26, 1934

Edwin Rolfe

These Men Are Revolution

I

These men are revolution, who move
in spreading hosts across the globe
(this part which is America), who love
fellow men, earth, children, labor
of hands, and lands fragrant under sun
and rain, and fruit of man's machinery.

These men are revolution even as
trees are wind and leaves upon them
trembling in a pattern which was
quiet a minute past, silent on stem,
immovable; just as all still things
grow animate like bow-stirred violin strings.

The power in men and leaves and all
things changeable is not within themselves
but in their million counterparts—the full
accumulation. These the world resolves
into men moving, becoming revolution
surely as blown seed takes root, flowers in sun.

2

These men are millions and their numbers
grow in milltowns, flow from coastlines,
buzz with the saws in lumber forests, rise
in cities, fields, to set the signal blaze.

Boys fresh from classroom, their professors,
bid farewell to books read well and loved,

join the hard climb, pick up friends on the way
to a rarer earth attuned to a newer day.

And soldiers down rifles as workingmen gather
in cities, on squares, at the most dismal corners:
no mourners, but grim with the task of the hour,
the conquest of industry, Soviet power!

Come brother, come millhand, come miner, come friend—
we're off! and we'll see the thing through to the end.
There's nothing can stop us, not cannon not dungeon
nor blustering bosses, their foremen and gunmen.

We will return to our books some day,
to sweetheart and friend, new kinship and love
to our tools, to the lathe and tractor and plow
when the battle is over—but there's fighting on now!

3

The tidal wave flowed first against the coast,
swept the Pacific, burst on Louisiana's gulf
bordering Mexico, and workmen's hearts glowed
with the fire of the fight.

The news spread eastward, dinned in Minnesota:
men wanted bread who strode across wheat fields.
Hands left the steering wheel, vehicle stalled
before filled granaries.

And southward; dusk-skinned men in Alabama
paralyzed plantation, joined with white brother,
emptied the mine shaft, silenced the clang
of pickaxe probing for ore.

Montana miners remembering Dunne
struck Anaconda, Rockefeller, copper;
and Foster's spirit in Pittsburgh, Gary, Youngstown,
swooped over steel mill.

Soon there will be no line on any map
nor color to mark possession, mean "Mine, stay off."

Brother, friend—and you, boss!—the tidal wave
sweeps coast to awakened coast.

4

You who would move, live freely among men,
regain lost grandeur, dignity and all
the varied riches of your worried toil:
observe America today: its fields
plowed under, trampled underfoot; its wide
avenues blistered by sun and poison gas,
its men grown reckless of bayonet and gun.
Regard the legion in your midst who hide,
hands twitching and empty, in hovels and see
their eyes grown dry, impotent of tears. . . .

Charter the next airplane, cross the continent,
see under you the colors of the map changing
as rivers crack the earth and bleak hills bulge,
their shadows darkening unlovely barren fields.
Heavy dust hugs the dry exhausted pastures;
chimney smoke rising from factory bears
the agonized sweat of driven men, it carries
the poison gas, it grasps their coughed-up lungs.
Their blood is dust now borne into the air—
the huge dark menacing cloud above our land.

Circling the tall peaks I dreamed I saw
your face, beloved, turned on leveled plains.
Clouds burst about you, fresh rain streamed
down mountainside, fed parched earth, bore
strength to shriveled root, food to buried tree,
swept drought of midsummer sun and autumn capitalism
away.
Fields ripened to fragrance and the world's wealth
turned soil aside, gleamed in the new kernel
till kinder sun speared cloud and earth returned
to joy, florescence in the harvest-dawn.

The plane zoomed under dust-cloud and I knew
this was mere mirage, saw dream as dream

but in it prophecy. Turned toward the real:
men fallen on field and wharf, shot down
at mine gate, trodden under horse's hoof.
Bullet in back, betrayer, jowled misleader
dealt death and sorrow, mangled limbs and tears
at empty chairs at frugal empty tables;
in a hundred beds the warm comforting body
sweet at your side at midnight, gone. . . .

O you who would live, revive the natural love
of man for fellow man for earth for toil:
commemorate these fallen men anonymous;
retrieve from rigid hands their strength, desire,
their vision from glazed eye, from dying brain their fire.
Mark the compass-toe—their last footprint—
and follow through! Precision now is needed
in limb, in sight, certainty in the heart.
Give meaning to these slain! Call no halt, sound
the siren for new striving, now clear, defined.

5

The line leaps forward on a hundred fields,
staggers—breaks—re-forms—returns
like molten steel to momentary molds
throughout America. The multimass learns
how desperate and doomed the enemy is,
how sure its own ascendant growing power.
Clear-eyed, alert, the stalwart legion grows
to recognize the imminent bright hour,
inevitable now. And time can but delay—
never impede—the winning of the world
by men for mankind. See approach the day
when millions merge and banner is unfurled!

Now the army moves, marks time, gives blow
for blow, sustains slain, shivers in retreat;
advances, counters thrust—and now moves . . . slow . . .
with lives, encounters lost. But never defeat.

September 9, 1934

Alfred Hayes

[1]

In Madrid

All day we heard the machine-guns rattle
Cavalry detachments thunder artillery roll
Above the public buildings government planes
Went zooming into the provinces
Heavy with bombs.

We were alone in the house we avoided the public squares
Cooked breakfast I read Calderon waited
They were blowing up railway depots shooting gendarmes
People were lying in their own blood in the gutters.
In Asturias they said in whispers the arsenals
Captured We feared for our lives.

While we were waiting we were alone in the house
Madame and I firing began again in the street
Then shots rang out in the hallway Madame shrieked
I rushed to the door quaking as a grenade roared
He came bursting into the house face like a gay fury
Bolted and barricaded the door jumped to the window
Sighted along the barrel of his pistol shouted fired
And clicked the shell out of his gun A revolutionist, I thought.

What were we to do? I am a peaceful man never mix
In politics the madness that infuriates the people
And shoots gendarmes Does it matter who rules?
I wished a peaceful life safe from catastrophe
With no violent death shielded from anger
The heart like a warm clock ticking in cotton
The brain wearing mufflers and a pair of goloshes
And there he was shouting Viva and firing the gun hot
And the shots from the police splintered our fine mirror

Buried themselves in the good furniture My wife wept
I distracted hid behind the armchair
Until a bullet plowed paper from the wall behind
Then I fell flat on the floor waiting his death.

He swore terribly when he was hit
The shoulder gushed blood;
Ripped his shirt with his teeth
Stuffed it into the wound and fired again
For you Lerroux he said firing
For you Gil Robles he said firing
Here's one in the gut for the priests he said
And fired
And with the last shot he stood up shouting
LONG LIVE right in the window.

Afterward they threw his body
Into the street Madame shrieked constantly
I picked up the poor shattered mirror
Swept the floor washed out the bloodstains
Calmed Madame but my own nerves were too wrought
I am a peaceful man I wish a calm death
We are not rich people ourselves
Madame will have my insurance the funeral will be small
Why must they come dying in blood under our windows?
There is still firing HUSH MY DEAR they say
In Barcelona Asturias and in the hills.

September 30, 1934

[2]

Success Story

Ride me around in your big blue car.
Where shall we eat tonight? At Maxie's.
Afterwards, the premiere. The dress-suit applause.
A quick scotch. And fast taxis.
Then Geraldine, smiling between the doors.
Thus our lives.

O the freedom of a thousand a week!

But those bigeyed on the curbs,
Those flattened against the restaurant windows,
Would they suspect
The agony of his wealth,
The soul hiding here and suffering under the starched shirt?
And the headaches, the constant depression,
The terrors of failure between rehearsal and opening night?

Of course there is my lawyer. 5 percent
    My agent. 10 percent
        My broker's fees.
The sleeplessness at night. I took a room with a river view.
    And the pains here, my heart, you know.
I'll leave. I must get away. What shall I do?
    Do you think I would like it in Mexico?

Let us unearth restaurants with mama's cooking
Drive the big cadillac through neighborhoods where we were
                                                young
Exercise the simple heart under the expensive tweed.
Nevertheless we must have twice a day
Nevertheless we must have three guest rooms and a car
Nevertheless, despising these,
    There are our agent's,
        Our lawyer's,
            Our doctor's,
                Our broker's fees.

                        January 24, 1939

Stanley Burnshaw

Mr. Tubbe's Morning Service
(Homage to T. S. Eliot)

The priceless Mr. Waldo Tubbe
And all his little Tubbes now dare
Approach the world they long to snub,
Well insulated with despair.

The junior Tubbes accost their sire:
"Haven't the masses gone too far,
Trying to soil us with the mire
Of vulgar, droll U.S.S.R.?"

Their ancient sage prepares to speak
In holy numbers presto-pronto:
Fused Hindu-Latin-Chinese-Greek,
The special Tubbey esperanto.

Whereon each pupil makes a wish.
And Bishop Tubbe prepares to drool
A priceless strain of gibberish
Concocted in the learned school.

While all the little Tubbes let pass
Secretions of orgasmic glee.
Tubbe father empties out a glass
Of quintessential poesy

Compounded by rare formulae
Of liquid siftings, while Laforgue's
And ghosts of other live men die
Once more in the scholastic morgues. . . .

But not to make small Tubbeys prate,
Hound, or horn him with discontent,

But wait—while father concentrate
In holy philosophic bent;

For he will find them magic toys—
This wizard of the cult, Despair—
Blinders for all his tender boys,
Protective from what's in the air.

While each one sobs in holy pains
Sweet inner masochisms storm,
And Waldo's philosophic strains
Of adolescence keep them warm.

November 13, 1934

H. H. Lewis

The Sweeter Our Fruits ...

It was said that oranges could not be
grown in the Soviet Union.
But there they are—
A new strain
Developed by cross breeding Horticulture to Socialism.

Where Wrangel's army was to defeat the Reds,
Now the citrus groves,
Triumphantly fruitful,
With golden death-rays,
Vanquish the ghouls of another wish-prediction.

There, O Massman,
Lift a festival beaker,
Drink
This tart sweetness of revenge
To the health of your comrades all over the world.

Behind clenched teeth
In hells of "democracy" and fascism,
We taste
What you taste,
Your joy
Is our joy—
Of the inspiriting example.

Before 1918 we were "visionaries,"
Socialism "against human nature,"
But now
We point
To Red Russia.

The sweeter our fruits,
The bitterer to profiteers.

March 9, 1937

James Agee

Sunday: Outskirts of Knoxville, Tenn.

*There, in the earliest and chary spring, the
    dogwood flowers.*

*Unharnessed in the friendly sunday air
By the red brambles, on the river bluffs,
Clerks and their choices pair.*

*Thrive by, not near, masked all away by
    shrub and juniper,
The ford v eight, racing the chevrolet.*

They can not trouble her:

*Her breasts, helped open from the afforded
    lace,
Lie like a peaceful lake;
And on his mouth she breaks her gentleness:*

*Oh, wave them awake!
They are not of the birds. Such innocence
Brings us whole to break us only.
Theirs are not happy words.*

*We that are human cannot hope.
Our tenderest joys oblige us most.
No chain so cuts the bone; and sweetest
    silk most shrewdly strangles.*

*How this must end, that now please love were ended,
In kitchens, bedfights, silences, women's pages,
Sickness of heart before goldlettered doors,
Stale flesh, hard collars, agony in antiseptic corridors,
Spankings, remonstrances, fishing trips, orange juice,*

Policies, incapacities, a chevrolet,
Scorn of their children, kind contempt exchanged,
Recalls, tears, second honeymoons, pity,
Shouted corrections of missed syllables,

Hot water bags, gallstones, falls down stairs,
Stammerings, soft foods, confusion of personalities,
Oldfashioned christmases, suspicious of theft,
Arrangements with morticians taken care of by sons in law,
Small rooms beneath the gables of brick bungalows,
The tumbler smashed, the glance between daughter and
      husband,
The empty body in the lonely bed
And, in the empty concrete porch, blown ash
Grandchildren wandering the betraying sun

Now, on the winsome crumbling shelves of the horror
God show, God blind these children!

September 14, 1937

David Wolff

A Summer Night

The wind wheels over Manhattan like an enemy
storming, and we wake before dawn in the midst of bombard-
*   ment,*
turning our heads from the beams of lightning, searchlight of
*   death.*

Then like newsreel on the flashing wall, from Shanghai
floating in conquered creek toward the dark ceiling, the eyes
* of uniformed soldiers, puffed with decay, the shocking smile.*

Long rains of childhood return in the hush of rain,
and the morning twenty years gone, the shouts in the wet
*   doorway:*
War At Last and our men over cloudy ocean marching in
*   parade.*

Wavering years: the mind burning and our hands unsatisfied
*   ever:*
gripping from job to job, in escape or search;
the children grown out of war and restless to return.

Helmet and muddy cheek, the grenade poised to throw,
natural we'll stand at last, watching in the man-deep furrow,
the explosive fountains, the shrapnel flowers with
*   instantaneous growth;*

The hateful stance, the habit of bayonets, the doomed
gasping in deadly landscape, and the imagined wound
darkening the sheets while the pulse of guns still thunders in
*   the shallow room.*

You gave no choice, Oh shouting rulers, so we learned none,
brave by routine, we'll come to pollute your brilliant guns,
your stadia, and your microphones—with your blood.
*   January 11, 1938*

Federico García Lorca

Translated by Langston Hughes

[1]

Ballad of One Doomed

Loneliness without end!
The little eyes of my body
and the big eyes of my horse
never close at night
nor look the other way
where sleep like three boats
tranquilly disappears
in the distance.

Instead, shields of wakefulness,
my eyes, clean and hard,
look toward a north of metals
and of cliffs
where my veinless body
consults frozen cards.
Heavy water-oxen charge
boys who bathe in the moons
of their waving horns.
And the hammers sing
on the somnambulous anvils
of the insomnia of the horseman,
and the insomnia of the horse.

The twenty-fifth of June
they said to Amargo,
    Now you can cut if you wish
    the oleanders in your courtyard.
    Paint a cross on the door
    and put your name beneath it,

for hemlock and nettle
shall take root in your side,
and the waters of wet lime
eat at your shoe-leather
at night in the dark
in the mountains of magnet
where water-oxen drink
of the dreaming reeds.
Ask for lights and bells.
Learn to cross your hands
and love the cold air
of metals and of cliffs
because within two months
you'll lie down shrouded.
Santiago moves his starry
sword in the air.
Heavy with silence, behind him
the bent sky flows.
The twenty-fifth of June
Amargo opened his eyes
and the twenty-fifth of August
he lay down to close them.
Men came down the street
to look upon the marked one
who hung on the wall
his loneliness without end.
And the impeccable sheet
with its hard Roman accent
gave death a balance
by the straightness
of its folds.

January 11, 1938

[2]

The Faithless Wife

I took her to the river
thinking she was single,
but she had a husband.

It was the night of Santiago
and almost because I'd promised.
They put out the street lights
and lit up the crickets.
At the farthest corners
I touched her sleeping breasts
and they opened for me
quickly like bouquets of hyacinths.
The starch of her underskirts
rustled in my ears
like a piece of silk
slit by ten knives.
With no silvery light on their crowns
the trees have grown bigger
while a horizon of dogs bark
off by the river.

Beyond the brambles,
the rushes and the hawthornes
beneath their mat of hair
I made a hole on the slippery bank.
I took off my tie.
She took off her dress.
I, my belt with the pistol.
She, the four parts of her bodice.
Neither lilies nor snail shells
have such lovely skin,
nor do the crystals of the moon
shine with such a light.
Half full of fire
and half full of cold,
her thighs slip away from me
like frightened fish.

That night ran off
down the best of roads
on a mother-of-pearl colt
with no bridle and no stirrups.
Being a man, I can't tell you
the things that she told me.
The light of understanding
has made me very careful.

Soiled with kisses and sand
I took her from the river
while the swords of the lilies
battled with the air.

I acted like the true
gypsy that I am,
and gave her a present of a work-box
of straw-colored satin,
but I didn't want to love her
because, being married,
she told me she was single
when I took her to the river.

January 11, 1938

[3]

The Gypsy Nun

Silence of lime and myrtle.
Mallow among the herbs.
The nun embroiders gilliflowers
on a straw-colored cloth.
Seven rainbow birds
fly through gray spider webs.
The church groans in the distance
like a bear on its back.
How well she embroiders!
With what grace!
On the straw-colored cloth
she puts flowers of her fancy.
What a sunflower!
What magnolias of spangles and ribbons!
What saffron and what moons
on the cloth for the mass!
Five grapefruits sweeten
in a nearby kitchen.
The five wounds of Christ
cut in Almeria.
In the eyes of the nun
two horsemen gallop.

A far-off final rumor
tears open her shirt-front,
and at the sight of clouds and mountains
in the distant stillness
her heart of sweet herbs and sugar
breaks. Oh!
What a steep plain
with twenty suns above!
What rivers stand on tiptoe
to glimpse her fantasies.
But she keeps on with her flowers
while the light in the breeze
plays a game of chess
at her high grilled window.

January 11, 1938

[4]

Ballad of the Spanish Civil Guard

Their horses are black.
Black are their iron shoes.
On their capes shimmer stains
of ink and wax.
They have, and so they never weep,
skulls of lead.
With patent-leather souls
they come down the road.
Wherever they pass they spread
silences of thick rubber
and rears of fine sand.
They go by, if they wish to go,
concealing in their heads
a vague astronomy
of abstract pistols.

Oh, city of the gypsies!
On the corners, banners,
The moon and pumpkins
preserved with gooseberries.
Oh, city of the gypsies!

Who could see you and not remember you?
City of grief and of musk
with towers of cinnamon.
When the night that came
nightly came nightly,
the gypsies in their forges
made suns and arrows.
A horse with a mortal wound
went from one door to another.
Glass roosters crowed
toward Jerez de la Frontera.
The naked wind turns
the corner in surprise
in the night-silver night
that nightly comes nightly.

San José and the Virgin
loose their castanets
and come looking for the gypsies
to see if they can find them.
The Virgin comes dressed
in her village finery
of chocolate paper
and necklaces of almonds.
San José swings his arms
under a silken cape.
Behind comes Pedro Domecq
With three sultans of Persia.

The half moon dreams
an ecstasy of cranes.
Banners and torches
invade the roof-tops.
In the looking glasses sob
dancers who have no hips.
Water and shadow, shadow and water
toward Jerez de la Frontera.
Oh, city of the gypsies!
On the corners, banners.
Put out your green lights
for the Civil Guards are coming.
Oh, city of the gypsies!

Who could see you and not remember you?
Leave her far off from the sea
with no combs for her hair.

Two by two they come
to the city of fiesta.
A rustle of siemprevivas
invades their cartridge belts.
Two by two they come.
A night of double thickness.
To them the sky is nothing
but a window full of spurs.

Fear ran wild in a city
that multiplied its door.
Through them came forty Civil Guards
bent on pillage.
The clocks all stopped
and the cognac in the bottles
put on their November mask
to invite no suspicions.
A flight of screams unending
rose among the weather-vanes.
Sabers cut the air
that the horses trampled.
Through the dusky streets
old gypsy women
flew with drowsy nags
and crocks of money.
Up the steep streets
the sinister capes mount,
followed by fugitive
whirlwinds of scissors.

At the Gate of Belen
the gypsies gather.
San José, full of wounds,
shrouds a young maiden.
All through the night
stubborn guns sound sharply.
The Virgin treats the children
with drops of small saliva.

But the Civil Guard
advances sowing fires
where imagination burns
young and naked.
Rosa de los Camborios
sobs on her doorstep
with two breasts cut away
and put on a platter.
And other girls flee
pursued by their tresses
through the air where the roses
of black dust explode.
When the roof-tops are no more
than furrows on the earth,
dawn rocks her shoulders
in a long profile of stone.

Oh, city of the gypsies!
As the flames draw near
the Civil Guard goes off
down a tunnel full of silence.
Oh, city of the gypsies!
Who could see you and not remember you?
Let them look for you on my forehead,
game of the sand and the moon.

March 1, 1938

Sol Funaroff

To the Dead of the International Brigade

Let me break down foundations of the earth
and speak to you in the dust
as the wind speaks in the dust,
as the dust is carried in the wind
and the wind makes a speech of it.

Listen to me who hold you in memory
as a sky holds a cloud, tenderly,
as the earth holds you, eternally,
bearing each Spring green remembrances.

January 3, 1939

Ruth Lechlitner

Forever This Spring

This Spring let the world keep out, we said, alone
Our feet to the path over the woodmint,
The red-tipped moss, and ours the single flower
Lovely under stone.

But here before us the hazel boughs are broken,
The coiled fern flattened by the invader's heel,
The hot spoor on the crushed leaf marking the course
That terror has taken.

When buds split and willow strikes like a whip at the heart,
When the hard fire at earth's core rolls
In green flame against the destroyers
How shall we walk apart?

The defenders too are among us; those who command
The blade of the quick fern, pattern the changing season,
Reshape the leaf and bind the bough
With a healer's hand;

And those who have fallen are with us: they shall inherit
Forever this Spring when the stars of bloodroot burn,
When light draws from the shadow of running water
The promised violet.

March 14, 1939

Judd Polk

Our House Divided by Itself

It's easy. This is how.
Count all the people, carefully, one at a time.
Ask questions. Record answers. For instance,
if they make less than a living, mark it.
Mark it if they make more.
If they have a radio, check radio.
If a house, check house.
Similarly rooms, bathrooms, frigidaires.
If they rent, how much?
How old a man is, whether he's married,
how many times he's been blessed with kids, etc.

All these things count. Count them.
Put them all into the machines.
Start the wheels working. Wait.
It will take a while, but wait.
It has to be coded, carded, counted, combed,
raised to the highest power, purged of mean roots.
The radical signs have to be removed.
In short, it has to be averaged, plain divided up.

No one will come off unfairly.
Names don't count, everyone is the same.
Nobody will be left aged or sick.
Everybody gets some kids.
Only an average hunger is left in the land.
Everybody gets a fraction of a job,
to support a fraction of a family,
in a good-sized fraction of a house.

No bloodshed, no plots, no hard feelings.
No taking over of the telephone exchanges.
This is the wisdom of the founding fathers.
It's right in the constitution.
It happens every ten years.
It's easy.

September 10, 1940

Genevieve Taggard

Ode in Time of Crisis

Now in the fright of change when bombed towns vanish
In fountains of debris
We say to the stranger coming across the sea
Not here, not here, go elsewhere!
Here we keep
Bars up. Wall out the danger, tightly seal
The ports, the intake from the alien world we fear.

It is a time of many errors now.
And this the error of children when they feel
But cannot say their terror. To shut off the stream
In which we moved and still move, if we move.
The alien is the nation, nothing more nor less.
How set ourselves at variance to prove
The alien is not the nation. And so end the dream.
Forbid our deep resource from whence we came,
And the very seed of greatness.

This is to do
Something like suicide; to choose
Sterility—forget the secret of our past
Which like a magnet drew
A wealth of men and women hopeward. And now to lose
In ignorant blindness what we might hold fast.

The fright of change, not readiness. Instead
Inside our wall we will today pursue
The man we call the alien, take his print,
Give him a taste of the thing from which he fled,
Suspicion him. And again we fail.
How shall we release his virtue, his good-will
If by such pressure we hold his life in Jail?
The alien is the nation. Nothing else.

And so we fail and so we jail ourselves.
Landlocked, the stagnant stream.
So ends the dream.

O countrymen, are we working to undo
Our lusty strength, our once proud victory?
Yes, if by this fright we break our strength in two.
If we make of every man we jail the enemy.
If we make ourselves the jailer locked in jail.
Our laboring wills, our brave, too brave to fail
Remember this nation by millions believed to be
Great and of mighty forces born, and resolve to be free,
To continue and renew.

(Written for the New York City Conference for Protection of Foreign Born.)

October 29, 1940

Henri Barbusse   GEORGES SCHREIBER

"We are gathered here to protest the unconstitutionality of the anti-lynching bill."

A job for United Labor

MISCHA RICHTER

2
Short Stories
and Sketches

FRED ELLIS

"They say he owns 25 sweatshops but he never perspires."

"Look glum, Everett—we're supposed to be making money!"

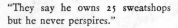

"Well! Well! And how's the Giant of Wall Street today?"

"Look, Humphries—the ideal type for the union organizer."

The Ruling Clawss

A. REDFIELD

M. Shulimson

On the Move

No snow fell and there was no wind. It was cold and it was all over. It was cold in doorways. It was consistent. You could not turn your back on it. There was no wind. There was just a little snow on the ground, but it was hard. No snow fell. You could not walk backwards against it. You could not escape it in the doorways. There was no changing in its intensity. It did not bite. It lay on you and around you and you could not run from it.

The old guy told me not to put on the light because a bunch of guys were sleeping inside. I came in and walked over to an empty cot. There was just enough light coming from the street to see it. I sat down and began unlacing my boots. A couple of them were whispering. One guy kept coughing and another was chewing tobacco. The fellow lying next to me said: "Better take another cot, bud, there's a suitcase under this cot and if it's missing they'll blame you for it." I said: "Thanks," and found another cot. I slept in my pants, holding my boots in one hand and coat in the other. In the morning as I was going out, one of the fellows, sleeping in the top bed of the double decker, said: "Ya mind passing up that butt?" There was a small butt laying on the floor with pools of spit around it. I gave him one of my cigarettes. He said: "Thanks, bud, mind passing up that butt, too?" I gave him the butt.

There was a bunch of us in the men's room in the railroad station. A couple of guys were trying to sleep on the benches. There was an old drunk who looked as if he'd had a couple of cuspidors emptied on him. I leaned against a radiator. After a while a couple of cops came in. One of 'em said: "All right, boys, break it up! Break it up!" and began pushing the guys out. I beat it into the can. I was pretty cold and wanted to stick around. One of the cops came in. I stood over a latrine. He stood behind me. After a while he said: "Okeh, bud, long enough, you've broken all the records already." I had to laugh at that. I buttoned my pants and went out of the station. I began walking again.

She was sitting on the stoop. When I walked by she crossed her legs showing her thighs and winked. I walked over to her. She said: "How about it, hon?" I said: "Christ, kid, if I had any dough I'd rather eat." She said: "Gee, it's tough to be hungry. If you want to come upstairs, I'll give you a cup of coffee and something." She was pretty bashful when she said that. I said: "Thanks, kid, I'd be glad to get a cup of coffee." She had a little kitchen and fixed me up a couple of eggs and a cup of coffee. She said: "I hate to rush you, kid, but somebody might be along soon." I ate fast and thanked her. She said: "You go downstairs first." When I came to the corner I turned and looked back. She was sitting on the stoop again. I waved to her and she waved back. I began walking again.

The little guy ran in, and the pastor hollered: "Louder." We began singing a little louder. His wife came in with three ladies and a guy in spats. They sat in the back awhile and listened. The little guy walked up the aisle whispering: "Don't look around." We sang four hymns and the pastor gave us a spiel with smiles. After a while the ladies and the guy with spats went out, and they let us flop.

The guy standing next to me against the radiator said: "I'm hopping the next train into the big city, kid. Want to come with me?"

I said: "No; it's too damn cold." A while after I heard some one say that a guy had just been killed in the yard. A redcap went into the can. I followed him and standing next to him with a partition between us so he couldn't see my clothes. I said: "What's this about a guy getting killed out in the yard, Redcap?"

He said: "Somebody hopped a freight and slipped between the cars, Mister. I've never seen anything like it. The train went right over him and cut him lengthwise, like this." He swept his hand down his body. "They don't know who he was," he said.

I didn't either.

I sat on a bench. They'd just swept the station. Some guy started looking for a butt. The floor was pretty clean. All of a sudden he dived under a bench and came up with a butt.

It was only about a half-inch long. He looked at it a while and threw it away. He was sore as hell and swore. I had to laugh. He looked at me. I said: "Tough, brother; tough." He smiled.

I was watching them. A cop knocked a sign out of a guy's hand. I picked it up. It said: "Work or wages." When I lifted it up some guy in plain clothes hit me on the head with a blackjack, and I went down. It felt funny, because I saw stars just like they have in the funny pictures. Then somebody kicked me. I started to get up and some girl helped me. The crowd had moved over a little. I got up and felt weak. We walked over a couple of blocks and I said: "I got to sit down." I sat down on a doorstep. My head felt swollen. I tried to vomit, but nothing came up. She tried to get my cap off and I hollered. The cap was stuck to my head by the blood. She said: "You shouldn't wear anything on your head, Comrade, it always gets stuck." I said: "I guess you're right, Comrade." And the sound of the word "Comrade" felt swell against my teeth.

You get shoved out early; you get your coffee and start walking. A couple of hours before noon you get in line. You eat and start walking. At night you flop where you can. You don't talk. You eat what you can. You sleep where you can. You walk. No one talks to you. You walk. It's cold, and you shiver and stand in doorways or sit in railroad stations. You don't see much. You forget. You walk an hour and forget where you started from. It is day, and then it's night, and then it's day again. And you don't remember which was first. You walk. There are men with fat on them, and you know it. There are lean men and you know it.

You walk. You are dead, and you know it. Something must happen and nothing does. Something must happen, and you know it. No one speaks to you. If you are to live again, something must happen, and you know it. If you are to live again, there must be revolution, and you know it.

You don't talk.

January 23, 1934

Langston Hughes

Mother and Child

"Ain't nobody seen it," said old lady Lucy Doves. "Ain't nobody seen it, but the midwife and the doctor—and her husband, I reckon. They say she won't let a soul come in the room. But it's still living, cause Mollie Ransom heard it crying. And the woman from Downsville what attended the delivery says it's as healthy a child as she ever seed, indeed she did."

"Well, it's a shame," said Sister Wiggins, "it's here. I been living in Boyd's Center for twenty-two years, at peace with these white folks; ain't had no trouble yet, till this child was born—now look at 'em. Just look what's goin' on! People acting like a pack o' wolves."

"Poor little brat. He ain't been in the world a week yet," said Mrs. Sam Jones, taking off her hat, "and done caused more trouble than all the rest of us in a lifetime. I was born here, and I ain't never seen the white folks up in arms like they are today. But they don't need to think they can walk over Sam and me—for we owns our land, it's bought and paid for, and we sends our children to school. Thank God, this is Ohio. It ain't Mississippi."

"White folks is white folks, honey, South or North, North or South," said Lucy Doves. "I's lived both places and I know."

"Yes, but in Mississippi they'd lynched Douglass by now."

"Where is Douglass?" asked Mattie Crane. "You all know I don't know much about this mess. Way back yonder on that farm where I lives, you don't get nothing straight. Where is Douglass?"

"Douglass is here! Saw him just now in the field doin' his spring plowin' when I drove de road, as stubborn and bold-faced as he can be. We told him he ought to leave here."

"Well, I wish he'd go on and get out," said Sister Wiggins.

"If that would help any. His brother's got more sense than he has, even if he is a seventeen-year-old child. Clarence left here yesterday and went to Cleveland. But their ma, poor Sister Carter, she's still trying to battle it out. She told me last night, though, she thinks she'll have to leave. They won't let her have no more provisions at de general store. And they ain't got their spring seed yet. And they can't pay cash for 'em."

"Don't need to tell me! Old man Hartman's got evil as de rest of the white folks. Didn't he tell ma husband Saturday night he'd have to pay up every cent of his back bill, or he couldn't take nothing out of that store. And we been trading there for years."

"That's their way o' striking back at us niggers."

"Yes, but Lord knows my husband ain't de father o' that child."

"Nor mine."

"Jim's got too much pride to go foolin' round any old loose white woman."

"Child, you can't tell about men."

"I knowed a case once in Detroit where a nigger lived ten years with a white woman, and her husband didn't know it. He was their chauffeur."

"That's all right in the city, but please don't come bringing it out here to Boyd's Center where they ain't but a handful o' us colored—and we has a hard enough time as it is."

"You right! This sure has brought the hammer down on our heads."

"Lawd knows we're law-biding people, ain't harmed a soul, yet some o' these white folks talking 'bout trying to run all de colored folks out o' de county on account o' Douglass."

"They'll never run me," said Mrs. Sam Jones.

"Don't say what they *won't* do," said Lucy Doves, "cause they might."

"Howdy, Sister Jenkins."

"Howdy!"

"Good evenin'."

"Yes, de meetin's due to start directly."

"Soon as Madam President arrives. Reckon she's having trouble gettin' over that road from High Creek."

"Sit down and tell us what you's heard, Sister Jenkins."

"About Douglass?"

"Course 'bout Douglass. What else is anybody talkin' 'bout nowadays?"

"Well, my daughter told me Douglass' sister say they was in love."

"Him and that white woman?"

"Yes. Douglass' sister say it's been going on 'fore de woman got married."

"Uh-huh! Then why didn't he stop foolin' with her after she got married? Bad enough, colored boy foolin' round a unmarried white woman, let alone a married one."

"Douglass' sister say they was in love."

"Well, why did she marry the white man, then?"

"She's white, ain't she? And who wouldn't marry a rich white man? Got his own farm, money and all, even if he were a widower with grown children gone to town. He give her everything she wanted, didn't he?"

"Everything but the right thing."

"Well, she must not o' loved him, sneaking round meeting Douglass in de woods."

"True."

"But what you reckon she went on and had that colored baby for?"

"She must a thought it was the old man's baby."

"She don't think so now! Mattie say when the doctor left and they brought the child in to show her, she like to went blind. It were near black as me."

"Do tell!"

"And what did her husband say!"

"Don't know. Don't know."

"He must a fainted."

"That old white woman what lives cross the crick from us said he's gonna put her out soon's she's able to walk."

"Ought to put her out!"

"Maybe that's what Douglass waitin' for."

"I heard he wants to take her away."

"He better take his fool self away 'fore these white folks get madder. Ain't nobody heard it was a black baby till day before yesterday. Then it leaked out. And now de folks are rarin' to kill Douglass!"

"I sure am scared!"

"And how come they all said right away it were Douglass?"

"Honey, don't you know? Colored folks knowed Douglass

been eyeing that woman since God knows when, and she been eyeing back at him. You ought to seed 'em when they met in de store. Course they didn't speak no more'n Howdy, but their eyes followed one another 'round just like dogs."

"They was in love, I tell you. Been in love."

"Mighty funny kind o' love. Everybody knows can't no good come out o' white and colored love. Everybody knows that. And Douglass ain't no child. He's twenty-six years old, ain't he? And Sister Carter sure did try to raise her three chillun right. You can't blame her."

"Blame that fool boy, that's who, and that woman. Plenty colored girls in Camden he could of courted, ten miles up the road. One or two right here. I got a daughter myself."

"No, he had to go foolin' round with a white woman."

"Yes, a white woman."

"They say he loved her."

"What do Douglass say, since it happened?"

"He don't say nothing."

"What could he say?"

"Well, he needn't think he's gonna keep his young mouth shut and let de white folks take it out on us. Down yonder at de school today, my Dorabelle says they talkin' 'bout separatin' de colored from de white and makin' all de colored children go in a nigger room next term."

"Ain't nothing like that ever happened in Boyd's Center long as I been here—these twenty-two years."

"White folks is mad now, child, mad clean through."

"Wonder they ain't grabbed Douglass and lynched him."

"It's a wonder!"

"And him calmly out yonder plowin' de field this afternoon."

"He sure is brave."

"Woman's husband liable to kill him."

"Her brother's done said he's gunning for him."

"They liable to burn Negroes' houses down."

"Anything's liable to happen. Lawd, I'm nervous as I can be."

"You can't tell about white folks."

"I ain't nervous. I'm scared."

"Don't say a word!"

"Why don't Sister Carter make him leave here?"

"I wish I knew."

"She told me she were nearly crazy."

"And she can't get Douglass to say nothin', one way or another—if he go, or if he stay—Howdy, Madame President."

"I done told you Douglass loves her."

"He wants to see that white woman, once more again, that's what he wants."

"A white hussy!"

"He's foolin' with fire."

"Poor Mis' Carter. I'm sorry for his mother."

"Poor Mis' Carter."

"Why don't you all say poor Douglass? Poor white woman? Poor child?"

"Madame President's startin' de meetin'."

"Is it boy or girl?"

"Sh-s-s-s! There's de bell."

"I hear it's a boy."

"Thank God, ain't a girl then."

"I hope it looks like Douglass, cause Douglass a fine-looking nigger."

"He's too bold, too bold."

"Shame he's got us all in this mess."

"Shame, shame, shame!"

"Sh-sss-sss!"

"Yes, indeedy!"

"Sisters, can't you hear this bell?"

"Shame!"

"Sh-sss!"

"Madame Secretary, take your chair."

"Shame!"

"The March meeting of the Salvation Rock Ladies' Missionary Society for the Rescue o' the African Heathen is hereby called to order.... Sister Burns, raise a hymn.... Will you-all ladies *please be quiet?* What are you talking 'bout back there anyhow?"

May 15, 1934

Albert Halper

A Morning with the Doc

The doc is a big, heavy man in his early forties and has a big, heavy face. He was in the Army during the war and something happened to his feet there in the trenches, and now when he walks it always looks as though his shoes are a bit too tight for him. Before the depression, he had a good neighborhood practice among the lower middle class on the West Side of the city, but since bad times had hit Chicago, his practice has fallen off to almost nothing, so that now in the afternoons he has a lot of time to read the sporting sections of all the evening papers and also glance through the medical journals which the association keeps on sending him.

In the morning, however, the doc is a busy man. He makes the rounds of about seven or eight public lower grade schools and also gives toxoids to infants. He works for the city in the morning. He's a health officer, a civil service man. He hasn't been paid for over nine months, but he keeps on the job. He keeps on the job, even though he grumbles. "I'm just an old draught horse," he told me. He and I have been good friends for a long time, ever since the old days when he lanced boils on the back of my neck and forgot to charge me, so when I returned to Chicago I went up to see him to find out how he was getting along.

I called early in the morning because it looked like rain, and his wife gave us breakfast and we sat around. We sat in his little office and I saw that dust had gathered on his books and on his furniture. The rug on the floor was old and the ribbon in his typewriter had frayed threads sticking out. I saw that he had changed a lot since I had seen him last. There was something heavy about him. His blond crinkly hair still frizzled up around his ears, his eyes were still small and blue, but his mouth was different. His mouth gave one the impression that he had been steadily smoking a lot of cheap, strong cigars.

Finally he looked at the little clock on his desk. "Well, I gotta get going," he said to me. "I've gotta make the morning rounds," and he stood up. "If you've got nothing to do, you can come along."

We went down to the street, got into his old 1928 Dodge sedan and the doc slammed the door. Just before he stepped in, I saw, as his big rear end raised high in the air, that the back of his overcoat was worn down as shiny as gloss.

The car bumped hard going up the street. There were huge holes in the asphalt and the doc told me they had been there for a long, long time. "You've come home to a bankrupt town," he told me and started cursing every politician who had ever put his foot inside the City Hall. In ten minutes, speaking grumpily, in snatches, he told me facts about departmental scandals which every civil service worker in Chicago knows, but which rarely gets into the Chicago papers. And when I mentioned the name of a high public official who had been assassinated down in the South, the doc laughed. "That crook? Did you ever hear of the deal he pulled off on the People's Forest Preserve? He made more than a million on it. And his relatives are sprinkled on every directors' board in town. That crook?" and he laughed again. The doc has a very expressive way of laughing sometimes which saves him a lot of talking.

He was still smiling hard about the mouth as we entered the first school on his list. We went through a side door and into the principal's office. "I'll have to fake your name," he told me, "because maybe it's against the rules to have you along." So when he went into the office he introduced me as Doctor Hall from New York. "He's an old friend of mine," the doc said to the principal.

As soon as we entered the office the principal's secretary got up and pressed a button and then I heard a bell ring through the building. The doc took a key from the wall and we went into another room. Pretty soon I heard a steady tramp of feet and in another minute a long line of little kids entered, forming quietly and standing without making any noise. There must have been about sixty of them. The doc took his hat off and sat down at a desk in his overcoat. As the kids approached, they stuck out their tongues, showed him their hands and waited for him to give them little slips of paper with his name signed on them. They were kids who had been absent from school on account of sickness and had to have the doc's okay.

They passed him slowly. The doc looked at their throats, their hands, behind their ears, their necks. Most of the kids were pale and scrawny. They came up quietly, a little frightened, holding out their little hands. The doc likes children and children like him, but as they came up to the desk I saw they were afraid of him. He passed a few on, then stopped one little kid.

"When did you eat last?" he asked. The doc has a low, gruff way of speaking and the kid couldn't talk. Finally he mumbled something. He had a large head which dropped like a heavy flower on a thin stem, and he looked very tired. The doc scribbled an address on a piece of paper and gave it to the kid. "Tell your mother to go to that address for relief tickets. You go home and stay home for three days. Understand?" The kid walked away and when he reached the door he started crying. The others stood more quiet than ever. I could see, as they stuck out their tongues, that most of the tongues were spotty. A great many kids had rashes behind their ears. The doc kept busy scribbling on the little pieces of paper.

When the last kid filed by, the doc closed the door, hung the key on the wall of the office and we went out. The principal, before we left, asked me how conditions were among the teachers and school doctors of New York. He told me that the Chicago teachers were way behind in their pay checks, and he looked sort of tired and helpless as he said it.

Our next stop was another school where the doc again introduced me as Doctor Hall from New York, and after the third or fourth school it got to be like a routine. Everything was the same. We came in, the doc took a key from the wall, the principal's secretary rang a bell and then the little kids came filing in, holding out their little hands for the doc to inspect, looking frightened and standing in line without making a noise. And the more I stared at them as I saw them coming up toward the desk, the more I felt I was looking at a bunch of little old people. It's hard to explain that feeling, but that's the best I can put it. I guess it was their skinny necks that gave me that impression.

At half past ten we had finished the schools, the doc sat down in his shiny overcoat and made out a report on three long sheets of paper, and then we started on the toxoid calls. During most of this time the doc didn't talk much to me. I hadn't seen him for over four years and you'd think he'd want to ask me questions and find out what was happening in the East, but he didn't seem much interested. He sat with his soft plump hands upon the steering wheel as the old Dodge went bumping along the street. He didn't feel like talking and he was honest enough not to fake conversation. I liked him for that.

Before we got out to make the first toxoid call, he opened his bag in his car and made sure he had all his supplies. We had stopped before a small, lopsided cottage near the rail-road tracks.

"Should I come in with you?" I asked the doc.

"Sure, why not?" he said.

So I went inside with him. A woman's face had appeared at a window and the door opened for us right away. The woman held a kid in her arms, a child of about three, a little girl. The woman was short and stumpy and looked Polish. As soon as we entered the kid began to scream. The doc didn't pay any attention to it. He walked past the woman and opened his bag in the kitchen where the light was good, and all the while the kid kept screaming. The doc was making his second appearance; he had given her the needle for the first time a few weeks ago, and the kid hadn't forgotten. The mother came back into the kitchen and, while the kid was screaming, she held its little arm firmly and the doc gave the shot quickly, expertly, drawing the needle out as only physicians who give hundreds of toxoids monthly know how to draw it out. We passed through the rooms, heading for the door. The woman thanked the doc in broken English, then patted her child who had calmed down to a whimper. It was all done briefly. The doc hadn't even taken his hat off.

We drove another block and made our second call. The second flat was full of babies and when we made our exit a trail of bawling kids was scattered throughout the rooms. The mothers couldn't bear the sight of the doc sticking in the needle, so I held the little arms while the doc turned the trick. The doc, glancing at my face, saw that I didn't care much for the job. I had begun to sweat, standing in hat and overcoat. I took my hat off, laid it on a table.

"Put it on again," he barked at me. "Put it on. Never take off your hat in these homes, you don't know what you'll pick up, bedbugs, lice, anything." I put my hat on again. When we went out the mothers, who had been standing in another room, thanked us, tears trembling in their eyes. "Are they all right, will they be safe from sickness now?"

"Sure, sure," said the doc gruffly and we went out.

We went from home to home, giving the toxoids. We cut down side streets and over carlines. Such unrelieved poverty I had never seen before, even in Manhattan's East Side tenements. I now knew why the doc's mouth looked as though he had smoked too many cheap, strong cigars. It was horrifying. We saw families living together, four or five pads and soiled mattresses lying on the floor, kids with that plump, humid, indoor look on their faces, their mouths slightly opened as if to suck in some air, a few scratches of firewood piled up in the corner, wrapping paper tacked up for window shades. We came in together, the doc and I, without saying a word, and the doc would lay out his bag upon a table, and as he'd measure out a shot and the kids saw the needle, the squalid rooms would fairly burst with screaming. It drove the mothers frantic, but when it was over they thanked us. They followed us to the door, asking if the children would be all right now, if they would be safe from sickness now. The doc never answered half of them. He merely gave a curt nod which they may or may not have seen. He went out, walking with that walk of his, as though his shoes were a bit too tight. Then he got into the car, slammed the door and we drove off.

In some of the homes we found men hanging around, though it was still fairly early in the day. As soon as we came in, the men would get up and go into another room and we wouldn't see them any more. They slunk off ashamed. They did not want us to see their defeat and unemployment. Most of them must have been out of work two, three, maybe four years, but they were still a bit ashamed of not being able to land a job. So they got up quietly when we came in, hid themselves in the bedrooms, and didn't come out until we were gone.

But though we left so much pain and wailing behind us,

there was no ill feeling toward us. The women would lift up their babies, crooning and soothing them. "It's good for you, the doctor has got to do it," and afterwards the kids would start their terrified screaming. Some of the women frankly could not stand the sight and left us, pressing their palms against their ears, until the job was finished. But I saw that all of them respected the doc. I saw it in their eyes. They saw his heavy, plodding, silent figure. They knew he was honest. They knew he was only doing what he thought was best. They read the papers and knew, also, that he hadn't gotten a cent in over nine months, and here he was plodding on, using up his tires and gasoline, walking up and down smelly hallways, brushing bugs from his coat as he passed their furniture.

At the last call we ran into a lot of trouble. It was almost noon and the doc, who is a regular eater, was getting grouchy. He still performed his job with all the skill at his command, but he always got tired out around a quarter to twelve or so.

The last toxoid we gave was to a boy of eight. He was a skinny gangling kid and he lay sick in bed. We had to climb four flights to get to him, and the doc was puffing when we reached the top. After all, he's over forty, weighs a full two hundred, and his service in France didn't do his feet any good. We went along a dark narrow hall and then the doc knocked. As soon as he knocked, we could hear the kid inside start screaming. We hadn't shown ourselves, but the kid, by some sixth sense, knew the doc had come. A little worried woman in her late thirties, her hair disordered, opened the door. She let us in. The kid, out of sight, began screaming louder than ever. As the doc laid out his bag, the woman went into another room and brought out another kid, a chubby little boy of two. The mother rolled the child's sleeve and the kid began to smile. The doc spoke soothingly. The kid's smile grew broader than ever. It was beautiful. He still was innocent. It was the first shot. He looked at the needle and began to gurgle. Then—zip, the job was done, as quick as a twinkling, and then he began to wail. Hearing him bawl, the older brother of eight began chewing on his bed sheets. The doc looked at him. I could see his jaw tighten. He went forward with another needle in his hand. I am not trying to make this gruesome. But there was something terrifying about the whole business. The kid, in bed, backed up against the wall like a cornered tiger.

The woman began to plead with him. "I'll give you a nickel, a nickel," she said. "Only let the doctor do it."

The kid backed further up against the wall and screamed bloody murder. It was terrible. He was such a young, gangly-looking terrified kid. As he rose, we saw his dirty underwear, his dirty drawers.

"I'll hold him," said his mother, but she couldn't. Then she lost her patience. She began to scream at him. "I'll give you a nickel, a nickel, a nickel!" She got her purse and opened it. She didn't have a cent. I reached down in my pocket and gave her a nickel. "See? The other doctor is giving you a nickel. A nickel, a nickel, a nickel!"

But it wasn't of any use. I reached down and gave the woman another nickel. "See? Two nickels, two nickels!" But you couldn't get around that kid. Where he got that lung capacity nobody knows. He was almost blue in the face. The doc saw he had to act fast. Besides, it was almost noon now and he was getting grouchy. He turned to me.

"You grab him," he said. "You used to be a wrestler, apply a hold he can't break."

So I grabbed him. He shouted and scratched out, but I grabbed him. He had the strength of ten fiends, but I grabbed him. I brought him forward, put a foot-lock about his legs to keep him from kicking me and a double arm-lock about his arms to keep his arms steady for the needle. The doc did it in a flash. The kid grew quiet. He began to whimper. The woman thanked me. She was perspiring all over. When we reached the hall, the kid realizing he had received the needle, began to scream harder than ever.

We rode home, the doc and I. The sun had gone. When we reached Ashland Avenue, a few drops of rain began to strike the car. The doc's quiet, plump hands lay heavy on the wheel. We were about four miles from his home. His wife had fixed him a lunch and he wanted to get there in a hurry. So he didn't talk much, not for the first mile or so. Then he began to open up. He spoke grumpily, in snatches. What he said came out of the depths of him. He was a big heavy man and he had a lot in his system. He cursed everything. He cursed quietly, savagely, and the fact that in rainy weather his feet hurt him more did not add to his good humor. The rain began to slant across the glass.

The car hit a deep hole and we both banged our heads against the top of the sedan. The doc swore. His face took on a slowly boiled look.

"They won't stand much more," he said. "You can't keep a rag over their eyes forever. There's too much surplus food and clothing lying around and some day they'll wake up to the fact that all they have to do is to reach out and take it."

Just then we hit another, deeper hole and the doc turned savagely on me. "Now a man doesn't have to be a prophet or a genius to guess what is going to happen! You can't keep stepping on people forever! They won't stand for it!"

May 15, 1934

William Saroyan

Prelude to an American Symphony

Sure he was bitter. Why shouldn't he be? All them fools talking their heads off, saying nothing. Them society people, burning him up. What the hell was he doing there in the first place? What the hell was he to them? A monkey maybe. A guy to be gawked at by society dames and their pals. All dressed up in slick black suits and patent leather shoes, dopes with dough, and no sense. The punks of the world, the rotten aristocracy. And he, he himself, standing in the God damn place, among all the cut glass and the sparkle, which stank, and taking it; not doing a thing about it.

Sure he was drunk. Why shouldn't he be drunk? What the hell was there to do in such a place? If you talked to one of them, anyone of them, it didn't matter who, why the crazy woman, or man, would make some flukey society remark in a society tone of voice and what the hell could you say back to them? You couldn't say anything to him. You could just be a little drunker than before and you could smile politely. They had him acting like a God damn monkey. Smiling when he didn't feel like smiling.

Maybe he was walking around like a fool, bumping into the big rumps of big ladies, the mamas, and bowing to the dull faces of the papas, but could he help it? What else was there to do? All they talked about was horse manure. It was worse and it smelled twice as lousy. Horse manure had a fine smell. He was a fellow from the street, why in Christ's name he had ever come to such a party he couldn't figure out. Not doing a thing about it. O no, not much, not for a while, maybe, but just wait till he got drunk enough. He'd do a thing or two. He'd make them shiver. He'd give them something to remember him by. The artistic people. They stank. He'd have four more drinks and ten minutes later he'd be ready to sail into them. Those young gals who were good for one thing, the what you call it, and for nothing else, and maybe not so very good for that either. Probably all dried-up anyway, most of them. Probably all worked out. Sure, they looked it. What eyes, what complexions, what hands, what bosoms, what wisdom. They were just plumb full of brilliance, and the way they laughed gave you a pain way down deep in the old pazaza.

Just one more drink and he'd be ready to let them know he came from the street and didn't care if he did because the street was a damn sight realer than they'd ever be. He'd tell them. Right up from the lousy gutter: no piano lessons, no fancy schools, just the old drive that got all the decent poor boys over: just the old anger and bitterness, and what he found out for himself. A fifty-dollar piano when he was ten, selling newspapers and playing all night, making up his own stuff, pounding hell out of the God damn thing, all out of tune, raising hell with the neighbors, keeping them awake, O'Hara's prelude, the Irishman's crazy overture, late at night, telling the old lady not to worry about him, he'd come out on top, he'd have them dizzy, he'd have them out of their senses with admiration, the stinkers, he'd have them inviting him to their swell parties, he'd be lying with their lovely daughters, his old woman wouldn't have to take in washing forever, her wild-eyed boy would turn part of the world up-side-down with his music, wait and see, ma, you just wait and see what I do before I get through with them punkos.

Playing his songs on every radio in the country, printing his picture in ten magazines every month, pouring gold all over him, offering him money for anything, any old thing you please, O'Hara, any old song you feel like writing, you're the boy who knows his stuff, you couldn't turn out a bad song if you tried, you got the stuff, and he was hauling it in: he was sitting on plenty: but they knew and he knew: he was from the street and what was more he wanted to remain that way. To hell with their horse manure.

Writing stories about him in the newspapers, in *Time*, in the *American Magazine*, that was the biggest laugh of all. Local boy makes good in Manhattan, ha ha. How I did it. Ha ha, I bought that piano with money I made selling papers and I didn't study a thing at school and I didn't obey my mother or my teachers and I told the whole world to take a flying you-know-what, and I learned to play the God damn thing like a baby learns to breathe after it is born, a good hard smack on the behind, and bingo, music, O'Hara's American Symphony, the real America at last, the only America, full of fire and insanity and rhythm, Negro, Jewish, Scotch, Irish, Bulgarian, German, ha ha, a little here, a little there, a little Brahms, a bit of a skyscraper, a little Bach, a little of Alabama, a little Beethoven, and a quart of gin, ha ha, and they went under it like the tunnel under the river, ha ha.

So they had him performing like a monkey, did they? They had him in fancy clothes, looking like another punko, did they? They had him in their fancy parlors, talking their horse crap, did they? Ha ha, he remembered the old lady, over the old washboard: a gangster to hang by his neck, or a genius: flip a coin, one or the other, trail along with the gang and wind up in the big house, or buy the piano and fight it alone: fight it in himself and in the old woman and in the world: make himself stand up big and make the woman believe and make the world bend: ten years old, fighting it out. The old woman thought he was nuts. A piano? Hardly enough to eat and he buys a piano. Wait, ma, for the love of Mike, wait: it won't take long: ten years, maybe twenty, but wait: you won't be over that God damn washboard all your life. I'll put you in the biggest house you ever saw. I'll buy you the finest car that's made. And he would have, too. Well, the old lady was dead. Maybe she was dead, but he wasn't. Maybe they killed her, but he was still alive, even if they were trying to make a monkey out of him. He was getting drunk enough to make them get things straight about him. He came from the street. He fought it out alone. Who in hell did they think *they* were?

This punko, for instance, talking with so much pride in himself, a wise guy, telling the ladies about business conditions. Stepped in what? He said. Got what in your eye?

O'Hara's such a comical fellow. Ha ha, they laughed. Stepped in what? They laughed.

N.R.A., he said. You know, bang bang, killing strikers. My next symphony, N.R.A. With a ballet of cooch dancers. You know, happy days with stomach wiggles. You know, capitalistic regeneration. One whole movement on the fatness of the rich. You know, a big belly laugh. Bang bang, killing the poor, so you can loll around in these dumps and arrange for sleeping together. One whole fornication movement: from A.

to Z. The way you do it. Funniest symphony ever composed. And a swell syphilitic movement, the rich walking carefully to science and invention. Part of it's already composed. Shall I play part of it? Would you society ladies like to hear the strike movement, with screaming N.R.A. eagles? It's very lovely, don't you know? It's full of death and blood and the running of workers and machine-gun fire. It's simply divine.

Sure he was bitter. It was their lousy party. Their idea. He came from the street. They were the ones who were always giving him a pain in the old pazaza, asking him to their lousy parties. The little boy made good, so they took him up. He became an aristocrat. He was in on the dough. He had talent. Maybe he was a genius. And they loved geniuses so much if they didn't turn out to be gangsters. They took geniuses right to their hearts and their beds. They loved poor boys who made the grade and did big things. It was their idea. You must come, Mr. O'Hara, you *simply* must come. So all right. So all right, he was in their dump. So what did he care if they were all looking at him as if he had just gone nuts and was about to run amuck? What did he care if he had shocked the fat ladies out of the room? What did he care if the well-dressed punkos were telling one another he must be ill, poor fellow? He was from the street and he was proud of it, only he didn't want them to get it wrong: he could have become something a little different like the other boys and end up in the big house: the other boys had as much of anything he had, and maybe more: so he couldn't be proud: all he wanted was to let them understand he could have been a gangster just as well, and would they invite a thief to their homes? Would they ask a murderer to their parties? He was no different from the others, so what did he care if they were scared out of their wits and didn't know what to do about him, swearing in front of the ladies and making everybody uncomfortable.

October 23, 1934

Albert Maltz

Man on a Road

At about four in the afternoon I crossed the ridge at Gauley, West Virginia, and turned the sharp curve leading into the tunnel under the railroad bridge. I had been over this road once before and knew what to expect—by the time I entered the tunnel I had my car down to about ten miles an hour. But even at that speed I came closer to running a man down than I ever have before. This is how it happened.

The patched, macadam road had been soaked through by an all-day rain and now it was as slick as ice. In addition, it was quite dark—a black sky and a steady, swishing rain made driving impossible without headlights. As I entered the tunnel a big cream colored truck swung fast around the curve on the other side. The curve was so sharp that his headlights had given me no warning. The tunnel was short and narrow, just about passing space for two cars, and before I knew it he was in front of me with his big front wheels over on my side of the road.

I jammed on my brakes. Even at ten miles an hour my car skidded, first toward the truck and then, as I wrenched on the wheel, in toward the wall. There it stalled. The truck swung around hard, scraped my fender, and passed through the tunnel about an inch away from me. I could see the tense face of the young driver with the tight bulge of tobacco in his cheek and his eyes glued on the road. I remember saying to myself that I hoped he'd swallow that tobacco and go choke himself.

I started my car and shifted into first. It was then I saw for the first time that a man was standing in front of my car about a foot away from the inside wheel. It was a shock to see him there. "For Chrissakes," I said.

My first thought was that he had walked into the tunnel after my car had stalled. I was certain he hadn't been there before. Then I noticed that he was standing profile to me with his hand held up in the hitchhiker's gesture. If he had walked into that tunnel, he'd be facing me—he wouldn't be standing sideways looking at the opposite wall. Obviously I had just missed knocking him down and obviously he didn't know it. He didn't even know I was there.

It made me run weak inside. I had a picture of a man lying crushed under a wheel with me standing over him knowing it was my car.

I called out to him "Hey!" He didn't answer me. I called louder. He didn't even turn his head. He stood there, fixed, his hand up in the air, his thumb jutting out. It scared me. It was like a story by Bierce where the ghost of a man pops out of the air to take up his lonely post on a dark country road.

My horn is a good, loud, raucous one and I knew that the tunnel would redouble the sound. I slapped my hand down on that little black button and pressed as hard as I could. The man was either going to jump or else prove that he was a ghost.

Well, he wasn't a ghost—but he didn't jump, either. And it wasn't because he was deaf. He heard that horn all right.

He was like a man in a deep sleep. The horn seemed to awaken him only by degrees, as though his whole consciousness had been sunk in some deep recess within himself. He turned his head slowly and looked at me. He was a big man, about thirty-five with a heavy-featured face—an ordinary face with a big, fleshy nose and a large mouth. The face didn't say much. I wouldn't have called it kind or brutal or intelligent or stupid. It was just the face of a big man, wet with rain, looking at me with eyes that seemed to have a glaze over them. Except for the eyes you see faces like that going into the pit at six in the morning or coming out of a steel mill or foundry where heavy work is done. I couldn't understand that glazed quality in his eyes. It wasn't the glassy stare of a drunken man or a wild, mad glare I saw once in the eyes of a woman in a fit of violence. I could only think of a man I once knew who had died of cancer. Over his eyes in the last days there was the same dull glaze, a far away, absent look as though behind the blank, outward film there was a secret flow of past events on which his mind was focussed. It was this same look that I saw in the man on the road.

When at last he heard my horn, the man stepped very deliberately around the front of my car and came toward the inside door. The least I expected was that he would show surprise at an auto so dangerously close to him. But there was no emotion to him whatsoever. He walked slowly, deliberately, as though he had been expecting me and then bent his head down to see under the top of my car. "Kin yuh give me a lift, friend?" he asked me.

I saw his big, horse teeth chipped at the ends and stained brown by tobacco. His voice was high-pitched and nasal with the slurred, lilting drawl of the deep South. In West Virginia few of the town folk seem to speak that way. I judged he had been raised in the mountains.

I looked at his clothes—an old cap, a new blue work shirt, and dark trousers, all soaked through with rain. They didn't tell me much.

I must have been occupied with my thoughts about him for sometime, because he asked me again. "Ahm goin' to Weston," he said. "Are you a-goin' thataway?"

As he said this, I looked into his eyes. The glaze had disappeared and now they were just ordinary eyes, brown and moist.

I didn't know what to reply. I didn't really want to take him in—the episode had unnerved me and I wanted to get away from the tunnel and from him too. But I saw him looking at me with a patient, almost humble glance. The rain was streaked on his face and he stood there asking for a ride and waiting in simple concentration for my answer. I was ashamed to tell him "no." Besides, I was curious. "Climb in," I said.

He sat down beside me, placing a brown paper package on his lap. We started out of the tunnel.

From Gauley to Weston is about a hundred miles of as difficult mountain driving as I know—a five mile climb to the top of a hill, then five miles down, and then up another. The road twists like a snake on the run and for a good deal of it there is a jagged cliff on one side and a drop of a thousand feet or more on the other. The rain and the small rocks crumbling from the mountain sides and littering up the road made it very slow going. But in the four hours or so that it took for the trip I don't think my companion spoke to me half a dozen times.

I tried often to get him to talk. It was not that he wouldn't talk, it was rather that he didn't seem to hear me—as though as soon as he had spoken, he would slip down into that deep, secret recess within himself. He sat like a man dulled by morphine. My conversation, the rattle of the old car, the steady pour of rain were all a distant buzz—the meaningless, outside world that could not quite pierce the shell in which he seemed to be living.

As soon as we had started, I asked him how long he had been in the tunnel.

"Ah don' know," he replied. "A good tahm, ah reckon."

"What were you standing there for—to keep out of the rain?"

He didn't answer. I asked him again, speaking very loudly. He turned his head to me. "Excuse me, friend," he said, "did you say somethin'?"

"Yes," I answered. "Do you know I almost ran you over back in that tunnel?"

"No-o," he said. He spoke the word in that breathy way that is typical of mountain speech.

"Didn't you hear me yell to you?"

"No-o." He paused. "Ah reckon ah was thinkin'."

"Ah reckon you were," I thought to myself. "What's the matter, are you hard of hearing?" I asked him.

"No-o," he said, and turned his head away looking out front at the road.

I kept right after him. I didn't want him to go off again. I wanted somehow to get him to talk.

"Looking for work?"

"Yessuh."

He seemed to speak with an effort. It was not a difficulty of speech, it was something behind, in his mind, in his will to speak. It was as though he couldn't keep the touch between his world and mine. Yet when he did answer me, he spoke directly and coherently. I didn't know what to make of it. When he first came into the car I had been a little frightened. Now I only felt terribly curious and a little sorry.

"Do you have a trade?" I was glad to come to that question. You know a good deal about a man when you know what line of work he follows and it always leads to further conversation.

"Ah generally follows the mines," he said.

"Now," I thought, "we're getting somewhere."

But just then we hit a stretch of unpaved road where the mud was thick and the ruts were hard to follow. I had to stop talking and watch what I was doing. And when we came to paved road again, I had lost him.

I tried again to make him talk. It was no use. He didn't even hear me. Then, finally, his silence shamed me. He was a man lost somewhere within his own soul, only asking to be left alone. I felt wrong to keep thrusting at his privacy.

So for about four hours we drove in silence. For me those hours were almost unendurable. I have never seen such rigidity in a human being. He sat straight up in the car, his outward eye fixed on the road in front, his inward eye seeing nothing. He didn't know I was in the car, he didn't know he was in the car at all, he didn't feel the rain that kept sloshing in on him through the rent in the side curtains. He sat like a slab of moulded rock and only from his breathing could I be sure he was alive. His breathing was heavy.

Only once in that long trip did he change his posture. That was when he was seized with a fit of coughing. It was a fierce, hacking cough that shook his big body from side to side and doubled him over like a child with the whooping cough. He was trying to cough something up—I could hear the phlegm in his chest—but he couldn't succeed. Inside him there was an ugly scraping sound as though cold metal were being rubbed on the bone of his ribs, and he kept spitting and shaking his head.

It took almost three minutes for the fit to subside. Then he turned around to me and said, "Excuse me, friend." That was all. He was quiet again.

I felt awful. There were times when I wanted to stop the car and tell him to get out. I made up a dozen good excuses for cutting the trip short. But I couldn't do it. I was consumed by a curiosity to know what was wrong with the man. I hoped that before we parted, perhaps even as he got out of the car, he would tell me what it was or say something that would give me a clue.

I thought of the cough and wondered if it were t.b. I thought of cases of sleeping sickness I had seen and of a boxer who was punch drunk. But none of these things seemed to fit. Nothing physical seemed to explain this dark, terrible silence, this intense, all-exclusive absorption within himself.

Hour after hour of rain and darkness!

Once we passed the slate dump of a mine. The rain had made the surface burst into flame and the blue and red patches flickering in a kind of witch glow on a hill of black seemed to attract my companion. He turned his head to look at it, but he didn't speak, and I said nothing.

And again the silence and rain! Occasionally a mine tipple with the cold, drear smoke smell of the dump and the oil lamps in the broken down shacks where the miners live. Then the black road again and the shapeless bulk of the mountains.

We reached Weston at about eight o'clock. I was tired and chilled and hungry. I stopped in front of a cafe and turned to the man.

"Ah reckon this is hit," he said.

"Yes," I answered. I was surprised. I had not expected him to know that we had arrived. Then I tried a final plunge. "Will you have a cup of coffee with me?"

"Yes," he replied, "thank you, friend."

The "thank you" told me a lot. I knew from the way he said it that he wanted the coffee but couldn't pay for it; that he had taken my offer to be one of hospitality and was grateful. I was happy I had asked him.

We went inside. For the first time since I had come upon him in the tunnel he seemed human. He didn't talk, but he didn't slip inside himself either. He just sat down at the counter and waited for his coffee. When it came, he drank it slowly, holding the cup in both hands as though to warm them.

When he had finished, I asked him if he wouldn't like a sandwich. He turned around to me and smiled. It was a very gentle, a very patient smile. His big, lumpy face seemed to light up with it and become understanding and sweet and gentle.

The smile shook me all through. It didn't warm me—it made me feel sick inside. It was like watching a corpse begin to stir. I wanted to cry out, "My God, you poor man!"

Then he spoke to me. His face retained that smile and I could see the big, horse teeth stained by tobacco.

"You've bin right nice to me, friend, an' ah do appreciate it."

"That's all right," I mumbled.

He kept looking at me. I knew he was going to say something else and I was afraid of it.

"Would yuh do me a faveh?"

"Yes," I said.

He spoke softly. "Ah've got a letter here that ah done writ to mah woman, but ah can't write very good. Would you all be kind enough to write it ovah for me so it'd be proper like?"

"Yes," I said, "I'd be glad to."

"Ah kin tell you all know how to write real well," he said, and smiled.

"Yes."

He opened his blue shirt. Under his thick woolen underwear there was a sheet of paper fastened by a safety pin. He handed it to me. It was moist and warm and the damp odor of wet cloth and the slightly sour odor of his flesh clung to it.

I asked the counterman for a sheet of paper. He brought me one. This is the letter I copied. I put it down here in his own script.

My dere wife

i am awritin this yere leta to tell you somethin i did not tell you afore i lef frum home. There is a cause to wy i am not able to get me any job at the mines. i told you hit was frum work abein slack. But this haint so.

Hit comes frum the time the mine was shut down an i worked in the tunnel nere Gauley Bridge where the govinment is turnin the river inside the mounten. The mine supers say they wont hire any men war worked in thet tunel.

Hit all comes frum thet rock thet we all had to dril. Thet rock was silica and hit was most all of hit glass. The powder frum this glass has got into the lungs of all the men war worked in thet tunel thru their breathin. And this has given to all of us a sickness. The doctors writ it down for me. Hit is silicosis. Hit makes the lungs to git all scab like and then it stops the breathin.

Bein as our hom is a good peece frum town you aint heerd about Tom Prescott and Hansy MCCulloh having died two days back. But wen i heerd this i went to see the doctor.

The doctor says i hev got me thet sickness like Tom Prescott and thet is the reeson wy i am coughin sometime. My lungs is agittin scab like. There is in all ova a hondred men war have this death sickness frum the tunel. It is a turible plague becus the doctor says this wud not be so if the company had gave us masks to ware an put a right fan sistem in the tunel.

So i am agoin away becus the doctor says i will be dead in about fore months.

i figger on gettin some work maybe in other parts. i will send you all my money till i caint work no mohr.

i did not want i should be a burdin upon you all at hum. So thet is wy i hev gone away.

i think wen you doan here frum me no mohr you orter go to your grandmaws up in the mountens at Kilney Run. You kin live there an she will take keer of you an the young one.

i hope you will be well an keep the young one out of the mines. Doan let him work there.

Doan think hard on me for agoin away and doan feel bad. But wen the young one is agrowed up you tell him wat the company has done to me.

i reckon after a bit you shud try to git you anotha man. You are a young woman yit.   Your loving husband,
                                                                Jack Pitckett

When I handed him the copy of his letter, he read it over. It took him a long time. Finally he folded it up and pinned it to his undershirt. His big lumpy face was sweet and gentle. "Thank you, friend," he said. Then, very softly, with his head hanging a little–"Ahm feelin' bad about this a-happenin' t'me. Mah wife was a good woman." He paused. And then, as though talking to himself, so low I could hardly hear it, "Ahm feelin' right bad."

As he said this, I looked into his face. Slowly the life was going out of his eyes. It seemed to recede and go deep into the sockets like the flame of a candle going into the night. Over the eyeballs came that dull glaze. I had lost him. He sat deep within himself in his sorrowful, dark absorption.

That was all. We sat together. In me there was only mute emotion–pity and love for him, and a cold, deep hatred for what had killed him.

Presently he arose. He did not speak. Nor did I. I saw his thick, broad back in the blue work shirt as he stood by the door. Then he moved out into the darkness and rain.

January 8, 1935

Thomas Wolfe

The Company

When Joe went home that year he found that Mr. Merrit also was in town. Almost before the first greetings at the station were over, Jim told him. The two brothers stood there grinning at each other. Jim, with his lean, thin, deeply furrowed face, that somehow always reminded Joe so curiously and so poignantly of Lincoln, and that also somehow made him feel a bit ashamed, looked older and more worn than he had the last time Joe had seen him. He always looked a little older and a little more worn; the years like the slow gray ash of time wore at his temples and the corners of his eyes. His hair, already sparse, had thinned back and receded from his temples and there were little webbings of fine wrinkles at the corners of his eyes. The two brothers stood there looking at each other, grinning, a little awkward but delighted. In Jim's naked worn eyes Joe could see how proud the older brother was of him, and something caught him in the throat.

But Jim just grinned at him, and in a moment said: "I guess we'll have to sleep you out in the garage. Bob Merrit is in town, you, you—or if you like, there's a nice room at Mrs. Parker's right across the street, and she'd be glad to have you."

Joe looked rather uncomfortable at the mention of Mrs. Parker's name. She was a worthy lady, but of a literary turn of mind, and a pillar of the Woman's Club. Kate saw his expression and laughed, poking him in the ribs with her big finger: "Ho, ho, ho, ho, ho! You see what you're in for, don't you? The prodigal son comes home and we give him his choice of Mrs. Parker or the garage! Now is that life, or not?"

Jim Doaks, as was his wont, took this observation in very slowly. One could see him deliberating on it, and then as it broke slowly on him, it sort of spread all over his seamed face; he bared his teeth in a craggy grin; a kind of rusty and almost unwilling chuckle came from him; he turned his head sideways, and said "Hi–I," an expletive that with him was always indicative of mirth.

"I don't mind a bit," protested Joe. "I think the garage is swell." And then—they all grinned at each other again with the affection of people who know each other so well that they are long past knowledge—"if I get to helling around at night, I won't feel that I am disturbing you when I come in . . . And how is Mr. Merrit, anyway?"

"Why, just fine," Jim answered with that air of thoughtful deliberation which accompanied most of his remarks. "He's just fine, I think. And he's been asking about you," said Jim seriously. "He wants to see you."

"And we knew you wouldn't mind," Kate said more seriously. "You know, it's business; he's with the Company, and of course it's good policy to be as nice to them as you can."

But in a moment, because such designing was really alien to her own hospitable and whole-hearted spirit, she added: "Mr. Merrit is a fine fellow. I like him. We're glad to have him anyway."

"Bob's all right," said Jim. "And I know he wants to see you. Well," he said, "if we're all ready, let's get going. I'm due back at the office now. Merrit's coming in. If you'd like to fool around uptown until one o'clock and see your friends, you could come by then, and I'll run you out. Why don't you do that? Merrit's coming out to dinner, too."

It was agreed to do this, and a few minutes later Joe got out of the car upon the Public Square of the town that he had not seen for a year.

The truth of the matter was that Joe not only felt perfectly content at the prospect of sleeping in the garage, but he also felt a pleasant glow at the knowledge that Mr. Robert Merrit was in town, and staying at his brother's house.

Joe had never known exactly just what Mr. Robert Merrit did. In Jim's spacious but rather indefinite phrase, he was referred to as "the Company's man." And Joe did not know exactly what the duties of a "Company's man" were, but Mr. Merrit made them seem mighty pleasant. He turned up ruddy, plump, well-kept, full of jokes, and immensely agreeable, every two or three months, with a pocket that seemed perpetually full, and like the Jovian pitcher of milk of Baucis and Philemon, perpetually replenished, in some miraculous way, with big fat savory cigars, which he was always handing out to people.

Joe understood, of course, that there was some business connection in the mysterious ramifications of "The Company" between his brother Jim and Robert Merrit. But he had never heard them "talk business" together, nor did he know just what the business was. Mr. Merrit would "turn up" every two or three months like a benevolent and ruddy Santa Claus, making his jolly little jokes, passing out his fat cigars, putting his arm around people's shoulders—in general, making everyone feel good. In his own words, "I've got to turn up now and then just to see that the boys are behaving themselves, and not taking any wooden nickels." Here he would wink at you in such an infectious way that you had to grin. Then he would give you a fat cigar.

His functions did seem to be ambassadorial. Really, save for an occasional visit to the office, he seemed to spend a good deal of his time in inaugurating an era of good living every time he came to town. He was always taking the salesmen out to dinner and to lunch. He was always "coming out to the house," and when he did come, one knew that Kate would have one of her best meals ready, and that there would be some good drinks. Mr. Merrit usually brought the drinks. Every time he came to town he always seemed to bring along with him a plentiful stock of high-grade beverages. In other words, the man really did carry about with him an aura of good fellowship and good living, and that was why it was so pleasant now to know that Mr. Merrit was in town and "staying out at the house."

Mr. Merrit was not only a nice fellow. He was also with "the Company." And since Jim was also a member of "the Company," that made everything all right. Because "the Company," Joe knew, was somehow a vital, mysterious form in all their lives. Jim had begun to work for it when he was sixteen years old—as a machinist's helper in the shops at Akron. Since then he had steadily worked his way up through all the states until now, "well-fixed" apparently, he was a district manager—an important member of "the sales organization."

The sales organization—or, to use a word that at this time was coming into common speech, the functional operation—of the Federal Weight, Scale & Computing Co., while imposing in its ramified complexity of amount and number, was in its essence so beautifully simple that to a future age, at least, the system of enfeoffments in the Middle Ages, the relation between the liege lord and his serf, may well seem complex by comparison.

The organization of the sales system was briefly just this, and nothing more; the entire country was divided into districts and over each district an agent was appointed. This agent, in turn, employed salesmen to cover the various portions of his district. In addition to these salesmen there was also an "office man" whose function, as his name implies, was to look after the office, attend to any business that might come up when the agent and his salesmen were away, take care of any spare sheep who might stray in of their own volition without having been enticed thither by the persuasive herdings of the salesmen and their hypnotic words; and a "repair man" whose business it was to repair damaged or broken-down machines.

Although in the familiar conversation of the agents, a fellow agent was said to be the agent of a certain town—Smith, for example, was "the Knoxville man," Jones, the Charleston one, Robinson, the one at Richmond, etc., these agencies, signified by the name of the town in which the agent had his office, comprised the district that surrounded them.

In Catawba there were six agencies and six agents. The population of the state was about three million. In other words, each agent had a district of approximately one-half million people. Not that the distribution worked out invariably in this way. There was no set rule for the limitation of an agency, some agencies were larger than others and considerably more profitable, depending upon the amount of business and commercial enterprise that was done in any given district. But the median of one agent to a half-million people was, in probability, a fairly accurate one for the whole country.

Now, as to the higher purposes of this great institution, which the agent almost never referred to by name, as who should not speak of the deity with coarse directness, but almost always with a just perceptible lowering and huskiness of the voice, as "the Company"—these higher purposes were also, when seen in their essential purity, characterized by the same noble directness and simplicity as marked the operations of the entire enterprise. This higher purpose, in the famous utterance of the great man himself, invariably repeated every year as a sort of climax or peroration to his hour-long harangue to his adoring disciples at the national convention, was—sweeping his arm in a gesture of magnificent and grandiloquent command toward the map of the entire United States of America—"There is your market. Go out and sell them."

What could be simpler or more beautiful than this? What could be more eloquently indicative of that quality of noble directness, mighty sweep, and far-seeing imagination, which has been celebrated in the annals of modern literature under the name of "vision"? "There is your market. Go out and sell them."

Who says the age of romance is dead? Who says there are no longer giants on the earth in these days? It is Napoleon speaking to his troops before the pyramids. "Soldiers, forty centuries are looking down on you." It is John Paul Jones: "We have met the enemy and they are ours." It is Dewey, on the bridge deck of the Oregon: "You may fire when you are ready, Gridley." It is General Grant before the works of Petersburg: "I propose to fight it out on this line if it takes all summer."

"There's your market. Go out and sell them." The words had the same spacious sweep and noble simplicity that have always characterized the utterances of the great leaders at every age and epoch of man's history.

It is true that there had been a time when the aims and aspirations of "the Company" had been more modest ones. There had been a time when the founder of the institution, the father of the present governor, John S. Appleton, had confined his ambitions to these modest words: "I should like to see one of my machines in every store, shop, or business in the United States that needs one, and that can afford to pay for one."

The high aims expressed in these splendid words would seem to the inexperienced observer to be far-reaching enough, but as any agent upon the company's roster could now tell you, they were so conventional in their modest pretentions as to be practically mid-Victorian. Or, as the agent himself might put it: "That's old stuff now—we've gone way beyond that. Why, if you wanted to sell a machine to someone who *needs* one, you'd get nowhere. Don't wait until he *needs* one—make him buy one now. Suppose he doesn't need one; all right, we'll make him see the need of one. If he has no need of one, why we'll create the need." In a more technical phrase, this was known as "creating the market," and this beautiful and poetic invention was the inspired work of one man, the fruit of the vision of none other than the great John S. Appleton, Jr., himself.

In fact, in one impassioned flight of oratory before his assembled parliaments, John S. Appleton, Jr., had become so intoxicated with the grandeur of his own vision that he is said to have paused, gazed dreamily into unknown vistas of magic Canaan, and suddenly to have given utterance in a voice quivering with surcharged emotion to these words: "My friends, the possibilities of the market, now that we have created it, are practically unlimited." Here he was silent for a moment, and those who were present on that historic occasion say that for a moment the great man paled, and then seemed to stagger as the full impact of his vision smote him with its vistas. His voice is said to have trembled so when he tried to speak that for a moment he could not control himself. It is said that when he uttered those memorable words, which from that moment on were engraved upon the hearts of every agent there, his voice faltered, sunk to an almost inaudible whisper, as if he himself could hardly comprehend the magnitude of his own conception.

"My friends," he muttered thickly, and was seen to reel and clutch the rostrum for support, "my friends, seen properly . . ." he whispered and moistened his dry lips, but here, those who are present say, his voice grew stronger and the clarion words blared forth ". . . seen properly, with the market we have created, there is no reason why one of our machines should not be in the possession of every man, woman and child in the United States of America."

Then came the grand, familiar gesture to the great map of these assembled states: "There's your market, boys. Go out and sell them."

Such, then, were the sky-soaring aims and aspirations of the Federal Weight, Scale & Computing Co. in the third decade of the century, and such, reduced to its naked and essential simplicity, was the practical effort, the concrete purpose of every agent in the company. Gone were the days forever, as they thought, when their operations must be confined and limited merely to those business enterprises who needed, or thought they needed, a weight scale or computing machine. The sky was the limit, and for any agent to have even hinted that anything less or lower than the sky was possibly the limit, would have been an act of such impious sacrilege as to have merited his instant expulsion from the true church and the living faith—the church and faith of John S. Appleton, Jr., which was called "the Company."

In the pursuit and furtherance and consummation of this grand and elemental aim, the organization of the Company worked with the naked drive, the beautiful precision of a locomotive piston. Over the salesmen was the agent, and over the agent was the district supervisor, and over the district supervisor was the district manager, and over the district manager was the general manager, and over the general manager was ... was ... God himself, or, as the agents more properly referred to him, in voices that fell naturally to the hush of reverence, "the Old Man."

The operation of this beautiful and powerful machine can perhaps best be described to the lay reader by a series of concrete and poetic images. Those readers, for example, with an interest in painting, who are familiar with some of the terrific drawings of old Pieter Breughel, may recall a certain gigantic product of his genius which bears the title *The Big Fish Eating Up the Little Ones*, and which portrays just that. The great whales and monster leviathans of the vasty deep swallowing the sharks, the sharks swallowing the swordfish, the swordfish swallowing the great bass, the great bass swallowing the lesser mackerel, the lesser mackerel eating up the herrings, the herrings gulping down the minnows, and so on down the whole swarming and fantastic world that throngs the sea-floors of the earth, until you get down to the tadpoles, who, it is to be feared, have nothing smaller than themselves to swallow.

Or, to a reader interested in history, the following illustration may make the operation of the system plain. At the end of a long line that stretches from the pyramids until the very portals of his house, the great Pharaoh, with a thonged whip in his hands, which he vigorously and unmercifully applies to the bare back and shoulders of the man ahead of him, who is great Pharaoh's great chief overseer, and in the hand of Pharaoh's great chief overseer likewise a whip of many tails which the great chief overseer unstintedly applies to the quivering back and shoulders of the wretch before him, who is the great chief overseer's chief lieutenant, and in the lieutenant's hand a whip of many tails which he applies to the suffering hide of his head sergeant, and in the head sergeant's hand a wicked flail with which he belabors the pelt of a whole company of groaning corporals, and in the hands of every groaning corporal, a wicked whip with which they lash and whack the bodies of a whole regiment of grunting slaves, who toil and sweat and bear burdens and pull and haul and build the towering structure of the pyramid.

Or, finally, for those readers with an interest in simple mechanics, the following illustration may suffice. Conceive an enormous flight of stairs with many landings, and at the very top of it, supreme and masterful, a man, who kicks another man in front of him quite solemnly in the seat of the pants, this man turns a somersault and comes erect upon the first and nearest landing and immediately, and with great decision, kicks the man in front of him down two more landings of these enormous stairs, who, on arriving, kicks the next incumbent down three landing flights, and so on to the bottom, where there is no one left to kick.

Now these, in their various ways, and by the tokens of their various ways, and by the tokens of their various imagery, fairly describe the simple but effective operations of the Company. Four times a year, at the beginning of each quarter, John S. Appleton called his general manager before him and kicked him down one flight of stairs, saying, "You're not getting the business. The market is there. You know what you can do about it—or else. . . ."

And the general manager repeated the master's words and operations on his chief assistant managers, and they in turn upon the district managers, and they in turn upon the district supervisors, and they in turn upon the district agents, and they in turn upon the lowly salesmen, and they in turn, at long and final last, upon the final recipient of all swift kicks—the general public, the amalgamated Doakses of the earth.

It is true that to the lay observer the operation did not appear so brutally severe as has been described. It is true that the iron hand was cunningly concealed in the velvet glove, but there was no mistaking the fact, as those who had once felt its brutal grip could testify, that the iron hand was there and could be put to ruthless use at any moment. It is true that the constant menace of that iron hand was craftily disguised by words of cheer, by talk of fair rewards and bonuses, but these plums of service could turn bitter in the mouth, the plums themselves were just a threat of stern reprisal to those who were not strong or tall enough to seize them. One was not given his choice of having plums or of not having plums. It is no exaggeration to say that one was told he must have plums, that he must get plums, that if he failed to gather plums another picker would be put into his place.

And of all the many wonderful and beautiful inventions which the great brain of Mr. John S. Appleton had created and conceived, this noble invention of plum-picking was the simplest and most cunning of the lot. For be it understood that these emoluments of luscious fruit were not wholly free. For every plum the picker took unto himself, two more were added to the plenteous store of Mr. Appleton. And the way this agricultural triumph was achieved was as follows:

Mr. Appleton was the founder of a great social organization known as the Hundred Club. The membership of the Hundred Club was limited exclusively to Mr. Appleton himself and the agents, salesmen, and district managers of his vast organization. The advantages of belonging to the Hundred Club were quickly apparent to everyone. Although it was asserted that membership in the Hundred Club was not compulsory, if one did not belong to it the time was not far distant when one would not belong to Mr. Appleton. The club, therefore, like all the nobler Appleton inventions, was contrived cunningly of the familiar ingredients of simplicity and devilish craft, of free will and predestination.

The club had the extraordinary distinction of compelling people to join it while at the same time giving them, through its membership, the proud prestige of social distinction. Not to belong to the Hundred Club, for an agent or a salesman, was equivalent to living on the other side of the railroad tracks. If one did not get in, if one could not reach high enough to make it, he faded quickly from the picture, his fellows spoke of him infrequently. When someone said, "What's Bob Klutz doing now?" the answers would be sparse and definitely vague, and, in course of time, Bob Klutz would be spoken of no more. He would fade out in oblivion. He was "no longer with the Company."

Now, the purpose and the meaning of the Hundred Club was this. Each agent and each salesman in the company, of no matter what position or what rank, had what was called a "quota"—that is to say, a certain fixed amount of business which was established as the normal average of his district and capacity. A man's quota differed according to the size of his territory, its wealth, its business, and his own experience and potentiality. If he was a district agent, his personal quota would be higher than that of a mere salesman in a district. One man's quota would be sixty, another's eighty, another's ninety or one hundred. Each of these men, however, no matter how small or large his quota might be, was eligible for membership in the Hundred Club, provided he could average 100 per cent of his quota—hence the name. If he averaged more, if he got 120 per cent of his quota, or 150 per cent, or 200 per cent of his quota, there were appropriate honors and rewards, not only of a social but of a financial nature. One could be high up in the Hundred Club or low down in the Hundred Club: it had almost as many degrees of honor and of merit as the great Masonic order. But of one thing, one could be certain: one must belong to the Hundred Club if one wanted to continue to belong to "the Company."

The unit of the quota system was "the point." If a salesman or an agent stated that his personal quota was eighty, it was understood that his quota was eighty points a month, that this was the desired goal, the average, toward which he should strive, which he should not fall below, and which, if possible, he should try to better. If a salesman's quota was eighty points a month, and he averaged eighty points a month throughout the year, he became automatically a member of the Hundred Club. And if he surpassed this quota, he received distinction, promotion, and reward in the Hundred Club, in proportion to the degree of his increase. The unit of the point itself was fixed at forty dollars. Therefore, if a salesman's quota was eighty points a month and he achieved it, he must sell the products of the Federal Weight, Scale & Computing Co. to the amount of more than three thousand dollars every month, and almost forty thousand dollars in the year.

The rewards were high. A salesman's commission averaged from 15 to 20 per cent of his total sales; an agent's, from 20 to 25 per cent, in addition to the bonuses he could earn by achieving or surpassing his full quota. Thus, it was entirely possible for an ordinary salesman in an average district to earn from six to eight thousand dollars a year, and for an agent to earn from twelve to fifteen thousand dollars, and even more if his district was an exceptionally good one.

So far, so good. The rewards, it is now apparent, were high, the inducements great. Where does the iron hand come in? It came in in many devious and subtle ways, of which the principal and most direct was this: once a man's quota had been fixed at any given point, the Company did not reduce it. On the contrary, if a salesman's quota was eighty points in any given year and he achieved it, he must be prepared at the beginning of the new year to find that his quota had been increased to ninety points. In other words, the plums were there, but always, year by year, upon a somewhat higher bough. "June Was the Greatest Month in Federal History"—so read the gigantic posters which the Company was constantly sending out to all its district offices—"*Make July a Greater One!* The Market's There, Mr. Agent, the Rest Is Up to You," etc.

In other words, this practice as applied to salesmanship resembled closely the one that has since been known in the cotton mills as the stretch-out system. June was the greatest month in Federal history, but July must be a bigger one, and one must never look back on forgotten Junes with satisfaction. One must go on and upward constantly, the race was to the swift. The pace was ever faster and the road more steep.

The result of this on plain humanity may be inferred. It was shocking and revolting. If the spectacle of the average Federal man at work was an alarming one, the spectacle of that same man at play was simply tragic. No more devastating comment could be made on the merits of that vaunted system, which indeed in its essence was the vaunted system at that time of all business, of all America, than the astounding picture of the assembled cohorts of the Hundred Club gathered together in their yearly congress for a "Week of Play." For, be it known, one of the chief rewards of membership in this distinguished body, in addition to the bonuses and social distinctions, was a kind of grandiose yearly outing which lasted for a week and which was conducted "at the Company's expense." These yearly excursions of the fortunate group took various forms, but they were conducted on a lavish scale. The meeting place would be in New York, or in Philadelphia, or in Washington; sometimes the pleasure trip was to Bermuda, sometimes to Havana, sometimes across the continent to California and back again, sometimes to Florida, to the tropic opulence of Miami and Palm Beach; but wherever the voyage led, whatever the scheme might be, it was always grandiose, no expense was spared, everything was done on the grand scale, and the Company–the immortal Company, the paternal, noble, and great-hearted Company– "paid for everything."

If the journey was to be by sea, to Bermuda or to Cuba's shores, the Company chartered a transatlantic liner–one of the smaller but luxurious twenty-thousand tonners of the Cunard, the German Lloyd, or the Holland-American lines. From this time on, the Hundred Club was given a free sweep. The ship was theirs and all the minions of the ship were theirs, to do their bidding. All the liquor in the world was theirs, if they could drink it. And Bermuda's coral isles, the most unlicensed privilege of gay Havana. For one short week, one brief gaudy week of riot, everything on earth was theirs that money could command. It was theirs for the asking–and the Company paid.

It was, as we have said, a tragic spectacle: the spectacle of twelve or fifteen hundred men, for on these pilgrimages, by general consent, women–or their wives at any rate–were disbarred–the spectacle of twelve or fifteen hundred men, Americans, of middle years, in the third decade of this century, exhausted, overwrought, their nerves frayed down and stretched to breaking point, met from all quarters of the continent "at the Company's expense" upon a greyhound of the sea for one wild week of pleasure. That spectacle had in its essential elements connotations of such general and tragic force in its relation and its reference to the entire scheme of things and the plan of life that had produced it that a thoughtful Martian, had he been vouchsafed but thirty minutes on this earth and could have spent those thirty minutes on one of the crack liners that bore the Hundred Club to tropic shores, might have formed conclusions about the life of this tormented little cinder where we live that would have made him sorrowful that he had ever come and eager for the moment when his thirty-minute sojourn would be ended.

III

It was a few minutes before one o'clock when Joe entered his brother's office. The outer sales room, with its glittering stock of weights, scales, and computing machines, imposingly arranged on walnut pedestals, was deserted. From the little partitioned space behind, which served Jim as an office, he heard the sound of voices.

He recognized Jim's voice–low, grave, and hesitant, deeply troubled–at once. The other voice he had never heard before.

But as he heard that voice, he began to tremble and grow white about the lips. For that voice was a foul insult to human life, an ugly sneer whipped across the face of decent humanity, and as it came to him that this voice, these words were being used against his brother, he had a sudden blind feeling of murder in his heart.

And what was, in the midst of this horror, so perplexing and so troubling, was that this devil's voice had in it as well a curiously human note, as of someone he had known.

Then it came to him in a flash–it was Merrit speaking. The owner of that voice, incredible as it seemed, was none other than that plump, well-kept, jolly looking man, who had always been so full of cheerful and good-hearted spirits every time he had seen him.

Now, behind that evil little partition of glazed glass and varnished wood, this man's voice had suddenly become fiendish. It was inconceivable and, as Joe listened, he grew sick with horror, as a man does in some awful nightmare when suddenly he envisions someone familiar doing some perverse and abominable act. And what was most dreadful of all was the voice of his brother, humble, low, submissive, modestly entreating. He could hear Merrit's voice cutting across the air like a gob of rasping phlegm, and then Jim's low voice–gentle, hesitant, deeply troubled–coming in from time to time by way of answer.

"Well, what's the matter? Don't you want the job?"

"Why–why, yes, you know I do, Bob," and Jim's voice lifted a little in a troubled and protesting laugh.

"What's the matter that you're not getting the business?"

"Why–why. . . ." Again the troubled and protesting little laugh. "I *thought* I was. . . !"

"Well, you're not!" That rasping voice fell harsh upon the air with the brutal nakedness of a knife. "This district ought to deliver 30 per cent more business than you're getting from it. And the Company is going to have it, too–or *else!* You deliver or you go right out upon your can! See? The Company doesn't give a damn about you. It's after the business. You've been around a long time, but you don't mean a damn bit more to the Company than anybody else. And you know what's happened to a lot of other guys who got to feeling they were too big for their job, don't you?"

"Why–why, yes, Bob. . . ." Again the troubled and protesting laugh. "But–honestly, I never thought. . . ."

"We don't give a damn what you never thought!" the brutal voice ripped in. "I've given you fair warning now. You get the business or out you go!"

Merrit came out of the little partition-cage into the cleaner light of the outer room. When he saw Joe, he looked startled for a moment. Then he was instantly transformed. His plump and ruddy face was instantly wreathed in smiles, he cried out in a hearty tone: "Well, well, well! Look who's here! If it's not the old boy himself!"

He shook hands with Joe, and as he did so, turned and winked humorously at Jim, in the manner of older men when they are carrying on a little bantering by-play in the presence of a younger one.

"Jim, I believe he gets better-looking every time I see him. Has he broken any hearts yet?"

Jim tried to smile, gray-faced and haggard.

"I hear you're burning them up in the big town," said Merrit, turning to the younger man. "Great stuff, son, we're proud of you."

And with another friendly pressure of the hand, he turned away with an air of jaunty readiness, picked up his hat, and said cheerfully: "Well, what d'ya say, folks? Didn't I hear somebody say something about one of the madam's famous meals, out at the old homestead. Well, you can't hurt my feelings. I'm ready if you are. Let's go."

And smiling, ruddy, plump, cheerful, a perverted picture of amiable goodwill to all the world, he sauntered through the door. And for a moment the two brothers just stood there looking at each other, drawn and haggard, with a bewildered expression in their eyes.

In Jim's decent eyes, also, there was a look of shame. In a moment, with that instinct for loyalty which was one of the roots of his soul, he said: "Bob's a good fellow... You... you see, he's got to do these things... He's... he's with the Company."

Joe didn't say anything. He couldn't. He had just found out something about life he hadn't known before.

And it was all so strange, so different from what he thought it would be.

January 11, 1938

Millen Brand

When You Spend a Dollar

Coyle, his wife, and daughter, Katy, lived in a tenement. Coyle was Irish; at one time he had lived in a better neighborhood but he was now working two days a week—he had found this apartment in a big tenement which housed for the most part Italian and Greek families. It was cheaper; he was glad now to have anything. The apartment, as it was called, had two small rooms—one was a nine-by-twelve bedroom, the other a six-by-nine kitchen. They had a toilet in a closet in the bedroom; in order to sit on it they had to leave the door open to make room for their feet.

But that was better than a common toilet in the hallway.

The worst time to be in a tenement is summer. The Coyles were on the next to the top floor and the heat of the sun came down and the heat of the building rose up to them. Heat and noise. But always heat.

As the days became really unbearably hot, the Coyles got into the habit of sleeping late, exhausted by the heat of the night before; they did this except on Thursday and Friday, when Coyle worked.

One morning, a Wednesday, they woke up at about quarter to nine. The heat of the day was now, just as they woke, as terrible as it had been when they fell into a fatigued sleep the night before. It was even worse. On the floor below they heard Mrs. Andriolo, one of their friends in the building, walking back and forth with her baby; the baby was crying— it seemed to be protesting against the furnace-like heat that Coyle, his wife, everybody in the building felt.

"The baby won't drink the bottle," Mrs. Coyle said.

"Why don't she nurse it?"

"She can't. She tried. Her breasts bleed."

Coyle lay silent. His wife lay beside him on her back, her half-hidden breasts—which had richly nursed their own baby—

with dark flattened nipples, like black roses on her skin. "Look at Katy," he said, "still sleeping. Asleep, Katy?" he said softly. There was no answer.

A canary began to sing in the Paraskevopoulos' apartment down the hall.

After an hour, Mrs. Coyle put her feet into slippers and stood up, shaking her long dark hair down her back and twisting it. "Come on, get up," she said. "You're gettin' lazy, my man."

"Me lazy?" he said. "And I work ten hours a day?"

"Twenty hours a week."

"Ah, but I wish it was sixty for your sake, Mary," he said.

Katy woke up. The first thing she said was, "It's so hot."

"All right, it's hot," Coyle said. "So what?"

"I wish we could go to the beach."

He said nothing. He felt angry. Katy should have more sense.

Mary went into the kitchen and Katy got up and went in too. He heard the two of them talking in low voices.

Why should he be angry? Why not? It was twenty hours, as Mary had said. Just twenty hours. No work for a man—only enough to keep from starving. No life; this was not living.

Well, if they were badly off, the Andriolos were worse. He had been talking to Andriolo—it was a wonder how they existed.

He lay thinking until breakfast was ready, then went into the kitchen in his pajamas. The room was airless; as he drank the coffee set out for him, beads of sweat came out on his forehead. His wife served some warmed-over potatoes and some bacon.

"Warm stuff," he said.

"It's all we have."

He ate without appetite and helped his wife with the dishes. The work was done; then his wife made the beds; then the day was ahead of them. The day and its heat.

At about eleven o'clock they were all three sitting around the one window they had on the courtyard. No air seemed to come in at all. Being a flight down from the top of the building, if there was any breeze, it would not reach as far down into the narrow court as to reach them.

"It's so hot," Katy said again. She leaned across the sill of the window; her arms stretched out as if imploring pity from the heat. But the heat, from the crowded buildings, the streets, the sweating pores of thousands of human beings, could not have pity. From other windows people reached too, like Katy, for some impossible coolness—in one window a man sat naked to the waist, his wife in a damp slip.

Italianos, Coyle thought. Hellaynays. But human beings. He was sorry for Andriolo, with four kids, with a brother hurt in the steel strike. He gave him a quarter sometimes for the Red Fighting Fund.

The sun was rising; it struck down straight on the roofs; the heat was more than blood temperature. There was no escape. Heat, death. . . . He looked at Katy. Her eyes seemed dull; her continual goodness, he thought, was more than half passivity. He was afraid; it was no good to see children become so good, so quiet. His wife too. She was too resigned, was—

A flood of canary song poured out of the Paraskevopoulos' apartment, first a few straight notes, then the bird's full repertoire.

"Mary," he said. He hesitated. "Mary," he said again, his voice unsure but hard, "let's go to the beach."

His wife turned and looked at him with shocked eyes. He might have proposed holding up a bank.

"Jim—" she said.

"Yes," he said, "why can't we go, Mary? In the name of God don't we deserve some happiness? Must we think about money always?"

"We need money for food."

"We have enough till Friday."

"Hardly enough."

"Enough, come, Mary, a dollar for everything—carfare, bathhouse, everything."

"And the rent?"

"I don't think anybody'll come."

They were two months behind in the rent. They had saved just fourteen dollars to pay one month's rent—if the landlord or his agent came.

"No, if they ain't come yet, they won't come till Friday," he said. On Friday he would be paid again.

"They might come."

"They won't."

"They might. Oh Jim, how can y' talk like that?"

"How can I talk like that! But it's the happiness of you and Katy I'm thinking of. Can't I–"

"No, Jim, no."

Both of them heard a funny sound and looked at Katy. She was hunched over the window sill, making a funny sound– when he turned her head up, he saw she was crying. "Katy!" He and his wife knelt down and he took the girl into his arms. "Katy," Coyle said, "Katy, don't you know we're going to the beach?"

Ahead of them they smelled the sea, a salt fresh smell they never smelled in the city; already the trip was worthwhile, to get that smell. As they came nearer, they began to hear the continuous thrashing of the surf–they could hear it past the stands of the concessionaires, the voices of people. . . . A year, Coyle thought, since they had been here.

The steady sound of the surf seemed to draw them; Katy became excited, wanted to hurry.

They went to the city bathhouses. As it was a weekday, they rented one for twenty cents. It was small and dark and there were only a few faint bars of light coming through a heavily latticed window at the back. Darkness was for the poor, he thought. He thought of the tenement with its interior rooms, its air shafts, its narrow courtyard, dark–why could he not escape even here, feel really free?

As he hung up his pants, he heard the silver jingling in his pocket; that was the dollar. They had rented suits, rough cheap suits of blue. Katy's was small for her; when she wriggled into it, it hugged her buttocks in a tight line.

"Well, Mary," he said, "how's it feel?"

His wife looked at him and smiled.

They went out and down to the beach. At first they could not see it because they were in a corridor of the bathhouses, then it came in view. The sea; there it was, the large fathomless element, blue, glittering, living. For a moment Coyle saw it as "the sea"; then he saw it only as a place to swim in, to get cool in, "the beach" they had come to for a day's relief from heat and the airless tenement.

Katy ran forward and into a wave that was coming in. The wave spread out over the almost level sand; first it rushed up at her ankles, then going out, it dug cups at her heels. She was excited, feeling the fine sand escaping under her heels and her heels sinking down.

They went in. Their suits turned from light to dark blue, the water streamed from their limbs. Up and down the beach were hundreds of other hot, exhausted city dwellers getting some of the natural health of the sea. There were screams, arms and heads floating, bodies intermingled. Katy churned her arms; she remembered the swimming lessons her father had given her the summer before. "Mary," Coyle said to his wife, "look at Katy. She's gonna make a swimmer."

After a half-hour they came out. They lay down feeling pleasantly tired. Coyle put his cheek against his wife's shoulder; together he and his wife looked at Katy. A little body that had come out of their own, a child, something to live beyond them. Yes, but into what kind of a world, Coyle thought. Unemployment. Depression. Well, it could change. At least now he felt good. Katy looked better—tired but with color, there was some animation in her stretched-out limbs.

After they had sprawled out resting a few minutes, Katy said, "Pop, the tide coming in?"

"Yeah, it's comin' in."

He knew that she wanted it to be coming in, but she said, "How can y' tell, Pop?"

"Look a' that pier down there, see the posts under it?"

"Yeah."

"Well, there's five posts outa water now. When we came, there was seven or eight outa water."

Then she said what he expected her to say, "Let's build a fort."

Obligingly he got to his feet and they went down just out of reach of the water and started a fort. They made a big one—a trench or moat first in front of the fort, then walls a foot and a half or more thick, packed hard, leveled smooth, then some outworks and towers. He made some imitation cannon with wet sand; Katy copied him with others; all the cannon pointed towards the menacing sea.

"Look," Katy said, running to her mother. "It's a good one, look."

Coyle came up again and lay down by Mary.

"Y' like it, Mama?" Katy said.

"I like it. It's fine."

"Now watch—"

As the three of them waited, under the sun somehow burning and cool at the same time, the sea began to come in. Wave after wave came up, ebbed out. At times there would be a long one and then several short ones so that it almost seemed as if the tide was going out. "You're sure the tide's comin' in?" Katy said.

"Yeah, it's comin' in."

Katy sat at her parents' feet. She watched patiently. At last a long wave rolled up and broke through one point of the outworks of the fort and ran into the moat where, as the wave ebbed out again, it was absorbed into the sand. This one long wave was the signal to others; soon they were coming stronger and they poured into and filled the moat.

With the gentle motion of the water rolling back and forth in the moat, a sliver was dislodged from the front wall and slid down and disappeared. Still the waves came slowly, gradually; the fort looked strong and Katy said, "It's strong enough, ain't it, Pop? It won't break, will it?"

"I don't know," he said. "Wait and see."

Now a long wave, with unexpected force, rolled in, crossed the moat, and hit the fort in a jet of thrown-up foaming water. "Oh," Katy said, as if she herself were hurt by this first mortal blow to the fort. Once the blow had been struck, there was no relaxing in the attack of the sea. More waves poured in, they hit and washed around the fort, huge slices of its walls—undermined—fell and crumbled away. The tide hurried on either side; the fort became a salient in the long line of the sea. Water in its mass was threatening, all the miles of the sea rose up. It now seemed unbelievable that the fort held at all. It held, then with a leap the sea was inside it; it pulled and thrust; everything went. The waves in a moment leveled and with steady suction erased the fallen walls, the sand, until nothing was left.

Sighing, Katy said, "I didn't think it could do it."

"You can't stop the sea," her father said.

They had to get up and sit further back. It was a defeat; he felt it. But man is not sand, something to be washed away. Man fights.

He looked out again over the sea; its mass was cool, calm, beautiful.

"Well, we're home," Coyle said to his wife as they stood outside the entrance to the tenement. It was only about seven-thirty; they came home early because Katy was tired—also they had no money to eat away from home. Still, it had been good, Coyle felt good. He had given his family a day at the beach as any family deserved—they had needed it and it had been good for them. Particularly it had been good for Katy. Weeks of being in this place, playing in the hallways and kitchens of neighbors— with Lily Andriolo—playing in the hot streets.

"Glad to get home?" he said to Katy.

She nodded.

Glad? he thought. They went into the building.

It was still far from sundown; the heat was almost as bad as at midday. In the papers on the way home he had seen that today was breaking records for heat. The heat closed like a furnace around them as they entered the building.

There was something else. Coming from the beach, with the clean smell of the ocean so late in his nostrils, Coyle particularly noticed, as he came in, the smell of the tenement. A peculiar unmistakable smell—rot, old paint, remnants of garbage falling from the pails left outside of doors, all the close packed human smell—from cooking, breathing, living in a space that was meant for half the number of people.

They started upstairs. Once they had gone up half a flight, although it was still full daylight outside, here it was almost pitch dark. No wonder he had noticed the darkness at the beach bathhouse—darkness, poverty. Instead of decent windows—air shafts, air shaft windows. Windows like the ones at each landing here, windows that out of the two-foot-wide air shaft dropped a spot of ghostly light on the landing platform. The light was invisible in the air, it could only be seen actually on the landing. Coyle was astonished—looking at it—to see that there could be light without illumination. The darkness of the stairway angered him. He had always hated to have Katy going up and down it. Even now, holding her mother's hand, she stumbled. It would be easy, by herself, to have a bad fall. But that was not the principal thing he feared. It was—

"You have the key?" his wife said.

They had reached the fifth floor, their floor, and Coyle got out his key and opened the apartment door for them. They were back. There were the same two rooms, the same stifling atmosphere, the same furniture, walls, life. Even the Andriolo baby was crying again; they could hear Mrs. Andriolo, who was still overweight from her pregnancy, walking back and forth with it. He turned and looked at his wife and Katy. In their eyes was no longer the happiness they had felt at the beach. They were oppressed; like him they knew their lives had little in them.

They ate supper, with a better appetite than they usually had. But Coyle noticed something. His wife was worrying. He knew what she was worrying about, whether anybody would come for the rent. Nobody would come; nobody would come before Friday. But he began to worry too.

When they had finished eating and cleaned up, they went to the window and sat down. It was just like the morning except that now there was not so long to wait for darkness, for possible coolness. He reached over and took his wife's hand; they sat without speaking. Katy leaned on the window sill and Coyle noticed that her arms were again outstretched; they seemed again to be imploring the heat as they had in the morning.

Other people sat at other windows; people came and went; voices called, changed, grew loud or soft.

When the sun finally set, it seemed to get dark quickly. They put Katy to bed and did not put on the light so that she would sleep. He knew now why tenement children stayed up late, why—

Yes, he knew plenty he had not known until the last two years.

He and Mary said nothing, but sat in silence by the window. The air had cooled a little, had to. A few lights came on around the courtyard, threw a faint radiance in their room. He heard a radio announce, faintly, "—nine o'clock." At almost the same moment he heard Andriolo.

Andriolo was talking in the hallway downstairs. He could tell his voice. There was another voice, under it—he knew that voice too. The two voices continued, one loud, the other less loud. He turned and looked at his wife.

What was there to say?

After a few minutes it was quiet; steps sounded on the stairs, then there was the expected knock on the door. He answered it. In order not to wake up Katy, he opened the door quickly, stepped into the hall, and closed the door behind him.

"What's the matter, don't I come in?" Mr. Regan said.

"The kid's asleep."

"Okay—well, what I want don't take long. You got the rent?"

"No, I'll have it Friday." Fourteen dollars. He had never offered less than at least one month's full rent, would not now.

"You're two months behind, y' know? Wha' d' y' expect me to do, come every day for it?"

"I'm sorry, but—"

"You think all I got to do is collect rent?"

Coyle held himself in. "It's the best I can do. Two days' work a week—"

"And maybe that's my fault. Coyle, if you wanta live here, pay. If you don't—"

"Live here," he said explosively. "Live."

"It's better than the street—"

Coyle got the hidden threat; his anger flared up.

"This tenement's better than the street. Stairs like sewers—"

"All right, I didn't come here to argue, Coyle. I been renting this place to keep it going; it's about time I made some money. Fourteen a month with a toilet, two rooms—it's cheap. I oughta get sixteen, eighteen. You don't pay your rent, I'll get somebody who'll pay it and pay more."

"So that's it, hey? You're getting the place filled up so now you raise the rent."

"Why not? Rents have gone up—"

"Listen, maybe I'm short today but I'll have it Friday. Before you talk about raisin' rent, why don't you fix some of the violations?"

"What violations?"

"You think I don't know? You think because there's a lot of Greeks and Italians here they don't know a few things? Fire escapes—the front door—does it lock? See that door over there? That's a dumbwaiter only it don't work an' it's filled up with paper an' garbage. Maybe you don't know about that—"

"All right, pay a couple more dollars and I'll put improvements in—"

"The house is lousy with violations. What you ever put into

it? If it was to fall apart, you wouldn't buy a nail to hold it together. Now you wanta raise the rent. Raise the rent outa what—food for my kid? Outa Andriolo's baby—?"

Without realizing it, his voice had risen. In the room behind him he heard something; Katy was beginning to cry. He knew what it was, she had heard him and was frightened. Her crying was muffled with sleep; in a minute she would be crying loud.

"Okay," he said, turning, "you'll get your rent Friday."

"Coyle, I don't like people that talk—"

Coyle went back into the apartment and closed the door. After a while his wife quieted Katy; afterwards Katy tossed restlessly. They kept the light off so that she would go back to sleep again.

"Nice, ain't it?" he said to his wife.

He wondered if his wife would throw the dollar up to him, but she did not. She was intelligent.

They went to bed. In bed, neither of them slept. At ten—it was still early—the doorway of the Paraskevopoulos' apartment opened; they heard the trill of the canary, three sweet sucking gasps.

"Jim," Mary said.

"What?"

"Regan gonna put us out."

Coyle said nothing. He got up and, pulling on his pants, said, "I'm going down an' talk to Andriolo. He's got ideas."

October 25, 1938

Meridel LeSueur

Salvation Home

The girls looked in at me and sometimes they came in and asked me what I was in for. How did it look outside? When was I going to pop? When they came in they had to watch for the matron, and run when she was coming up the stairs. Alice, the deaf girl, and I wrote notes and looked out the black bars at the snow.

In the cold mornings I could see the girls about to deliver walk slowly down the hall. Every night you could hear screams from someone in labor and day and night the kids squalled in the nursery and the girls would go down the halls trying to see their babies but they couldn't.

At night the policewoman sat up all night at the bottom of the stairs. Every half-hour she went through the halls with a flashlight. She was a great, strong woman and the girls said she pinched and bent your arms when she got hold of you.

I couldn't sleep in there for thinking they would sterilize me. When I went to the bathroom and back I could see in the open doors and the beds would be drawn close together and I could hear the girls laughing and whispering. Alice said there were electric alarms at the windows. There was certainly no way to escape. I couldn't sleep so I began dreaming about trying to get something to eat again, and it would make me very sick and I would vomit. I asked the matron for a doctor because I didn't want to lose the baby but she said, You are all right, there is nothing the matter with you, you just want to get out of working in the laundry.

Alice told me that somebody was leaving the next day and I wrote a letter to Amelia and this girl I didn't know took it out for me and in about two days I got an answer from Amelia. I read it over and over and I showed it to Alice and she knew Amelia. It seems just about everybody knew her. The letter said:

Don't be afraid, baby. U are a maker now. U are going to have a good child, very good child, young dater or son. The day is near. Take hope, comrade. Dr. will see u soon. We see to that. Take sum hope. Workers Alliance meet nex day frum this. Have child happy demand ther be no so bad misry for our peepl like we hev so we can hev our childs in gret city with sum joy. See u very soon, deerhart. Amelia.

On Easter we had chicken for dinner and we could stay downstairs one hour longer and talk. There were hundreds of funny papers for us to read sent by some woman's club, and also jigsaw puzzles. Alice showed me all the people, writing funny things on her pad. There was a pretty girl with blonde hair named Julia who made all the jokes. Nobody could get her down. She said last Easter she spent in a beer joint getting stiff with a guy she had never seen before. Couldn't we have a swell time, she said, if we could push all the tables together and have a beer and something to spike it, with a couple of cartons of cigs, we wouldn't even need any tails.

The radio played "I Love You Truly," and everyone laughed, and a girl who had one glass eye she lost in a munitions factory said, You son of a bitch if you loved me truly I wouldn't be here—and we all laughed.

I'll be glad to get out of here, Julia said, I'll be glad to say good-bye to this. She said to me very polite, I hope you have your kid here, I think we're gonna pop about the same time.

We'll all go nuts together in this joint, the girl with the glass eye said bitterly.

When are you going to deliver, I asked her.

Hell, she said, if you work nine hours a day and no fresh air you're too damned tired to deliver.

A girl with yellow hair like straw came in and everyone was quiet.

Alice wrote on the pad, A stool.

We all began to read the funny papers. The bed bell rang and the major came in to lead us in prayer. She read from the Bible. Some of the girls could talk together on their fingers, clasped behind their backs. The major talked about the great divine joy of Easter and of motherhood and prayed asking the deity to forgive us for the great sin we had committed and be lenient with us and help us lead better lives in the future. Somebody must have made a mistake about the song because it was "Hark, the Herald Angels Sing," which is a Christmas song, but everyone sang as loud as they could because it's a pleasure to sing and everybody sang it,

> *Hark, the herald angels sing*
> *Wally Simpson stole our king*

and Julia began to giggle so that the major said, You may go Julia—and Julia turned at the door and thumbed her nose at the major and I felt an awful tickle of laughter like I was going to hoot and howl. Alice pinched me and smiled and pretended she was singing.

We marched upstairs. You could see all our gingham dresses exactly alike. I undressed and got in the gunny sack and big shoes and I could hear somebody crying in their pillow from the next room and the cries of the hungry babies in the nursery. Alice touched my cheek and showed me a tiny flashlight she had under her pillow. I didn't feel sleepy so we began to "talk."

She wrote, Don't cry. We, the common people, suffer together.

I didn't know what she meant. How did she know I felt sad? She nodded and wrote again. Nothing can hold us apart . . . See . . . even deafness; then she wrote, Or loneliness. And then—Or fear.

I looked at her. I nodded. She held the flashlight cupped by her hand so it couldn't be seen from the hall.

I wrote, How?

We are organizing, she wrote.

I read it.

Then she wrote, Nothing can stop us.

The matron came down the hall and her face went dark and you couldn't hear a sound. When she had passed, the light went on again and Alice was leaning over the pad.

I read, I am with the Workers Alliance.

I looked at it a long time. I wrote, Amelia too?

She nodded and smiled.

I chewed the pencil and then I wrote, I worked all my life.

She read it and nodded and pointed to herself, shaking her head in a quick joyful way, and pointed to her own breast. She grabbed the pad. She looked at me like she loved me, then she wrote swiftly.

I took the pad. I was excited. I read, We are both workers!

She rolled over, the light went out, and I could hear her laughing. I began to laugh too. When she turned on the light again we could not write fast enough.

I wrote, What does it do, the Workers Alliance?

They demand food, jobs, she wrote quickly.

I looked at the word demand. It was a strong word. I didn't know what to write. I looked at it a long time. She looked at me and when I looked at her she smiled and nodded like she was going through a woods and I was following her. She leaned over and the light shone through her thin hand. She put her hand under her cheek, closed her eyes, which I saw meant sleep, and then she wrote in a bold hand and turned the tiny light on it.

Wake tomorrow!

January 10, 1939

Alvah C. Bessie

Solo Flight

The plane rolled to a stop, my instructor released his safety belt, stood up in the front cockpit and stepped out onto the wing. My God, I thought, it's come! (Twenty years ago I wrote a letter.) He bent down over me in a confidential manner, as though he were about to impart a piece of information intended for my ear alone, and he said: "O.K. You can go alone now." He stepped down off the wing onto the ground. "I'll be right here when you get back," he said.

"Hey, wait a minute," I said. "I don't feel at all confident about this."

"Nuts," he said. "Remember what I told you. There's a stiff breeze; you'll probably need the engine till you're most of the way down. Don't level off the way you've been doing. Bring it right down to the ground. Go ahead." Tachometer, I thought; climb at 1,600, turn at 1,550, cruise at 1,500. Five hundred feet.

I looked at him, but he turned away. I jerked the throttle open, and snapped it closed again. I turned to him (he'd swung on his heel toward me with an angry expression), and I said, "I'm sorry." I wanted to get off the ground; I wanted to get away from there before I lost... (Twenty years ago...)

The plane rolled; I made a special effort with that throttle, pushing it forward slowly, infinitely slowly and with a steady pressure. The grass moved by swiftly, the engine was roaring. I held the stick forward, enjoying the pressure necessary to hold it against the airstream. The nose was down now and I eased back a bit on the stick, gently, gently. We were rolling fast now and I eased the stick a trifle farther back toward me, felt the excitement of the lift in the wings, held the stick toward me, my left hand on the throttle, my feet against the rudder pedals. I felt it lift, it was lifting now, it was off the ground, the ground was slipping by under me; it was dropping away. I enjoyed, for a second, the memory of many hours of maddening self-disgust, when I had had to fight the ship, fight my fear, fight my body to keep the plane running in a straight line across the ground. It had been impossible. But now I was climbing steadily; the earth was fifty feet below; the Coast Guards' squat military planes were beneath me, warming their engines on the ground; I shot a swift glimpse ahead, above, to both sides; there were no other planes in sight. I was rising diagonally across Flatbush Avenue, saw the toy cars going through the toll gate at the bridge, saw the green piers of the new bridge I had used so many times as a guide when I was trying to fly straight and level. A straight line is the shortest distance... (Twenty years ago...) *The fascists, the flight commander said, are sixteen miles due south.*

I remembered, and glanced at the tachometer; it was at 1,800 r.p.m. and with a feeling of deep regret I eased the throttle back a little till it fell to 1,600. ("Listen to the goddam engine!" he had said at least a hundred times. "Listen to it; don't fly so mechanical.") It made me sore that I had not heard the difference between 1,800 and 1,600. But I hated to ease it off; I hated to lose those 200 r.p.m. on the climb.

The bay was below me now, the shoal waters and the clean rippling surface, like watered silk. I could see the hundreds of parked cars in Riis Park, and on the far side, the beach, black with people safely on the earth. *Sixteen miles due south, under the baking sun, the enemy. Do you love peace? Do you love freedom? Do you love human dignity?* There was a small steamer far out on the horizon, and I suddenly recalled with a shock entirely unwarranted by the importance of the phenomenon, the fact that there really was no horizon; that was mist. That meant that when I got to the top, I would have to hold the nose above the point that looked like the horizon.

Exhausted, I reached the top of the climb (the altimeter on the underside of the upper wing read 500) and cautiously, as though I were handling eggs, reaching down a box from a high shelf, I pulled the stick slightly toward me and brought the throttle back a trifle. I leaned out to the left and looked at the tachometer in the front cockpit–1,550–and nodded my head. Slowly, cautiously, I brought the stick a trifle to the left and pressed gently on the left rudder pedal, saw the horizon tip, and then remembered that I had forgotten to look to the left before I turned. I cursed. The nose was swinging slowly around and when the field came into sight on my left, I brought the r.p.m. to 1,500, felt myself shaking as though I had the ague, and consciously relaxed. My legs ached; my knuckles were white with the grip I'd had upon the stick; I relaxed my throttle hand, took it off the lever for an instant, and then hurriedly put it back again.

"By Christ!" I said aloud, "that's funny." I laughed. I said, "Ha! ha!" as loud as I could say it, and then consciously relaxed again. My flesh was wet; there were beads of perspiration on the backs of my hands; my back ached and my neck was stiff. I said aloud, "Well, you're flying." I said, *"Well, you're flying!"* I shot a swift glance down at the field, but I couldn't see him: I looked for him anxiously for a moment, felt the left wing go down, and hurriedly, my heart in my throat, looked forward and corrected the unintentional bank. The shadow of the plane moved under me across the earth, a dark cloud scudding, man's shadow on the earth he'd left behind.

Wind rising. A gust of wind struck us and the plane rose ten feet, dropped five, fell off on the left wing, and righted itself before my mind got round to directing my hand to correct the error. I could feel that I was tightening up again, and relaxed. "Relax!" I said aloud, *"Relax, you damned fool, relax!"* ("You'll either fly it yourself," he said, "or it'll fly *you*. I want *you* to do the flying, not the ship.") Twenty years ago I wrote a letter. . . .

There was something in my mind trying to get my attention, but I purposely refused to think of it; I knew what it was, but I rejected it, I held it off without too much effort; I knew it would worry me. Time enough. Across the field I could see long lines of cars parked, and a thin edge of people standing at the wire fence before the concrete apron. There were three people there I couldn't see. My wife was there, and my two small sons; one four and a half years old, one two years and three months. Maybe they're having a cocoamalt, I thought, not watching at all. How would they know he'd got out of the plane; they couldn't see across the field. The thought of them sitting calmly on the veranda of the restaurant, the kids having a cocoamalt, not watching, annoyed me. Don't they know? Can't they tell? Don't they feel it. . . . No, my mind said; it doesn't matter; I want this for you all; I want *you* to handle this, and not the enemy. (Twenty years ago:

To: Master Alvah C. Bessie
From: Chief of the Signal Corps
In Re: Riding in Government Airplanes

1. Your recent letter to the President has been referred to me.

2. I regret to say that it will not be possible for the President to grant you permission to ride in a government airplane.

3. If we gave permission to all boys your age to ride in government airplanes, there would be no planes available to train pilots for France.

4. If you wish to see an airplane, you may go to the nearest army flying field and ask for the commanding officer; and he will be willing to show you an airplane.)

This is no place for you, my mind said. This is no place to be; what are you doing here? The kids . . . the older boy has been up five times now; it doesn't mean a thing to him. "Poppy," he said, "if I jumped out of the airplane, would it hurt me?" "Yes," I said, "I suppose it would." "Poppy," he said, "if I jumped out of the airplane with a parachute would it hurt me very much?" Four and a half; thirty-three. What did I say, the kid? Dear President Wilson, did I say? Honorable Sir, did I say? I am a young boy thirteen years of age, and I would like to ride in an army airplane twenty years ago. Now, now.

Suddenly I knew I was in the air, that I was flying, that the earth was below me, that the water was down there on my right, the field on my left, and millions were walking the earth, in Brooklyn, in Manhattan, in Chicago, and in Spain. The front cockpit looked empty for the first time, and I fought off the thing my mind wanted to tell me; just a little while longer now, just a little longer. Let them all fly; let all of them soar on stiff wings above the earth. Man made this thing for all, this was made for man and who is keeping it from him; who is keeping the shattering joy of flight from the multitudes of the earthbound? Who will give it to them? I put my left hand out and felt the solid rush of the airstream. I looked to the left, and with my heart pounding, my body awake for the first time in my life, I eased the stick off to the left, gave it left rudder, felt the seat tip under me, saw the horizon tip. There were wings over the earth, moving swiftly from point to point, seeking out the distant places of the earth. Over the North Pole, the broad Atlantic, bringing peace and happiness and the exultation of accomplishment.

Below me there were some fishermen's huts on the edge of the swampy land; there were rivulets running out into the bay. *Basque.* There was a rowboat moored a few feet offshore, its shadow on the water. There were gulls below me, wheeling over the surface. The nose swung gently across the slanted horizon, Flatbush Avenue came into my field of vision, and the cars moving slowly on it, crawling like army ants on the march. There was a ship coming into the field ahead of me, and I banked to keep an eye on him and let him have all the time he needed. I remembered my instructor in the front cockpit, his goggled profile, pointing at his own eye, then at another plane in the air, then at his eye, then at the plane. Below me, the fishermen's huts; poor people. *Suddenly I released the bombs, saw them melting away below as they fell, twisting, saw the soundless detonation and the flash, the smoke, and the geyser of earth and broken wood and broken water. I thought of Guernica, of Madrid, of Durango, of Bilbao, and shut the sight out of my mind, the hate out of my heart.* . . . Who is keeping them all (the poor) upon the ground? Why can't they soar, why can't they stretch their wings? There are wings over the earth, moving swiftly, point to point, bringing death and grief and pain and the horror of man's ingenuity.

I leveled the wings with the horizon and looked down. The wind sock on the little signal tower was plain, and as I watched I could see him, he was standing there, just where I had left him. My heart rose into my throat and my mind acknowledged the thought it had been shunting off as a football player stiff-arms interference. I banked to the left again and slowly pulled the throttle toward me, heard the engine idle down, shoved the nose down, and waited. It was *now*.

"Do it!" I said aloud, and was astonished by the sound of my own voice. The wires were whistling and the plane rocked and rolled under me. I corrected a bit for the wind, gave it a little right rudder and brought it into the breeze. *For a brief moment, the machine guns rattled, two through the propeller, one on either wing, and the fascist troops threw themselves flat on the road, rolled into the ditches, their hands above their heads.* I could see him now, he was waving his arms to show me where he was. The wires were screaming and I pulled the nose up a trifle. I could feel I was undershooting the field, opened the gun for a few seconds, closed it again. There was nothing to do but wait—"Don't sit there like a *dummy*; keep your wits about you; you can't fall asleep in an airplane," he said. "What the hell do you want to do, dive it into the ground!"

The earth was rising, the soft green field was swelling under me, I corrected for the gusts of air nearer the ground, keeping the wings level, holding the nose along the line I had determined to land on, parallel to the concrete runway. My voice was in my ears.

"Wait. Wait.

"All right now, soon; all right now, soon. Don't level off too soon.

"Don't level off too soon. Bring it right in.

"Now," my voice said, and I eased back on the stick. He was standing to my left, his hands at his sides, watching. His goggles gleamed on his forehead and I had a momentary image of my own serious face, the sinister face of the pilot, helmeted and goggled, like some monster, like an insect under a microscope, the clean sweep of the skull, the enormous eyes, the firm mouth with the lips in a thin line; watching alert, the eyes moving behind the lenses. *Machine guns rattle for the poor.*

"Now," my voice said again, "take it easy; take it easy take it easy take it easy."

The ground was rushing past me; the individual grass blades could be seen; I felt like bursting.

"*Now,*" I shouted, pulled the stick into my lap, and felt the ship sit down, felt the dull shock of the solid earth vibrate through the fuselage, kicked the rudder right and left to keep the plane rolling straight across the grass, my chest aching with desolation, the joy and the agony of flight.

He was running up to me and I could feel my face cracking with the smile, my jaws aching from the pressure of my teeth against each other. I wanted a drink of water; my throat was bone-dry; my eyes felt as though they were bursting from their sockets; my head ached. The strap of the goggles cut into my scalp. (Twenty years ago I wrote a letter.)

"That was ridiculous!" he shouted. "The whole thing was ridiculous! Your takeoff stank, you climbed too fast—do you want to stall and crash! You yanked it through the turns, the approach was absolutely absurd, you bounced when you landed. Didn't I *tell* you not to dive the wings off it! Do I have to *teach* you to glide all over again? Do I!!!!"

"I don't remember bouncing," I said.

He put his hands on his hips. "You don't remember?" he said gently, as though he were talking to a four-year-old. "Do you want me to hold your hand? I'm perfectly willing to hold your hand. I say it *stank*!"

He turned away from the plane, and without looking back at me he said, "Go ahead; do it again, and stop *dreaming*."

January 24, 1939

3
Reportage

"Couple of guys named Marx and Engels. Find 'em and give 'em the works."   NED HILTON

Monopolies

Hearst Over America

The Cradle Will Rock

Bank Night

BILL GROPPER

Erskine Caldwell

"Parties Unknown" in Georgia

Will Walker was shot to death a month ago on the streets of Bartow, Georgia; Ernest Bell was beaten to death with an iron pipe and his body thrown into a well near Bartow; and an unidentified man about thirty-five years of age was shot in the head and breast six times and, apparently because he did not die quickly enough, his head was almost severed from his body with a knife. This body was found in a field near Bartow.

Sam Outler would be dead now, too, if Sheriff Jim Smith had not put him in the Jefferson county jail for protection against the gang of white men who killed the three others. Sam sits in his cell, his head swollen and sore from the beating he received the night his friend Ernest Bell was lynched.

You can climb the cell block stairs and find Sam Outler sitting on his iron bunk waiting–he does not know what he's waiting for, and after you have talked to him a while, you yourself begin to wonder what there is for him to wait for. If Sam goes back to Bartow, he will be killed. If he leaves the state, his family will never see him again. And so, while you sit there looking at Sam and listening to him, you cannot keep from feeling uncomfortable; because your skin is white, and Sam Outler is an accusing finger pointing at the white men of your country who butcher hogs with more humaneness than they kill Negroes.

Last night I revisited Bartow, Georgia. It was not quite midnight when I got there. The town appeared to be as peaceful as the starry sky overhead. There were lights in some of the big white houses on the hill above the stores and railway station. Two or three men were hurrying along the streets. A night watchman sat on the steps of a ginnery. Behind the town the South Branch of the Ogeechee River flowed as smoothly and as silently as a stream of crude oil.

Hoar frost was forming on the roofs of buildings bordering the lowlands of the river.

Walking up the unpaved main street that had dried out after a week of rain, you cannot help stopping in front of the drug store and looking at the window display. Costly cosmetics and cheap ones are piled side by side, and behind them all is a seven-color cardboard poster displaying three naked girls and the name of a perfume manufacturer. All around you are signs repeating the magic phrase: "Drink Coca-Cola." You move on before the aromatic drug store smell gains possession of your senses.

Across the river is the well where Ernest Bell was thrown. I stumbled around in the darkness trying to locate it. I found a well beside one of the numerous sites where houses have been burned. Sam Outler had said the well was only a few steps from the road, and the one I found may or may not have been the one I was looking for. Anyway, it was like most wells in Jefferson County. It was about twenty feet deep and three feet in diameter. It had the well-stand rope and bucket. The stone I dropped into it struck a board floating in the water.

Recrossing the creaking iron bridge to the town, you hear a girl laughing somewhere in the darkness. You know she is not far away, because the sound of voices reaches your ear distinctly. While waiting at the end of the bridge, a Negro boy comes out of the darkness and dodges you. When you speak to him, he darts into the swamp beside the road.

I stood on the road, listening to sounds in the Ogeechee swamps to the right and left and in the rear, and watching the lights of the town spread over the hillside, and I could not forget what Sam Outler had said. He was speaking of the night he was beaten with the pipe and Ernest Bell was thrown into the well.

"The white men came up to where we was and said Ernest was a son-of-a-bitch. Ernest told them, 'White-folks, I ain't no son-of-a-bitch, and I don't want to be called one.' Then this young Bradley boy steps out and hits Ernest with something he had in his hand, and Ernest told him not to do that no more.

"Then I said, 'Look here, white-folks, me and Ernest don't want to make trouble.' Some of the white men went to a automobile and took some short pieces of iron pipes out and came back where we was. I heard Ernest saying to them, 'I don't mind being called any other name you can think of, but don't call me a son-of-a-bitch.' Just then I saw them coming at us, and the next thing I knew was the next day. I reckon the only reason why they didn't shoot me and throw me in the well with Ernest was because I didn't do much talking like Ernest did. I saw that Bradley boy run up and hit Ernest on the head with the pipe, and that's the last I remember, because somebody started beating me on the head with the other pipes about the same time."

The main street at midnight was deserted, but three weeks ago there was a milling mob crowding the narrow unpaved thoroughfare. Nobody was lynched that day, because the Negro whose life the mob demanded died in the hospital from bullets pumped into his body by a local policeman. Will Walker would have been lynched by this mob of several hundred men and boys armed with pistols, rifles, shotguns, and cane knives if the shooting at the hands of the policeman had not been fatal. Walker had tried to protect his life, and he was killed for his pains.

The Negro whose mutilated body was found in a field near Bartow today lies buried in an unmarked grave in an abandoned field. Nobody knows his name; nobody cares. But the men who killed him, like those who killed Ernest Bell and Will Walker, walk the streets in heroic strides. Their names are known; they will even boast of their crimes. But the coroner's jury washed its hands of the deeds when it returned the verdict: "Death at the hands of parties unknown."

The number of other Negroes who have been killed in the vicinity of Bartow during the past twelve months, as well as the number killed during the past three decades—is unknown. One man's guess apparently is as good as another's. A farmer living three miles from town will tell you that "there must have been ten or twenty put to death last year." A Negro living on the edge of the Ogeechee swamp near Bartow will say: "White-folks—only the devil himself knows how many."

Two weeks ago Will Jordan was killed by two white men who went to his house after midnight and shot him while he was asleep in bed with his wife. His six children were in the room with him. The next day the two men admitted that they had killed the wrong Negro—they were after someone else and had gone into the Jordan house by mistake. The killers were acquitted. They promised the jury they would kill the "right" Negro the next time they went out shooting.

But this killing took place in another section of Jefferson County. I was standing in the main street of Bartow trying to wonder what I was doing there. I was trying to reason why three Negroes could be put to death in such a quiet, peaceful town by white men who were at that moment in their homes asleep. Nobody was disturbed. Nobody was walking around in the dark with a flashlight trying to find evidence to convict the killers. Nobody was abroad offering protection to Negroes who wished to come out of their cabins. Bartow was as calm as any Georgia town at midnight. Georgia was as peaceful as any Southern state in January. Sam Outler, sitting in his cell in the county jail ten miles away, was wondering what was going to happen to him. If Sheriff Jim Smith turned him loose, he knew the Bartow mob would get him before he could walk a mile; if he was to be taken to the state line and released, he would never again see his family in Bartow. I walked once more up the street and looked at the display of perfumes, soaps, and powders in the drug store window. The drug store odor again filtered through my senses and I turned away wondering if I could ever forget the association in my mind of perfumed women and brutal men.

Half a mile from the main street, on the Augusta highway, I stopped and looked for a while at the swollen and bloated carcass of a mule that had been killed by an automobile or truck. The mule was lying on the shoulder of the highway, and it appeared to have been dead a week or ten days. It will probably remain there until the swamp rats and buzzards finish removing it bite by bite.

Somewhere in the South Branch of the Ogeechee River above the town or below it, some people will tell you that the bodies of two Negroes lie. When you stop and ask a storekeeper or farmer if he thinks the rumor true, he will squint at you for a moment or two and then say that what he knows he found out himself and if you wish to find out anything you will have to do likewise. You can do as the Bartow storekeeper suggests, or you can go along with Sheriff Jim Smith while he is dragging the stream, and after a day's search you can say that probably the rumor has no truth in it.

But nonetheless the rumor continues to persist, just as did those rumors that preceded the finding of one body in a well and another in an abandoned cotton field.

After leaving the town of Bartow and the Ogeechee swamps and the partly devoured mule, you begin a gradual climb to the Georgia uplands, the sand hills west of Augusta. Up there the air is clear and sweet with the odor of pine. When you stop and look back over the lowlands where you have spent most of the night, you cannot help wondering anew if the fate that awaits Sam Outler will be death at the hands of the Bartow gang, or a life torn from his family in a strange country.

Back in Augusta in the early hours of the morning, I stop and enter a drug store for a pack of cigarettes, and the startling odor of perfumes and cosmetics does something to me. The clerk thinks I am drunk; I am unable to ask for what I wish, and I have to cling to the tobacco counter for support. He takes me by the arm and leads me to the sidewalk, and with a gentle shove, starts me on my way. Partly revived by the night air, I realize that, after a night spent in the Ogeechee swamps, perfumery and brutality will ever plague me.

January 23, 1934

John L. Spivak

A Letter to President Roosevelt

Fresno, Calif., 1934

Dear Mr. President:

I don't suppose you will ever see this but I am writing to you
to keep a promise I made to a little fifteen-year-old Mexican
girl. She wanted to write to you because she had heard you
were doing things for poor workers. She didn't write because
she did not have three cents for a stamp and because she
never went to school to learn how to write. Her earliest
memories are of wandering about in an old, rattling, wheezing Ford from vegetable field to fruit field, from fruit field
to vegetable field, and you can't go to school if your father
needs your labor in the fields as soon as you are seven years
old.

I cannot give you her name because when I told her I
would write to you for her she became frightened and
pleaded with me not to mention her name. She was afraid
maybe you'd write the boss and her family would be denied
the privilege of working in the fields all day for thirty-five
cents. She said it was all right, so I'll tell you how to find
her.

Just take the main highway from Fresno, Calif., to Mendota which is about thirty miles away and turn west at Mendota for about four miles. You can't miss it because you'll
see a big sign "Land of Milk and Honey." When you've
passed this sign you'll see against the horizon a cluster of
houses and when you come to the sign "Hotchkiss Ranch–
Cotton Pickers Wanted" turn up the side road a few hundred
yards beyond the comfortable farmhouse with its barns and
cotton shelters. There's a row of fifteen outhouses along the
road. That is where the migratory workers and this little girl
live, Mr. President.

There are two more outhouses a little way from these and

those are the ones actually used for outhouses. You can tell that by the odor and the swarms of flies that hover around these two especially. This is a typical migratory workers' camp, only some have five outhouses for the workers and some have thirty. It depends upon the size of the farm.

You'll recognize a migratory workers' camp because each outhouse—"homes" they call them out here—is made of plain wooden boards, dried by years of tropical sun.

The little girl lives in the third house from the front as you approach. You can't miss it. It has a large sign: SCARLET FEVER.

But don't worry about that because the health authorities here are not worrying. They just tacked up the sign on this outhouse door and on that one there near the end of the row and went away. They didn't tell anyone to be careful about a contagious disease because that might have had the camp quarantined and the whole crop lost to the farmer, for all the cotton pickers and their children have been in that outhouse. I don't imagine it's very dangerous though for only two more children have caught it. If it had been dangerous I'm sure the health authorities would have warned them.

In this outhouse where a baby girl has scarlet fever you'll find an iron bedstead. That's where the baby sleeps, the one that's tossing around in fever while the mother tries to shoo the flies away. That's the only bed and it's one of the five in the whole camp, so you can't miss it. The other six in this family sleep on the floor huddled together; father, mother, two grown brothers, a little brother, and the fifteen-year-old girl. They sleep like most everybody else in the camp: on the floor.

That barrel and rusty milk can in the corner of the room where everybody sleeps on the floor holds the water they bring from Mendota to cool the child's fever. It is four miles to Mendota and four miles back and eight miles costs a little for gas so they have to be very sparing with the water. That's why they all look so dirty—it's not because they don't like to wash. It's because it costs too much to get water—water needed for cooking and drinking. You can't waste water just washing yourself when it costs so much to get. After all, when you make thirty-five cents for a full day's work and spend of that for gas to get water it leaves you that much less for food.

The mother isn't in the field today because the baby is

pretty sick and those children playing in and out of the houses marked with SCARLET FEVER signs are too young to go into the field but everyone else is there. That's where I found the little girl for whom I am writing this letter.

Perhaps I had better tell you exactly how I found her and what we talked about so you can understand just what she wants. It would be a big favor, she said, and she would be very grateful.

She doesn't mind picking cotton bolls for thirty-five cents a day and she doesn't mind the filth and dirt and starvation but she is worried about that electric light in the shack. You noticed it, didn't you? The one with the dusty bulb right in the middle of the outhouse they live in. Well, you have to pay twenty-five cents a week if you want to use that electric light and twenty-five cents is a lot of money when you get only thirty-five cents a day and you need that twenty-five cents for food and for gas for the car so you can go get water.

It's not that she wants the light at night. She and her family get along without it but you see they've discovered that it's awfully hard to tend the sick baby in the darkness. And it's always dark when the baby seems to cry the most. And in addition, this little girl is worried about herself. She is going to have a baby and suppose it comes at night and there is no light? She is going to have a baby in this little outhouse where her mother and father and brothers live, this little outhouse with the sign SCARLET FEVER over its door.

What she wanted to ask you is if you could possibly get in touch with somebody and have them not charge them twenty-five cents for the use of the electric light–especially when somebody's sick or expecting a baby. It's not so bad when you're well, but it's awfully hard when you have a little sick sister tossing and crying and you yourself are expecting a baby.

I explained to this little girl that you would understand about her not being so moral. She is such a frail little thing working so hard in the fields all day and you know after you get through working and you just don't know what to do with yourself and your youth just cries out to forget the days that have gone and the long years that stretch ahead of you, well–you sort of forget that maybe it isn't just quite moral to have a baby when you're not quite fifteen.

I told the little girl that you had a daughter, too, grown

up now of course, and she thought that if your girl had gotten into trouble when she was fifteen that you wouldn't have liked her to have a baby in a little wooden outhouse with another baby tossing in fever and no light to see anything by. I told her I didn't think you would, either, and so sitting there in the cotton field in this "Land of Milk and Honey" she cried.

But I started to tell you what we talked about and here I've gone telling you what she wanted me to write. You see, when I walked out in the field there was this little girl dragging a huge sack along the furrow, and stuffing the brown bolls into it. She looked so tired, so weary and then I noticed that she was with child.

"How old are you?" I asked.

She looked up and smiled pleasantly.

"Fifteen."

"Working in the fields long?"

"Uh-uh."

"How old were you when you started?"

She shrugged shoulders. "Dunno. Maybe eight. Maybe nine. I dunno."

"What do you make a day?"

"Sometimes in first picking dollar and a half. We get seventy-five cents a hundred. Used to get sixty cents but red agitators got us fifteen cents raise. But for third picking get only forty cents a hundred and there ain't so much to pick."

You may be interested in her phrase "red agitators." That's what the Communists were called here by the newspapers, so now everybody calls a Communist a "red agitator." This little girl didn't know what a "red agitator" was; she knew only that "red agitators" got them a raise of fifteen cents on the hundred pounds by organizing them and calling a strike.

Forty thousand out of the 250,000 agricultural workers in California have taken out cards in the Communist union. They call it the Cannery and Agricultural Workers Union. And most of the 40,000 are from the 100,000 migratory workers—those who live in the camps like this little girl. They don't pay dues often but they carry their cards and they are strong on organization and very militant, especially the Mexicans.

You probably read in the papers about the fruit and vegetable pickers' strike in the Imperial Valley and around

Sacramento and Alameda and in the San Joaquin Valley right here in Tulare and Kern counties. There have been violence and killings but the strikes were almost always won. That's because the workers felt a lot like this little girl: no matter what happened it couldn't be worse than it was. If the Communists would help them then they would be Communists. Nobody else seemed to care for them, nobody ever tried to organize them until the "red agitators" came. Businessmen and bankers and farmers are terrified by "red agitators"; you understand, of course, why when you read this letter that the little girl wanted me to write you.

"Last year when 'red agitators' make strike in Tulare and get seventy-five cents a hundred so we get seventy-five cents here, too," she added laughing.

Her father, a tall, dark-skinned man with a week's growth of black beard, saw me talking to her and came over.

"Somet'ing wrong, eh?" he asked.

"No. Nothing wrong. Just talking to your daughter. I want to find out how much you people make a week."

A slow smile spread over his features.

"We make nodding," he said definitely.

"How much?"

"Me, my wife, my girl here. Last week we work from Monday to Thursday night and make $2.50—all of us."

"Your daughter is only fifteen. I thought there was a law against child labor."

He shrugged his shoulders.

"Nobody come here. All children work in field soon big enough. Only time man come here is when put up sign 'Scarlet Fever.' Nobody care."

"Things any better now than they were last year or two years ago?"

"No. No better. Lots worse. Last year we buy 100 pounds cheapest flour for $2.45. Now I pay $3.10 same kind. Last year before President make N.R.A. I make more money dan I make now. Made lots more in '32, less in '33, in '34 hardly don't make nodding."

"I thought you fellows got a raise for picking cotton?"

"Yes. But we no get it. We make strike before we get it. 'Red agitators.' They make for us."

"How about before the depression?"

"Good times. Get $1.50 a hundred. Very bad now. Yes, sir. Very bad."

"Now that you've finished picking these acres what do you do?"

"Go to peas field. Everybody go in car or truck. We take everything except house. We get nodding but house when we come. When finished peas fields we come back for grapes."

"What do you make a week when the whole family is working? In good times?"

"In good times? Oh, sometimes make $8, maybe if work very hard, make $10."

That seemed to be the height of his earnings and he sounded very pleased that he and his family were able on occasions to earn that much.

"Well, I got go back pick bolls." He said something to the girl in Spanish. She flushed and started picking again.

"My father he say better work," she said.

"Yes; well, you go ahead and work while I walk alongside and talk to you. Are you married?"

She flushed again and shook her head.

"No. No marry."

"Looks like things are not so good for you people, eh?"

"Oh, they awright. Things gettin' better–everybody say. The President, he take care of poor people."

"Is he taking care of you?"

"No, sir. Not yet. Things very bad for us. But he got lots to do and he never hear about cotton pickers. I wanted write and tell him hurry up because I going to have a baby and things very bad for us. He do something for poor people if he know how things very bad, eh?"

"Why didn't you write to him, then?"

She blushed again.

"No got stamp."

"Oh," I said, "I'll give you a stamp."

"Thank you but no can write."

"Sure, you go ahead. The President will be glad to hear from you."

"No can write," she repeated. "No go school; work in fields all the time."

"If you'll tell me what you want to write, I'll do it for you."

She looked at me with a swift smile and giggled.

I took out a pencil and some paper and asked her name.

A look of terror spread over her face.

"No! No! No write the President!" she begged.

"Why not? Didn't you want to write to him?"

"No! No! I just talk. Just talk."

"What are you afraid of?"

"No write the President, Mister, please." She straightened up and looked at me pleadingly. "If you write for me to the President my father get in trouble. Maybe the President get mad and my father, he no get no more work."

"I don't think so," I assured her. "But if you don't want me to tell who you are I can write to him and tell him about it without mentioning your name."

She looked up with a sudden hope.

"You do that?"

"Sure. I don't have to give your name. I'll just say a little Mexican girl in a cotton field four miles from Mendota."

She looked earnestly at me for a moment.

"Please, you write the President. Tell him my baby is coming," she said in a low tone. "I dunno when the baby come. Maybe at night and we got no light. Please, you tell the President things very bad. We no make maybe nothing. My little sister sick and if baby comes I no can have bed. I got to have baby on floor and if it come in night how I have baby?"

I nodded, unable to speak.

"You please tell the President maybe he tell boss here not charge us twenty-five cents a week for electric light so I can have my baby."

"I'll tell him exactly what you said," I promised.

"You no fool me?"

"No, I'm not fooling you. I promise."

That is all, Mr. President. I don't know whether you will ever see this but I just wanted to keep my promise; and if you do see it you'll know why "red agitators" are making more headway here than anywhere I've been so far in this country.

March 20, 1934

Joseph North

Taxi Strike

So you ride the streets all day long and at five o'clock you look at the meter and what do you see? A soldier. [$1] "Good Christ," you say, "you gotta make three bucks more before you turn in." So you cruise the streets round and round and finally you get desperate and you open the door and say, "Come on in. Anybody." And who should walk in? A ghost. So you say to the ghost, "Where to?" And the ghost says, "Drive me around Central Park." So you drive the ghost around Central Park till the meter hits four bucks. Then you ask him for the dough. Then the ghost tells you he's broke. So you t'row him out and you go back to the garage. You shell out t'ree bucks of your own so you don't get the air. When you get home, the wife says, "Where's the dough?" Then you tell her, "Today I gave it to the company to keep the job." So she says, "Keep your job, hell. You're keeping the company. Well pick. Who's it you gonna keep? Me or the company?" So you gotta pick. Who you gonna keep, men, the wife or the company?

Hackie's Fable

Men who ply the streets for their livelihood develop a characteristic attitude: the highways belong to them. When they go on strike, be they taxicab drivers, or traction employees, the authorities may well expect the major pyrotechnics of revolt. The police nightstick can flail from day to night, it cannot dislodge the idea. The Mayor may cajole and storm in turn from dawn to dusk but the men of the streets stay on the streets. The streets are theirs—not only the gutters. As the New York cabbies say in their juicy lingo that springs partly from their slum derivations, partly from their enforced association with the night-life characters of a big city, and partly from the peculiar conditions of their trade: "What? Them weasels tell us to get off the streets? Spit on them! Push me off, rat!"

The strike of the New York cabmen stands unique in American labor history: it is, to date, the biggest in the industry and possesses connotations of great importance to all

American workingmen. Forty thousand cabmen abandoned their wheels for the sake of an independent union, and against the strait jacket of a company union. They symbolize most spectacularly the rebellion of the American workers—700,000 of whom have been weaseled into company union-ism under the pressure of finance capitalism and the N.R.A.—against the flumdummery of "employee-representation" organizations.

The trio of policemen bivouacked across the street and dawn found them cracking slats to heap on the fire. Three ruddy faced cops—"mugs"—pretended to ignore the hackies picketing the Parmelee garage at 23rd Street and Eleventh Avenue. One patrolman picked a carrot from the gutter and fed a blanketed horse, deliberately turning his massive blue-coated back on the strikers. Across the street this hackie, Leo Chazner, strike placards flapping against his chest and back, eyed him obliquely. "I been in the racket seventeen years," he told me. "I never seen a strike like this one. The beauty part of it is, kid, we're making history for the whole woild. The eyes of the woild is on us—the New York hackies."

He marched up and back, hackman's cap and worn overcoat. Every time he passed the garage entry he peeped inside. "What a sight! Look at them, kid, look at them! Two hundred and fifty of 'em crowding the walls." Within, shiny cabs, row on row, stretched a full block to the next wall—phalanxes of beautiful cars—eerily silent, something uncanny about them like all machines when the human factor is extracted. He boasted of the Parmelee cab. "Wonderful engine. Hums like a boid. Don't know you're riding. No bumps." We had tramped all over lower Manhattan that morning from garage to garage, picketing and checking up on the turnout. Radio police cars swept up and down West Street. Across the boulevard, ocean liners trumpeted in from the harbor. The first trucks lumbered their route, but no taxis rolled. "Look at the avenoo," Cabby Chazner gloated. "Clean as a whistle."

That was Saturday morning. The previous night the strikers had swirled across Broadway, leaving a wake of wreckage which plunged the iron deep in the Parmelee, Radio, and Terminal fleet operators. Cabs lay on their sides, the wheels grotesquely whirling; here and there they burst into flames, scabs fled down the street pursued by strikers, while mounted police picked their way through the streets at the fore and rear of the demonstrations. The cabbies' "Educational Committee" was on the job. Parmelee, Radio, and Terminal fleet owners spent thousands of dollars for full-page advertisements in the commercial press moaning "Vandals!" and calling for the military. "Take the scabs off the street and there won't be no violence," the hackies responded. "Who's driving them cabs? Chicago gunmen wit' soft hats: say, did you ever see a hackie on duty wit' a soft hat? That's the Parmelee Chicago gunmen...."

The next day when the strikers took a night off, I heard a detail of mounted police at Fifteenth Street and Irving Place taunt a crowd of hackies, "Well, well, them Chicago boys got you on the run now, ain't they?" The strikers retorted, "Say, mug, look, look–there goes Dillinger! See if you can catch Dillinger."

The New York hackie is a man in whom revolt has been festering for many years. Every policeman has the right to commandeer his cab at any moment without compensation–for police duty. The city officialdom has raised his tax, his license fee, forced him to plaster his photo in the cab in a sort of Bertillon system, libeling him a semi-underworld man. Pugnacious and independent by nature, he has resented the need to live off the tip, which always carries with it a smack of mendicancy. He found redress nowhere; neither the press which he has learned belongs to those who "give him the woiks"; nor the government, for why had they elected Fiorello, the self-announced hackies' "friend," they ask.

The hackies are bad men when riled. Like all long-enduring workers, they are not finicky about scabs or company property. They have developed a technique in this strike: the Education Committee–("Better teachers than Yale professors")–which is a guerrilla picket line well adapted to the needs of a big city strike of this sort.

Scab drivers halted by a red light often find the committee of "professors" waiting on them. To the epithet "Rat!" or "Mouse!" or "Weasel!" the scab finds his car doorless or even in flames–a lit match flicked into the engine beneath the hood does the trick.

How race hatred melts in the crucible of class struggle was poignantly evidenced when a Negro hackie from the Harlem detachment of strikers addressed the strikers at Germania Hall. "Boys," he said, "when you say you're with us, mean it. Mean it from the bottom of your hearts! We been gypped ever since 1861 and we're from Missouri. If you show the boys up in Harlem you mean what you say, then you're getting the sweetest little bunch of fighters in the world: for them spades driving the Blue and Black taxis up there can do one thing—and that's fight!" The hats began to fly in the air. He gestured for silence. "And when we fights together, us black and white, man, they ain't nobody can stop us!" The ovation he received from these recently politically uneducated workers was tremendous; it signified to me how deeply inured prejudices and hatreds fostered among the proletariat can vanish overnight when solidarity is needed in common struggle.

Returning to strike headquarters after the meeting (it was necessary to run a gauntlet of files of bluecoats, mounted horsemen, radio cars, and riot trucks), Hackie Chezar clapped his hand to his forehead. "Oh, for a couple hours of shut-eye," he groaned. "I been up three days straight now." At leaflet-littered strike headquarters on 42nd Street I read the placard in rude hand-printed letters, "Watch Out for These Cars: Yellow Cab Large Sedan—Penna Plates; Terminal Cab 021-644; Coupé N. Y. Plates I-T-5469." Chezar watched me. "Gangsters and dicks riding them cars," he commented.

A massive youth, pug-nosed and Irish, they called him Pondsie, was recounting the demonstration the delegation of cabbies received at the Communist district convention in the Coliseum the other night. "We walks in and the Communists go crazy. They stand up, about a million of 'em, and start singing. We go up on the platform and they give us the spotlight." The crowd about him listened intently. "Then when they come to the chorus of the song they're singing they give us the Communist salute." His left fist—a huge affair—goes up in a sort of short uppercut. "Know what their salute is?" he asks, looking around the room. "The left hook." And he demonstrates it again and again. The others in the room watching him, try the salute, too. I notice a youth with a palm cross on his lapel, giving the left hook. (It was Palm Sunday.) "And then," Pondsie finishes his story, "they have a collection. Man, they raked the coin in wit' dishes on broomsticks. 'Bout three hundred bucks them Communists give us."

The lad with the palm cross on his lapel raises his eyebrows. "Three hundred bucks!" He shoots a few left hooks in the air. "If them Communists are wit' us, I'm wit' them. Left hook!" he shouts. The others chorus, "Left hook ... left hook ..."

April 3, 1934

Josephine Herbst

A Passport from Realengo 18

On the earthen floor of the house of the poet of Realengo 18, one of the Realengo men draws with a stick a map of Cuba. The hard-baked earth swept clean with a broom makes a good blackboard. He shapes the island and we stare at its smallness that is now being related to the world. Outlines of the United States take shape roughly. There is an ocean, Europe and a sudden great bulge of the stick moved by an inspired curve makes the Soviet Union. Everyone in the room smiles. Jaime, the actor, turned Realengo farmer these ten years, says excitedly that in my pocketbook I carry a passport that has a visa from the Soviet Union upon it. Two little girls sitting together on a narrow bench keep their seats, everyone else crowds forward. The passport goes from hand to hand.

Through the doorway is a view down the valley. We are very high on top of the world in Realengo. We are in the midst of steep cultivated mountains with banana and tobacco growing in regular rows. Around these cultivated patches virgin forest bristles in tough areas. Realengo 18 feels somewhat protected by its location, by its difficult trails too narrow for the artillery of an army. Last August airplanes whirled overhead looking for places to drop bombs. Now four men of Realengo are gravely studying the map of Cuba on the floor and they are looking at my visa from the Soviet Union.

They stare slowly at the visa and pass it from hand to hand. Someone picks out the tiny hammer and sickle on the seal. Jaime says that there ought to be a visa from the Soviet of Realengo 18. He says there are plenty of blank pages and I should certainly have a visa from the first Soviet on the North American continent. The visa has changed the atmosphere of the room in a moment. Realengo 18 is a small spot on a small island and we have been discussing the problems of this island, its relation to the world. Every person in the room has been weighed down with the great bulk of the United States pressing from above on that map drawn upon the floor. We have been looking at the map and feeling the powers that are against this small island in its battle for freedom. The visa is a kind of magic that restores everyone.

The wife of the poet gets up briskly and makes some coffee. She serves it in tiny cups with sugar-cane juice. Though this island is devoted to sugar, there is no sugar here, only the juice of the cane pressed out with a rude handmade machine of logs. Sugar sells, is not eaten, is not made in Realengo. Jaime, who has traveled in his day and knows the ports of South America, loves my passport. He keeps looking at it and insisting that I get a visa from Realengo. They are now discussing it gravely and the question is to be taken up with the secretary. After that it will be taken up with the president, Lino Alvarez. A stir and bustle of business and the relation of this tiny spot to the great one-sixth of the world where the Soviet Union flourishes changes the entire mood of the party. We get on horseback again and start out over the trails.

In Realengo 18 it is not possible just to travel. In every hut is a Realengo man who wants the news. I am a stranger in a pair of overalls and a blue workshirt sitting astride a very bony and mangy horse. This only lasts a moment. The next moment I am in the house, we are smiling and talking. The man of the house may be very ill of malaria. This sickness is a terrific scourge in Realengo where the outside world seems never to have come except for plunder. Agents from the big sugar mills below penetrate Realengo 18 on horseback wearing very white starched clothes, riding haughtily with whips in their hands and guns on their hips. Realengo men passing on their own humble horses never speak to these emissaries. The silent procession goes past the rider whose spying eyes look sharply. Contempt is thick in the air as the invader disappears. Realengo men exchange glances; someone spits loudly and with fury. Not a word may be spoken until we are in the house of the sick man whose bright feverish eyes want all the news. From what deep source does this talk about politics and history come? Their own struggle to hold the land to which they have given so much labor is the answer.

There isn't a hut that must not have a look at the visa. It

is taken out, passed shyly, delightedly; again the question of putting a Realengo visa in the book is seriously pondered. An old woman cannot stop her tirade against the spies sent in by the sugar companies long enough to look but her son thrusts it under her nose. She cannot read, few can, yet those who do read talk much. They explain, going over and over the situation in the world, relating it to this little world of Realengo 18. They are practical people, not romanticists, not Rousseaueans. They know that they need more than the fighting men of Realengo to keep their land and be free, they need more than Cuba.

Doves strut around cooing. The little pigs hunt frantically for bits of food, nuzzle each other's hide searching for crumbs. A lean and hungry look is in this fertile land. A fire is made on the pile of stones that makes a hearth and the very sight of the crude fire makes fierce talk bubble up about the day that will some day come when they will have electricity, radios and their children will not need to pause on the long toil up the hill from the stream with the heavy water jug. So much tiredness in children, so many thin bodies, yet the little girl in the house where I spend a night hunts for a tiny bit of a broken comb to comb out lovely hair. She takes a morsel of soap from its place behind a splinter on the wall, delicately washes her hands in a tin basin, laughing. "Some day we will have lots of water, lots of soap."

They believe in that *some day* and they believe in their *today* and are proud of their struggle. They should take their place beside the great of the world, they have fought well. Everyone agrees on the necessity of the visa. So it is no surprise that night, very late, with the darkness heavy with the scent of many flowering herbs, to hear footsteps coming along the banana path. Under the banana leaves they are carrying a typewriter and Lino Alvarez their leader is coming with many papers to show me. We go through these papers first, with a tiny oil lamp flickering and the owner of the house sitting upright in a hammock very excited and happy at all the company that has suddenly filled the room. The wife has made a wonderful drink out of oranges yanked hastily from a tree by the children and she has brought out a treasure, a tiny round tin box the size of a silver dollar, with a white powder in it. It turns out to be nothing more extraordinary than soda, a pinch of which makes the drink foam up in a way to delight everyone. Lino Alvarez, with his white clothes and blue shirt and the sword of the Spanish general that he wears since his days as a soldier in the Spanish-American war, wants the entire background of the struggle in Realengo understood. His stubborn integrity makes the trickery of the companies who have tried to defraud these people seem even more shameful. We are going over the papers and it is only toward the finish that the matter of the visa is again brought up. The question has been threshed out long before the trip to this house was made, it seems, because the visa is now ready. Lino Alvarez did not think a visa should be placed in the book but he thought a paper of some kind was fitting. The paper was already in an envelope and as it is laid down the whole scheme of these mountain lives resolves itself more clearly. Not only miles but steep mountains apart, they must have been busy all that day hurrying up and down, consulting, carrying messages, by some secret telegraphy of the mountains transmitting news.

They are very proud as I read the visa. The secretary and one of the vice presidents sign. Lino Alvarez, the president, signs slowly. He is only learning to write now. Little pigs grunt for food and in the excitement of signing, a huge pan of corn that had been painfully shelled that day by the entire family so that on the next day it could be ground up for Realengo bread, a thick corn mush, fell to the floor. All the children scrambled to save it from the assault of the greedy pigs. The mother pig outside with a brood of very thin tiny young, screams for her share. A horse sensing food, whinnies. Doves begin chortling and bristling around one's very legs. The whole room is humming and what kernels are not saved, are scooped up and guzzled by the noisy pigs. Hunger is here, it was here all during the evening meal of ñame and malanga but no one is paying attention to it. Bright eyes are looking at the paper and as I put it in my pocketbook they take seats again gravely.

This is a small hut. The district of Realengo is small in comparison to Cuba and Cuba is only a tiny island but no one in Realengo feels alone in the fight for freedom. They talk too much of what is going on in the world. They know too much to be alone.

I am writing this many weeks later than the visit yet it is impossible not to write of it as if it were in a continuous present. This is Pennsylvania farming land. On May Day the farmers of this community had May Day in Doylestown. A woman told of the effort to evict her family of eight children. It took many hours to get her off the land. They had to pay her a dollar apiece for five pigeons before she would go and the little humble triumph sounded good to every farmer. The meeting on the courthouse lawn closed with singing the *Internationale* and I remembered one Sunday afternoon in Realengo 18 where it rained hard on the palm roof all day and little boys played a game with beans on the earthen floor. The calf stepped inside out of the rain and a parrot screamed on its hoop swung from the roof. After a while it got dark. We had been talking about the problems of Realengo and some of the men had again drawn maps to show the relation of this district to Santiago and Havana where workers had gone on strike in sympathy with Realengo last August. Soon it was too dark to make maps and we began singing, first the *Marseillaise* and then the *Internationale*.

Everyone knows that since that time much blood has been shed in Cuba; the iron military rule has tried to crush strikes, stifle protests. Neither jail nor guns can completely silence such singing.

July 16, 1935

Richard Wright

Joe Louis Uncovers Dynamite

(When Joe Louis knocked out Max Baer September 24, he touched off celebrations in every Negro community in the nation. Something of the same emotional release occurs whenever a Negro triumphs in competition with a white person: it was present last spring when Jesse Owens was piling up track records, and its reverse was shown when Negroes gathered in groups to mutter against adverse decisions in the Scottsboro trials. In the following article, the author, a young Chicago Negro poet, shows that Negroes considered the Louis victory more than a victory for a prize fighter; to them it was a refutation—a decisive, smashing one—of the theory that Negroes are inferiors who inevitably fail when they match skill or knowledge with whites. This theory of the inferiority of Negroes has been cultivated by the dominant classes in America for centuries for it redounded to their economic advantage by splitting asunder the masses of laborers; it is the final excuse given to justify discrimination, lynching and exploitation. Normal and natural social intercourse between Negroes and whites is forbidden by both law and custom, and Negroes cannot fail to see that those who make and enforce these prohibitions are whites. Hatred and distrust flourish; nor do harassed Negro workers always distinguish between whites who make these rules and the great mass of white people, who though induced to acquiesce in them, are their natural allies against all upper-class tyranny. The triumph of one Negro, as in Louis' case, releases the hatred that Negroes feel for those who are guilty of setting them apart and for those who brand them as pariahs.

The celebrations following the Louis victory were not only tributes to the man who the celebrants believed had proved Negroes are not inferiors; they were also demonstrations against the whole system of white chauvinism. Anything that

tends to widen the breach between the Negro and white mas-
ses is, of course, dangerous, but the group-solidarity felt by
Negroes cannot be wished out of existence. They are not only
workers, they are black workers—hence doubly exploited. The
Negroes are a people, a nation within this nation, and this
cannot, must not, be overlooked. It must be taken into ac-
count and the burden of removing this distrust felt by
Negroes for whites must be borne chiefly by the latter. The
Communist Party, consisting of Negroes as well as whites,
has made valiant beginnings—the Scottsboro defense, the
demonstrations against Italian fascism and in scores of other
instances. But much remains to be done. It is apparent too
that if the feelings vented by Negroes after the Louis triumph
can be directed against their real enemies, the Bourbons of
North as well as South, they will prove valuable in the com-
mon struggles of all oppressed, white and black, that lie
ahead.–The Editors)

"*Wun-tuh-threee-fooo-fiiive-seex-seven-eight-niine-thuun!*"
Then: "JOE LOUIS—THE WINNAH!"

On Chicago's South Side five minutes after these words were yelled, and Joe Louis' hand was hoisted as victor in his four-round go with Max Baer, Negroes poured out of beer taverns, pool rooms, barber shops, rooming houses and dingy flats and flooded the streets.

"LOUIS! LOUIS! LOUIS!" they yelled and threw their hats away. They snatched newspapers from the stands of astonished Greeks and tore them up, flinging the bits into the air. They wagged their heads. Lawd, they'd never seen or heard the like of it before. They shook the hands of strangers. They clapped one another on the back. It was like a revival. Really, there was a religious feeling in the air. Well, it wasn't exactly a religious feeling, but it was *something,* and you could feel it. It was a feeling of unity, of oneness.

Two hours after the fight the area between South Parkway and Prairie Avenue on 47th Street was jammed with no less than twenty-five thousand Negroes, joy-mad and moving to they didn't know where. Clasping hands, they formed long writhing snake-lines and wove in and out of traffic. They seeped out of doorways, oozed from alleys, trickled out of tenements, and flowed down the street; a fluid mass of joy. White storekeepers hastily closed their doors against the tidal wave and stood peeping through plate glass with blanched faces.

Something had happened, all right. And it had happened so confoundingly sudden that the whites in the neighborhood were dumb with fear. They felt—you could see it in their faces—that *something* had ripped loose, exploded. Something which they had long feared and thought was dead. Or if not dead, at least so safely buried under the pretence of goodwill that they no longer had need to fear it. Where in the world did it come from? And what was worst of all, how far would it go? Say, what's got into these Negroes?

And the whites and the blacks began to *feel* themselves. The blacks began to remember all the little slights, and discriminations and insults they had suffered; and their hunger too and their misery. And the whites began to search their souls to see if they had been guilty of something, some time, somewhere, against which this wave of feeling was rising.

As the celebration wore on, the younger Negroes began to grow bold. They jumped on the running boards of automobiles going east or west on 47th street and demanded of the occupants:

"Who yuh fer—Baer or Louis?"

In the stress of the moment it seemed that the answer to the question marked out friend and foe.

A hesitating reply brought waves of scornful laughter. Baer. Huh? That was funny. Now, hadn't Joe Louis just whipped Max Baer? Didn't think we had it in us, did you? Thought Joe Louis was scared, didn't you? Scared because Max talked loud and made boasts. We ain't scared either. We'll fight too when the time comes. We'll win, too.

A taxicab driver had his cab wrecked when he tried to put up a show of bravado.

Then they began stopping streetcars. Like a cyclone sweeping through a forest, they went through them, shouting, stamping. Conductors gave up and backed away like children. Everybody had to join in this celebration. Some of the people ran out of the cars and stood, pale and trembling, in the crowd. They felt it, too.

In the crush a pocketbook snapped open and money spilled on the street for eager black fingers.

"They stole it from us, anyhow," they said as they picked it up.

When an elderly Negro admonished them, a fist was shaken in his face. Uncle Tomming, huh?

"Whut in hell yuh gotta do wid it?" they wanted to know.

Something had popped loose, all right. And it had come from deep down. Out of the darkness it had leaped from its coil. And nobody could have said just what it was, and nobody wanted to say. Blacks and whites were afraid. But it was a sweet fear, at least for the blacks. It was a mingling of fear and fulfillment. Something dreaded and yet wanted. A something had popped out of a dark hole, something with a hydra-like head, and it was darting forth its tongue.

You stand on the borderline, wondering what's beyond. Then you take one step and you feel a strange, sweet tingling. You take two steps and the feeling becomes keener. You want to feel some more. You break into a run. You know it's dangerous, but you're impelled in spite of yourself.

Four centuries of oppression, of frustrated hopes, of black bitterness, felt even in the bones of the bewildered young, were rising to the surface. Yes, unconsciously they had imputed to the brawny image of Joe Louis all the balked dreams of revenge, all the secretly visualized moments of retaliation, AND HE HAD WON! Good Gawd Almighty! Yes, by Jesus, it could be done! Didn't Joe do it? You see, Joe was the consciously felt symbol. Joe was the concentrated essence of black triumph over white. And it comes so seldom, so seldom. And what could be sweeter than long nourished hate vicariously gratified? From the symbol of Joe's strength they took strength, and in that moment all fear, all obstacles were wiped out, drowned. They stepped out of the mire of hesitation and irresolution and were free! Invincible! A merciless victor over a fallen foe! Yes, they had felt all that— for a moment. . . .

And then the cops came.

Not the carefully picked white cops who were used to batter the skulls of white workers and intellectuals who came to the South Side to march with the black workers to show their solidarity in the struggle against Mussolini's impending invasion of Ethiopia; oh, no, black cops, but trusted black cops and plenty tough. Cops who knew their business, how to handle delicate situations. They piled out of patrols, swinging clubs.

"Git back! Gawddammit, git back!"

But they were very careful, very careful. They didn't hit anybody. They, too, sensed *something*. And they didn't want to trifle with it. And there's no doubt but that they had been instructed not to. Better go easy here. No telling what might happen. They swung clubs, but pushed the crowd back with their hands.

Finally the streetcars moved again. The taxis and automobiles could go ahead. The whites breathed easier. The blood came back to their cheeks.

The Negroes stood on the sidewalks, talking, wondering, looking, breathing hard. They had felt something, and it had been sweet—that feeling. They wanted some more of it, but they were afraid now. The spell was broken.

And about midnight down the street that feeling ebbed, seeping home—flowing back to the beer tavern, the pool room, the cafe, the barber shop, the dingy flat. Like a sullen river it ran back to its muddy channel, carrying a confused and sentimental memory on its surface, like water-soaked driftwood.

Say, Comrade, here's the wild river that's got to be harnessed and directed. Here's that *something,* that pent up folk consciousness. Here's a fleeting glimpse of the heart of the Negro, the heart that beats and suffers and hopes—for freedom. Here's that fluid something that's like iron. Here's the real dynamite that Joe Louis uncovered!

October 8, 1935

Jack Conroy

A Groundhog's Death

> *Near the little town of Moberly*
> *In Dear Old Missouri State*
> *There four brave miners labored*
> *And their lives were all at stake;*
> *It was in the month of August*
> *On one Tuesday afternoon*
> *That they were all imprisoned*
> *There within this gassy tomb.*

(From "The Moberly Mine Disaster," composed by Carl Haden and sung by him from Station WIBW, Topeka, Kan.)

The lean old miners of Moberly remember the good old days when the UMWA was strong and the veins of coal rich and deep, free from soapstone and sulphur. It's hard to make a mine pay these days. Most of the rich and high veins have been gutted long ago, and in the slope mines you have to wriggle on your belly in pursuit of the dwindling streaks, pushing a low flatcar before you or dragging it behind you. Two years ago there was an attempt at a revival of the union. The deep shaft and slope diggers marched on the strip mine, intending to sign it up or close it down. But the militia was there with modern machine guns, tear gas, and trucks that could tear up and down the roads lickety-split. The miners had only pick handles and stones.

Last summer Ed Stoner opened an abandoned shaft near Moberly. He couldn't afford the proper fans, air shafts, and so on, but the state mine inspector and his deputies, lenient fellows, knew that enforcing the safety regulations would mean the closing of most small mines. In some of the hollows nobody had seen hide nor hair of a mine inspector for years. So the groundhogs were not bothered.

Ed Stoner hired Jack McCann, Demmer Sexton, George

Dameron, and another fellow to help him. They wouldn't get rich, but they might sell enough of the coal to buy corn bread on weekdays, sow tits and hominy on Sunday.

The old mine was full of gas and falling in where the timbering had rotted away. McCann and Sexton were experienced miners, knew when to jump from beneath a falling rock, could tell where the deadly pockets of white damp and black damp gas might be located. The miners did need, most of all, a barrel of water to set on the tipple, for the wheezing Buick engine used in hoisting belched sparks that lived an ominous length of time on the greasy planks. Stoner didn't have the $1.65 required to fill the barrel, so there was no use worrying one's head over it.

On the afternoon of August 17 the tipple caught fire and the shaft caved in with Stoner, McCann, Sexton, and Dameron entombed a hundred feet below the grass roots; another man, who was operating the hoist, led the alarm.

> Their friends and loved ones labored
> Thru the night the same as day,
> Trying to move the mighty timbers
> And clear the stumps away
> To save the lives of their beloved ones,
> This was their battle's aim;
> They knew well that those embedded
> If were them would do the same.

Before another twenty-four hours had passed, thousands of people had gathered around the caved-in shaft. Many of them were experienced miners, and they set to digging in an abandoned air shaft with only a short distance to go until the main shaft could be reached. When the state mine inspector arrived, he decided it was too dangerous to dig any longer in the air shaft. The main shaft must be dug out, said the inspector, and he was *giving* orders, not *taking* them. Movie cameramen arrived, the rescuers having to stumble over them and push them out of the way. Newspaper men darted about like beetles on a mill pond. C.C.C. boys directed traffic; the American Legion served sandwiches and coffee. Enterprising boys hawked soda pop from tubs in which chunks of ice were floating. The state mine inspector read prepared manuscripts over the radio. He posed in a tub for the benefit of the sound cameras, and told his men he was descending into perhaps deadly damps but he insisted upon taking the first risk. There was almost no chance the men below would be unearthed alive, he said.

All this time the old-timers who had flocked in with their tools from every camp within a score of miles cursed loudly and bitterly. There were muttered threats of pushing the inspector down the shaft, or at least knocking him cold so that the work might proceed without wasted time in grandstanding for the newspapers, radio, and movies.

> *There were dear old gray-haired mothers.*
> *All their heads in sorrow hung,*
> *Awaiting news from down below them*
> *Of their own, beloved sons.*
> *Three long days and nights they waited*
> *Until Friday afternoon*
> *When the rescue parties entered,*
> *Found that two had met their doom.*

A newspaper man is calling in to Kansas City over the phone line strung through the scrub-oak brush to a rural line half a mile away. The rewrite man on the other end is both sore and playful, insists upon playing knock! knock! "Aw right," says the youth covering the mine disaster, "Who's there? ... Sheba who? ... Now, listen, Ches ... Hey!" Jiggling the receiver hook. "Hey, Ches! Get some of this color here. A truck pulling the tub up and down. Pulley on a tripod over the hole. Guess you'd call it a tripod ... Three legs, yeah, and made of telephone poles. Yeah! Yeah! ... Listen, grimy fiends in an inferno toiling like mad ... Tub comes up, exhausted men step out, are quickly replaced by a new crew ... Got it? Okay! ... Mothers, wives, and sweethearts, clutching shawls around their throats, babies clinging to their skirts. No babies clinging to the sweetheart's skirts? That's what *you* think. Okay, for our refined readers, no babies a-holt of sweetheart's skirts ... Go to hell, you bastard! Maybe I ain't pooped out, too; my tail is dragging my tracks out ... Torches like fireflies in the brush, like a lynching scene, like a, what-ya-call-it, Walpurgee Night, look that up and check on it ... Hey, you bastard! Hey, Ches, for Chrissakes! Okay! Okay! Who's there? ... Frieda who? ... This is the last one, now. I'm gonna take my step-ins and go home, the party's gettin' too rough . . . Something in the air here, see? Tenseness, determination, the will of men of iron, dark men out of the womb of Mother Earth . . . Listen, Ches! Hey! Hey!" Jiggling the hook and scratching his behind. . . .

On a mound of soapstone and slag beside the shaft, movie cameramen and newspaper men and women are rolling in the gray dust, heads jerking with drowsiness. They reach for gin and cigarettes, swear piteously. There is a blonde bedraggled sob-sister snoring on the flat of her back, legs wide apart, skirts high. Every time a party of rescue workers ascend in the tub, they sweep her with a glance. The rescuers work silently but swiftly.

There is an ambulance hearse waiting, and inside it is a pile of the brightly artificial grass used to disguise raw grave mounds. The green stuff looks queer among the blasted buck brush and scrub oaks. The dead wagon is needed for two of the men when they're finally brought up. McCann is able to wave to the madly cheering crowd. Sexton is unconscious but alive. Stoner and Dameron have been dead since a few hours after the cave-in.

> *Another one had fell unconscious*
> *Only one had stood the test*
> *Even Spot, their faithful pony,*
> *Lay beside them, cold in death.*
> *And so must we all heed warning*
> *All precautions we must take*
> *And get right with our Dear Maker*
> *Now before it is too late.*

The people around Moberly collected about $600 for McCann, Sexton, and the widows of Stoner and Dameron. McCann spoke at a few of the small theaters, but the story was soon an old one that no one would pay a cent to hear about. Sexton and McCann have bad lungs from the gas and exposure, and the hospital bills were high. A week or so after the Moberly mine disaster, four brothers were entombed near Fulton, and all of them killed. The state mine inspector has issued a warning that all safety regulations must be strictly observed from now on. But other groundhogs are working in perilous holes in the hollows around Moberly. How in the world is a man who has been a miner all his life going to eat if he doesn't dig coal? How are the small operators to observe the regulations? The mine inspectors are good fellows, men of understanding, and most of them have been miners at one time or other. They won't make it too hard on a man who has to root hog or die.

January 12, 1937

Albert Maltz

"Bodies by Fisher"

On Monday evening, January 11, when the sit-down strike in the Fisher Body plants in Flint, Mich., had reached its tenth day, General Motors gave the order to attack. Fisher No. 1 plant had about six hundred men inside, on the first floor. Fisher No. 2, in another section of town and connected by a bridge to the main Chevrolet plant had only about one hundred. In addition the strikers were on the second floor, a position strategically much less favorable than the first.

General Motors began its offensive by these steps: at noon the heat was shut off in the plant; at six o'clock company guards barricaded the first-floor entrance through which the sit-downers had been getting their food. Then the police and the so-called "Flint Citizens' Alliance," a company vigilante organization, were mobilized.

After ten days of sitting down, the strikers were without heat or food—and ten days and nights are a long time to be shut up away from home and family, with a vicious press to read and a vicious radio to listen to, with stool pigeons, provocateurs, paid company whisperers, and with the whole uncertainty of the struggle at work to break down morale. Their morale was not broken. At the end of ten days they faced a fight, they fought it out and today they are flaming with a spirit of solidarity which is much greater than they have had before.

The purpose of General Motors in taking these steps was purely to be provocative. They had prepared for violence and they wanted it. They wanted a chance to use their vigilantes. And they wanted martial law established if possible; as I write, the militia is waiting in the armory.

At seven o'clock, the union had a picket line before the entrance to Fisher No. 2. There were only about three hundred men. They circled around and around in front of the doors.

It was bitter cold. Over a loudspeaker attached to an auto-mobile, Victor Reuther, local organizer of the Auto Workers' Union, kept up a steady stream of talk about the strike. Occasionally, some music was switched on and the men sang. The auto was guarded by a wall of bodies—a few days before a union loudspeaker was smashed by a group of Chevrolet foremen.

On the second floor the windows were open and the strikers had their heads out. They sang, they shouted slogans, they called, "Let's have some action," they called for food and heat, they wisecracked, they laughed, they yelled out, "Hey, Bob, if you see ma, you tell her I'm fine." They were mostly young men.

Through a window down the line, a rope went up and down with a bucket on its end, bringing in a little food. No one stopped it. There were only a few policemen visible. And on the opposite side of the street there was a steadily increasing crowd of citizenry—union men, reporters, plain-clothes men, relatives of the sit-down strikers, one or two children bawling from the cold, thugs, vigilantes, company whisperers, middle-class sightseers, and all those others who make up the varied crowd that assembles on such an occasion.

At about eight o'clock, several of the company guards, who had been barricading the entrance, were detailed off to capture a ladder which the strikers had begun to use as a supplement to the bucket. The company tactician may be considered to have made a mistake. As the guards went up, the strikers came down. The few guards who remained were brushed aside. The doors were opened. A cheer went up. First skirmish to the strikers.

About five minutes passed. The scene was comparatively quiet. The loudspeaker kept going, the picket line circled, and on the enclosed bridge which connected Fisher No. 2 to the building opposite, a large C-H-E-V-R-O-L-E-T sign winked on and off, on and off, regularly, quietly, definitely, telling all concerned who owned what, who gave the orders, who was running the works.

It started then. The picket line suddenly stopped. The men moved back at a walking pace. Six policemen came out of the darkness. They were dressed for a tear-gas attack—masks, guns, helmets, shell vests. The strikers closed the doors. The policemen walked forward. One stepped up, smashed twice at the glass door with the end of his gun and then, without pause, fired point-blank at the men inside.

A gas gun sounds like a jumbo sky rocket. There is a burst of flame and an instantaneous cloud of smoke. It is more effective than a bomb: it can be aimed, it bursts full without any delay, it cannot be picked up and flung back. And it is a violent chemical. At close quarters, temporary blindness is possible with severe after effects to eyes and lungs; at a distance a faint whiff of it makes one's eyes burn and tear immediately.

When the first shells were fired into the plant, the men on the picket line rushed forward. The policemen turned on them and fired point-blank. This was how some of the casualties occurred, at this time and later. Men were struck by the shells themselves. But the most serious injuries to the strikers, and the greater number, came from steel-jacketed bullets from service revolvers or buckshot from riot guns.

Three things happened then: the men outside fell back twenty or thirty feet. From the inside there came three powerful streams of water, from the downstairs doors and from the upper windows—the sit-downers had turned on the fire hoses. They struck full force at the policemen. The cops fell back. And then the strikers charged—with tin cans, with chunks of frozen snow, with fists—they had no prepared ammunition, and there were no brickbats lying around.

The police kept shooting. There were twenty to thirty reports, only some of which were followed by bursts of flame. The others were riot guns at close quarters. But the gas had less effect than hoped for. Three things were against its success: the water from the fire hoses, which cleaned the air; a cold night with a slight wind so that the gas did not rest heavy on the ground; and, most of all, the flaming courage of two hundred men who didn't care a damn about gas or police.

And through the twenty minutes or so that the attack lasted, there was one steady, unswerving note: the strikers' loudspeaker. It dominated everything! The voice of Victor Reuther, organizer of the union, rose to a tremendous pitch. It was like an inexhaustible, furious flood pouring courage into the men. That voice never stopped for breath, for thought, to escape gas or bullets. And it won. The strikers won. The police ran back.

The crowd of bystanders had increased. They were now divided into two opposite groups. The police had fired tear gas at them, too, and forced them back. As a body, they did not join into the fight, although as more and more union men came onto the scene, volunteers slipped into the center group of pickets. There was no question of the basic sympathy of the crowd. What was lacking was a uniform passion, a measure of final solidarity sufficient to make them join in the fight, to join the little group of men who were facing the police isolated, unprotected, alone.

And in addition there were varied elements in that crowd. There were those who immediately jumped into their cars and went home—out of the way. There were the company men who began instantly to circulate a story that the fight had started between strikers and non-strikers and that the police had come in only to pacify both sides. This, too, was carefully prepared beforehand. It is part of the general fraud that General Motors is trying to put over on the public—that this nationwide strike is a struggle not between capital and labor, but between strikers and non-strikers. There was the woman who runs a restaurant a little down the street, who said after it was all over: "Isn't it terrible—I mean about the Mattson boy?" And there were the men like the young, white-faced worker who ripped off his leather jacket. His wife locked her arms around his neck and she cried over and over in a voice that was curiously soft and passionate at the same time: "No, no, I won't let you. I won't let you." He was silent, struggling with her. She kept crying out in her soft, frightened voice. He tore her hands away and ran into the fight.

That was the first attack. It was cold-blooded, murderous, carefully calculated, precisely carried out. The cops retired. The strikers held their ranks and the doors. The ambulances came down and bleeding men were carried out—wounds in the leg, the back, the shoulder, the face, one man with four wounds and a bullet in his bowel.

About twenty minutes later, the gas squad returned. But this time the strikers had some ammunition: rubber hoses, bricks torn up from the floor of the plant, a section of curbstone, and, mostly, heavy automobile door hinges carried down from upstairs. And when the cops attacked, more of them this time, the men advanced to meet them. And again the loudspeaker kept up its furious, torrential cry. It could not be stopped and the men would not be driven back. And again they held and again the cops retired, this time with some casualties amongst them. They had been battered by bricks and hinges—one of them had been struck over the head by a milk bottle and had had his gas gun and mask taken away from him. Today's papers report eleven policemen with injuries.

Now the pickets built a barricade. They drove autos into a solid line across the street. This prevented squad cars from coming through. Neatly in its place in the barricade was a squad car which they had overturned and captured. And a hundred and fifty yards down the street was another barricade held by the police to prevent sympathizers from coming through to the pickets.

And again, for the third time, the gas squad came back. This time they fired directly at the bystanders as well as at the pickets. They fired into a restaurant where wounded men were waiting for ambulances and where men and women had run for protection. They fired into the building where sit-downers were, but the men ran up to the windows and a hailstorm of bolts, hinges, and anything throwable rained down upon them. And again they were driven back—this time pursued by strikers to the door of the plant they were stationed in.

The attacks stopped. Thirteen strikers had been shot. General Motors against the auto workers. Property rights against the rights of people. But the workers held the plant.

From then on, the strikers took over completely. They stationed their barrels of ammunition, they patrolled, they kept the picket line circling. They kept the loudspeaker going. Food was brought in. Forces were added to the men in the plant. The picket line kept going all night. Overhead the Chevrolet sign was winking, telling who was who. But down below, the strikers were running things. The situation remains very critical. The militia are likely to be used and used against the strike although many of the union men have faith in Governor Murphy and his alleged labor sympathies. But General Motors showed its face and shed blood. And the strikers showed what they meant by their slogan: *Till hell freezes over.*

January 26, 1937

Dorothy Parker

Incredible, Fantastic ... and True

I want to say first that I came to Spain without my ax to grind. I didn't bring messages from anybody, nor greetings to anybody. I am not a member of any political party. The only group I have ever been affiliated with is that not especially brave little band that hid its nakedness of heart and mind under the out-of-date garment of a sense of humor. I heard someone say, and so I said it too, that ridicule is the most effective weapon. I don't suppose I ever really believed it, but it was easy and comforting, and so I said it. Well, now I know. I know that there are things that never have been funny, and never will be. And I know that ridicule may be a shield, but it is not a weapon.

I was puzzled, as you may have been, about Spain. I read in our larger newspapers that here was a civil war, with the opposing factions neatly divided into Reds and Whites—rather as if they were chessmen. Even I could figure out that there is something not quite right when Moors are employed to defend Christianity. Since I have been here, I have heard what the people in the streets say. Not many of them call it the "war." They speak of it as the "invasion." Theirs is the better word.

There cannot be, in all the world, any place like the city of Madrid today. It has been under siege for nearly a year. You read about besieged cities in medieval days and you say, how awful things must have been, thank goodness they don't happen now. It has happened in Madrid and it goes on happening. In a city as big and as beautiful and as modern as Washington, D.C.

The dispatches say that there is not much doing on the Madrid front now—there is very little activity. It is what is called a lull. But all day long you hear the guns, the dull boom of the big guns and the irritable cackle of machine guns. And you know that gunners no longer need to shoot just for practice. When there is firing, that means there is blood and blindness and death.

And the streets are crowded, and the shops are open, and the people go about their daily living. It isn't tense and it isn't hysterical. What they have is not morale, which is something created and bolstered and directed. It is the sure, steady spirit of those who know what the fight is about and who know that they must win.

In spite of all the evacuation, there are still nearly a million people here. Some of them—you may be like that yourself—won't leave their homes and their possessions, all the things they have gathered together through the years. They are not at all dramatic about it. It is simply that anything else than the life they have made for themselves is inconceivable to them. Yesterday I saw a woman who lives in the poorest quarter of Madrid. It has been bombed twice by the fascists; her house is one of the few left standing. She has seven children. It has often been suggested to her that she and the children leave Madrid for a safer place. She dismisses such ideas easily and firmly. Every six weeks, she says, her husband has forty-eight hours' leave from the front. Naturally, he wants to come home to see her and the children. She, and each one of the seven, are calm and strong and smiling. It is a typical Madrid family.

There are fifty thousand babies still there. All food is scarce, and dairy products are almost memories. But the Republican government has stations all over the city where a mother may get milk and eggs and cereals for her baby, regularly, without delay. If she has any money, she may buy them at cost. If she hasn't any, she is given them. Doctors say that the little children of Madrid are better nourished than they ever were in the old days.

The bigger children play in the streets, just as happily and just as noisily as the children in America. That is, they play after school hours. For during siege and under shell fire, education in Republican Spain goes on. I do not know where you can see a finer thing.

Six years ago, when the royal romp, Alfonso, left his racing cars and his racing stables and also left, by popular request, his country, there remained twenty-eight million people. Of them, twelve million people were completely illiterate. It is said that Alfonso himself had been taught to read and write, but he had not troubled to bend his accomplishments to the reading of statistics nor the signing of appropriations for schools.

Six years ago almost half the population of this country was illiterate. The first thing the Republican government did was to recognize this hunger, the starvation of the people for education. Now there are schools even in the tiniest, poorest villages; more schools in a year than ever were in all the years of the reigning kings. And still more are being established every day. I have seen a city bombed by night, and the next morning the people rose and went on with the completion of their schools. Here in Madrid, as well as in Valencia, a workers' institute is open. It is a college, but not a college where rich young men may go to make friends with other rich young men who may be valuable to them in business with them later. It is a college where workers, forced to start as children in fields and factories, may study to be teachers or doctors or lawyers or scientists, according to their gifts. Their intensive university course takes two years. And while they are studying, the government pays their families the money they would have been earning.

In the schools for young children, there is none of the dread thing you have heard so much about—depersonalization. Each child has, at the government's expense, an education as modern and personal as a privileged American school child has at an accredited progressive school. What the Spanish Republican government has done for education would be a magnificent achievement, even in days of peace, when money is easy and supplies are endless. But these people are doing it under fire. . . .

The government takes care, too, of the unfortunates of war. There are a million refugee children in Spain. A million is an easy number to say. But how can you grasp what it means? Three hundred thousand of them are in the homes of families and seven hundred thousand are in children's colonies. When it can, the government wants to have all in colonies. I hope that will happen, because I have seen some of the colonies. There is no dreadful orphan-asylum quality about them. I never saw finer children—free and growing and happy. One colony was in a seaside resort, near Valencia. There were sixty children, from four to fourteen, who had been going to school in Madrid. And the fascist planes had bombed the school.

It was amazing to see how many of these children could draw and draw well–and it was heartening to see how their talent was encouraged by the teachers. When they first came to the colony, the children drew the things that were nearest and deepest to them–they drew planes and bursting bombs and houses in flames. You could see by the dreadful perfection of detail, how well they knew their subjects. Now they are drawing flowers and apples and sailboats and little houses with smoke coming out of the chimneys. They are well children now.

And in Valencia, a few miles away, the fascist planes come over and the bombs drop, and so there will be more children who will draw planes and flames and fragments of bodies blown in the air. That is if there are any children left.

I can't get any pleasing variety into this talk. I can't tell you amusing anecdotes of the boys in the trenches. I don't think there are any such stories. The men who fight for Republican Spain, the men, who in less than a year have come from a mob wearing overalls and carrying sticks to a formidable disciplined army, are no gangling lambs, endearingly bewildered as to what is which front and who is on whose side. These are thinking men, knowing what they do, and what they must go on doing.

They are fighting for more than their lives. They are fighting for the chance to live them, for a chance for their children, for the decency and peace of the future.

Their fight is the biggest thing, certainly, that we shall see in our time, but it is not a good show. This is no gay and handsome war, with brass bands and streaming banners. These men do not need such assurances. They are not mad glamorous adventurers, they are not reckless young people plunged into a chaos. I don't think there will be any lost generation after this war.

But I, as an onlooker, am bewildered. While I was in Valencia the fascists raided it four times. If you are going to be in an air raid at all, it is better for you if it happens at night. Then it is unreal, it is almost beautiful, it is like a ballet with the scurrying figures and the great white shafts of the searchlights. But when a raid comes in the daytime, then you see the faces of the people, and it isn't unreal any longer. You see the terrible resignation on the faces of old women, and you see little children wild with terror.

In Valencia, last Sunday morning, a pretty, bright Sunday morning, five German planes came over and bombed the quarter down by the port. It is a poor quarter, the place where the men who work on the docks live, and it is, like all poor quarters, congested. After the planes had dropped their bombs, there wasn't much left of the places where so many families had been living. There was an old, old man who went up to every one he saw and asked, please, had they seen his wife, please would they tell him where his wife was. There were two little girls who saw their father killed in front of them, and were trying to get past the guards, back to the still crumbling, crashing house to find their mother. There was a great pile of rubble, and on the top of it a broken doll and a dead kitten. It was a good job to get those. They were ruthless enemies to fascism.

I have seen the farms outside of Valencia—the lovely green quiet farms. There is soil so fertile, since the government has irrigated it, that it yields three harvests a year. So hospitable that oranges and beans and potatoes and corn and pomegranates all grow in one field. I have seen the people in the country and in the cities wanting only to go about their lives, only to secure the future of their children. They ask only as much as you have, because they are people like you—they want to get up from their tables and go to their beds, to wake to a quiet morning, and the sending of their children off to school. They don't think of accumulated money. They want to do their own work in self-respect and peace. They want the same thing that you have—they want to live in a democracy. And they will fight for it, and they will win.

But in the meantime it makes you sick to think of it. That these people who pulled themselves up from centuries of oppression and exploitation cannot go on to decent living, to peace and progress and civilization, without the murder of their children, and the blocking of their way because two men—two men—want more power. It is incredible, it is fantastic, it is absolutely beyond all belief . . . except that it is true.

November 23, 1937

Barrie Stavis

Barcelona Horror

Barcelona

At twelve noon–you could set your watch by it–the first
bomb hit Barcelona. A dull thundering rumble all around
me. A hail of splintered windows. From the terrific impact
I knew it was a heavy one–later they told me it was 500 kilos.
I race to the spot–already police lines are established– I show
my card–I'm passed through the lines. Talk about the easy-
going Spanish and their *mañana*–I've never seen anything
move so disciplined and fast. Half a dozen ambulances already there–more coming–each with a man on the running
board, shrill whistle in his mouth, to clear the way. Lorries
speeding in–whistles on board them, too–each lorry jammed
with men and rescue equipment. Almost complete silence–
from much practice everyone knows his job–dozens of
stretchers laid out–Red Cross men working in and out of the
debris–quick examination of sprawling figures–separation of
wounded from dead–"This one's still alive; on the stretcher
with him"–a clean gray stretcher quickly blotting up a red
stain–"Leave that one alone, he's finished"–"Lorry man,
here's one for you"–two lorry men pick up the body and de-
posit it in a lorry–they find another–another–more dead than
wounded–and another whose head is a pulp–a great square
of stone squashed it–a doctor says, "Get this one, he's all
right"–nearly all the stretchers are now red-stained–an ambulance fills up–shrill whistle of the running board man–it's
gone and another takes its place–the cleanup group is busy
at work–they're the "Defensa Pasiva"–they form a long file
of men starting at the lorry and ending in the heart of the
wreckage on the third floor–they pass the debris down from
hand to hand like a relay team–a piece of table, plaster, a
quarter of a bed, bricks, a kitchen pot–a straw hat, for some
crazy reason undamaged–a ball of wool with two knitting

needles stuck through and a partly finished sweater–they relay with a speed that comes from much practice–lorry for
debris full up–another takes its place–a third–choking
cementy dust floats over everything–the sun through it
orange–handkerchiefs over mouths and noses, banditwise,
making emergency gas masks–whistles–more ambulances–
more lorries–a relay man tugs at a chunk of wall–something
under it–he calls, "Stretchers"–two men climb up and
blanket the mutilation and bring it in the lorry for bodies–
I'm in the way–I stand to one side–I step on something slippery–it gives way, soft and spongy–I look down at the thigh
of man–just the thigh–nothing else–and my weight has made
it ooze–my knee caps dance up and down doing a mad jig–
I look around to lean against something–I pass a tree blown
away at its roots and lean against another–something on my
sleeve dropping soft, like rain–I look up–caught in a branch
a woman's arm dangling, her fingers still clutching her purse–
another man sees it–together we shake the tree and the arm
comes slithering down, landing at my feet–the purse caught
in a branch swings back and forth in a slow arc–a blanket
spread on the ground–in it a piece of a woman, a breast and
a leg–the man shovels the woman's arm into the blanket and
drags the whole business to the lorry for pieces–more whistling–two people arguing, one says the bomb was five hundred
kilos, the other a thousand–a shopping bag with a few
oranges flattened out against a wall–a fistful of flesh pasted
on the same wall–an auto was passing by, the windshield
minced the driver's face into bits–two men shove the car
away–they have to steer it between two dead horses still in
their shafts–that's about all that's left of the wagons and the
drivers–except a strip of harness–there's another horse there–
his two back legs are cut badly–his flanks jerk up and down
like crazy jack-in-the-boxes–big drops of steaming liquid
rheum come from his nose–his eyes are crying–a man pats his
head and says quiet words to him–whistles–another ambulance–no end to the dead? To the wounded? Lorry after
lorry filling up with rubble–a pool of jelled blood with a
footprint dented in it–a man with a pail of dirt covers it–a
grilled iron gate–someone flung into it so badly that body,
clothes and all, is cut into two-inch squares–you'd have to
pick the pieces out with a nail file–or burn it all away with
a blowtorch–a woman breaks the police lines–I see her run-

ning down the street–she runs, hoping it isn't her house–but she knows–and when she sees, she stops dead still–she could have been a statue–and then she screamed–not loud, just low and with pain–maybe you'd call it moaning instead of screaming–suddenly tears zigzag down her old face–and she rocks from side to side–and her hands fumble at her clothes– and her mouth is away wide open in a grimacing circle–have you ever seen anyone like that? Something grotesque in that great big, open mouth–the hair sticking out in points–hands pulling at clothes–or sawing the air. Grotesque! Maybe–but her pain makes me cry out in pain–hers was the dolor of the world–a soldier, with a son's gentleness, leads her away– lorries running in and out–whistles–the hoarse cry of a relay worker–another body uncovered–two stretcher bearers go after it–it's the body of a man blown out of his shoes, as if his bones were water–an ambulance–whistles–a streetcar rail torn out and twisted into the shape of a giant clip–a gas main smashed open–the place stinks–I met a New York friend whom I haven't seen for over a year–he calls to me, "Hey, Barrie, when did you get here?"–neither of us surprised–we sort of take it for granted that we meet in Barcelona–"Two weeks ago. And you?"–"I've been with the International Brigade for over ten months." Then he says, "This is worse than the front." "Than the front–why?" "At the front it's only dirt. There aren't so many pieces of stone flying around to clip you. And at the front we're soldiers"–he points to a stretcher–a dead girl of ten or eleven on it–"What's she got to do with this war?"–I lose him in the crowd–I go to see how the horse is getting on–his legs are squirting red–pieces of muscle and tendon coil out of his back legs–a man says, "We must kill him," and he draws a heavy-barreled revolver –the second man, the one patting his head, says, "All right, I'll hold his head"–he points to the horse's throat–"You must send the bullet in here; be sure it doesn't hit me coming out" –the barrel right up against the horse's windpipe–two fast revolver shots–a fountain spurts out of the horse's mouth, and the men are drenched red to their elbows–the horse buckles under and sinks to the ground–someone brings a rope and ties it to the right hind leg–he yanks at the rope, and the leg swings back and forth–and with each jerk a thin, squirt-ing fountain of vermilion from the gaping throat–minutes and minutes it takes–I never knew a horse had so much blood in him—a man, cigarette in mouth, fussing a couple of times with a stubborn cigarette lighter—he curses, sticks lighter and cigarette in pocket—another body uncovered—more lorryfuls of rubble—meanwhile, the horses have been derricked up on a lorry and driven off—they're food for tomorrow—the light fades away—night comes on—electric lights are strung around —a new shift of relay workers replaces the first—they're still working there—and they'll work till they're replaced—and it will be three or four days before they clear everything and only the steel skeleton remains—and gradually more bodies will be uncovered.

And now it's late at night and I'm in my room writing this out.

I'd like to get some sleep, or walk in the still nightness of Barcelona, or get drunk. What I want is to forget. To blot out images. And yet—maybe it's better to keep them fresh in mind—yes—all of them! The piece of thigh under my shoe— the blood on my coat—the horse fountaining a jet of blood— the body twisted into the iron grill gate. Better to keep it all fresh before me and to know that this is not an isolated, unfortunate accident of war, but a definite part, a vital part of the technique of fascist aggression. To know that this has happened in Guernica—in Bilbao—in Durango—in Malaga. To know that this goes on now, day after day, in Madrid—in Barcelona—in Valencia—in Tarragona—in Lerida—in Guadalajara.

March 29, 1938

Ernest Hemingway

Who Murdered the Vets?
(A First-Hand Report On The Florida Hurricane)

I have led my ragamuffins where they are peppered; there's not three of my hundred and fifty left alive, and they are for the town's end, to beg during life.

Shakespeare

Yes, and now we drown those three.

Whom did they annoy and to whom was their possible presence a political danger?

Who sent them down to the Florida Keys and left them there in hurricane months?

Who is responsible for their deaths?

The writer of this article lives a long way from Washington and would not know the answers to those questions. But he does know that wealthy people, yachtsmen, fishermen such as President Hoover and President Roosevelt, do not come to the Florida Keys in hurricane months. Hurricane months are August, September and October, and in those months you see no yachts along the Keys. You do not see them because yacht owners know there would be great danger, unescapable danger, to their property if a storm should come. For the same reason, you cannot interest any very wealthy people in fishing off the coast of Cuba in the summer when the biggest fish are there. There is a known danger to property. But veterans, especially the bonus-marching variety of veterans, are not property. They are only human beings, unsuccessful human beings, and all they have to lose is their lives. They are doing coolie labor for a top wage of $45 a month and they have been put down on the Florida Keys where they can't make trouble. It is hurricane months, sure, but if anything comes up, you can always evacuate them, can't you?

This is the way a storm comes. On Saturday evening at

Key West, having finished working, you go out to the porch to have a drink and read the evening paper. The first thing you see in the paper is a storm warning. You know that work is off until it is past, and you are angry and upset because you were going well.

The location of the tropical disturbance is given as east of Long Island in the Bahamas, and the direction it is traveling is approximately toward Key West. You get out the September storm chart which gives the tracks and dates of forty storms of hurricane intensity during that month since 1900. And by taking the rate of movement of the storm as given in the Weather Bureau Advisory you calculate that it cannot reach us before Monday noon at the earliest. Sunday you spend making the boat as safe as you can. When they refuse to haul her out on the ways because there are too many boats ahead, you buy $52 worth of new heavy hawser and shift her to what seems the safest part of the submarine base and tie her up there. Monday you nail up the shutters on the house and get everything movable inside. There are northeast storm warnings flying, and at five o'clock the wind is blowing heavily and steadily from the northeast. They have hoisted the big red flags with a black square in the middle, one over the other that means a hurricane. The wind is rising hourly, and the barometer is falling. All the people of the town are nailing up their houses.

You go down to the boat and wrap the lines with canvas where they will chafe when the surge starts, and believe that she has a good chance to ride it out if it comes from any direction but the northwest where the opening of the sub-basin is; provided no other boat smashes into you and sinks you. There is a booze boat seized by the Coast Guard tied next to you and you notice her stern lines are only tied to ring-bolts in the stern, and you start belly-aching about that.

"For Christ sake, you know those lousy ringbolts will pull right out of her stern and then she'll come down on us."

"If she does, you can cut her loose or sink her."

"Sure, and maybe we can't get to her, too. What's the use of letting a piece of junk like that sink a good boat?"

From the last advisory you figure we will not get it until midnight, and at ten o'clock you leave the Weather Bureau and go home to see if you can get two hours' sleep before it starts, leaving the car in front of the house because you do not trust the rickety garage, putting the barometer and a flashlight by the bed for when the electric lights go. At midnight the wind is howling, the glass is 29.55 and dropping while you watch it, and rain is coming in sheets. You dress, find the car drowned out, make your way to the boat with a flashlight with branches falling and wires going down. The flashlight shorts in the rain, and the wind is now coming in heavy gusts from the northwest. The captured boat has pulled her ringbolts out, and by quick handling by José Rodriguez, a Spanish sailor, was swung clear before she hit us. She is now pounding against the dock.

The wind is bad and you have to crouch over to make headway against it. You figure if we get the hurricane from there you will lose the boat and you never will have enough money to get another. You feel like hell. But a little after two o'clock it backs into the west and by the law of circular storms you know the storm has passed over the Keys above us. Now the boat is well-sheltered by the sea wall and the breakwater and at five o'clock, the glass having been steady for an hour, you get back to the house. As you make your way in without a light you find a tree is down across the walk and a strange empty look in the front yard shows the big old sappodillo tree is down too. You turn in.

That's what happens when one misses you. And that is about the minimum of time you have to prepare for a hurricane; two full days. Sometimes you have longer.

But what happened on the Keys?

On Tuesday, as the storm made its way up the Gulf of Mexico, it was so wild not a boat could leave Key West and there was no communication with the Keys beyond the ferry, nor with the mainland. No one knew what the storm had done, where it had passed. No train came in and there was no news by plane. Nobody knew the horror that was on the Keys. It was not until the next day that a boat got through to Matecumbe Key from Key West.

Now, as this is written five days after the storm, nobody knows how many are dead. The Red Cross, which has steadily played down the number, announcing first 46 then 150, finally saying the dead would not pass 300, today lists the dead and missing as 446, but the total of veterans dead and missing alone numbers 442 and there have been 70 bodies of civilians recovered. The total of dead may well pass a thousand as many bodies were swept out to sea and never will be found.

It is not necessary to go into the deaths of the civilians and their families since they were on the Keys of their own free will; they made their living there, had property and knew the hazards involved. But the veterans had been sent there; they had no opportunity to leave, nor any protection against hurricanes; and they never had a chance for their lives.

During the war, troops and sometimes individual soldiers who incurred the displeasure of their superior officers, were sometimes sent into positions of extreme danger and kept there repeatedly until they were no longer problems. I do not believe anyone, knowingly, would send U.S. war veterans into any such positions in time of peace. But the Florida Keys, in hurricane months, in the matter of casualties recorded during the building of the Florida East Coast Railway to Key West, when nearly a thousand men were killed by hurricanes, can be classed as such a position. And ignorance has never been accepted as an excuse for murder or for manslaughter.

Who sent nearly a thousand war veterans, many of them husky, hard-working and simply out of luck, but many of them close to the border of pathological cases, to live in frame shacks on the Florida Keys in hurricane months?

Why were the men not evacuated on Sunday, or, at latest, Monday morning, when it was known there was a possibility of a hurricane striking the Keys *and evacuation was their only possible protection?*

Who advised against sending the train from Miami to evacuate the veterans until four-thirty o'clock on Monday so that it was blown off the tracks before it ever reached the lower camps?

These are questions that someone will have to answer, and answer satisfactorily, unless the clearing of Anacostia Flats is going to seem an act of kindness compared to the clearing of Upper and Lower Matecumbe.

When we reached Lower Matecumbe there were bodies floating in the ferry slip. The brush was all brown as though autumn had come to these islands where there is no autumn but only a more dangerous summer, but that was because the leaves had all been blown away. There was two feet of sand over the highest part of the island where the sea had carried it and all the heavy bridge-building machines were on their sides. The island looked like the abandoned bed of a river where the sea had swept it. The railroad embankment was gone and the men who had cowered behind it and finally, when the water came, clung to the rails, were all gone with it. You could find them face down and face up in the mangroves. The biggest bunch of the dead were in the tangled, always green but now brown, mangroves behind the tank cars and the water towers. They hung on there, in shelter, until the wind and the rising water carried them away. They didn't all let go at once but only when they could hold on no longer. Then further on you found them high in the trees the water had swept them. You found them everywhere and in the sun all of them were beginning to be too big for their blue jeans and jackets that they could never fill when they were on the bum and hungry.

I'd known a lot of them at Josie Grunt's place and around the town when they would come in for payday, and some of them were punch drunk and some of them were smart; some had been on the bum since the Argonne almost and some had lost their jobs the year before last Christmas; some had wives and some couldn't remember; some were good guys, and others put their pay checks in the Postal Savings and then came over to cadge in on the drinks when better men were drunk; some liked to fight and others liked to walk around the town; and they were all what you get after a war. But who sent them there to die?

They're better off, I can hear whoever sent them say, explaining to himself. What good were they? You can't account for accidents or acts of God. They were well-fed, well-housed, well-treated and, let us suppose, now they are well dead.

But I would like to make whoever sent them there carry just one out through the mangroves, or turn one over that lay in the sun along the fill, or tie five together so they won't float out, or smell that smell you thought you'd never smell again, with luck when rich bastards make a war. The lack of luck goes on until all who take part in it are gone.

So now you hold your nose, and you, you that put in the literary columns that you were staying in Miami to see a hurricane because you needed it in your next novel and now you were afraid you would not see one, you can go on reading the paper, and you'll get all you need for your next novel; but I would like to lead you by the seat of your well-worn-by-writing-to-the-literary-columns pants up to that bunch of mangroves where there is a woman, bloated big as a balloon and upside down and there's another face down in the brush next to her and explain to you they are two damned nice girls who ran a sandwich place and filling station and that where they are is their hard luck. And you could make a note of it for your next novel and how is your next novel coming, brother writer, comrade shit?

But just then one of eight survivors from that camp of 187 not counting 12 who went to Miami to play ball (how's that for casualties, you guys who remember percentages?) comes along and he says, "That's my old lady. Fat, ain't she?" But that guy is nuts, now, so we can dispense with him, and we have to go back and get in a boat before we can check up on Camp Five.

Camp Five was where eight survived out of 187, but we only find 67 of those plus two more along the fill makes 69. But all the rest are in the mangroves. It doesn't take a bird dog to locate them. On the other hand, there are no buzzards. Absolutely no buzzards. How's that? Would you believe it? The wind killed all the buzzards and all the big winged birds like pelicans too. You can find them in the grass that's washed along the fill. Hey, there's another one. He's got low shoes, put him down, man, looks about sixty, low shoes, cop-per-riveted overalls, blue percale shirt without collar, storm jacket, by Jesus that's the thing to wear, nothing in his pockets. Turn him over. Face tumefied beyond recognition. Hell, he don't look like a veteran. He's too old. He's got grey hair. You'll have grey hair yourself this time next week. And across his back there was a great big blister as wide as his back and all ready to burst where his storm jacket had slipped down. Turn him over again. Sure he's a veteran. I know him. What's he got low shoes on for then? Maybe he made some money shooting craps and bought them. You don't know that guy. You can't tell him now. I know him, he hasn't got any thumb. That's how I know him. The land crabs ate his thumb. You think you know everybody. Well you waited a long time to get sick brother. Sixty-seven of them and you get sick at the sixty-eighth.

And so you walk the fill, where there is any fill and now

it's calm and clear and blue and almost the way it is when the millionaires come down in the winter except for the sand-flies, the mosquitoes and the smell of the dead that always smell the same in all countries that you go to—and now they smell like that in your own country. Or is it just that dead soldiers smell the same no matter what their nationality or who sends them to die?

Who sent them down there?

I hope he reads this—and how does he feel?

He will die too, himself, perhaps even without a hurricane warning, but maybe it will be an easy death, that's the best you get, so that you do not have to hang onto something until you can't hang on, until your fingers won't hold on, and it is dark. And the wind makes a noise like a locomotive passing, with a shriek on top of that, because the wind has a scream exactly as it has in books, and then the fill goes and the high wall of water rolls you over and over and then, whatever it is, you get it and we find you, now of no importance, stinking in the mangroves.

You're dead now, brother, but who left you there in the hurricane months on the Keys where a thousand men died before you when they were building the road that's now washed out?

Who left you there? And what's the punishment for man-slaughter now?

September 17, 1935

Liberal at the Crossroads   CROCKET JOHNSON

The Hire Learning   MACKEY

4
The Writer
and Society

AD REINHARDT

The Hoochy-Coochy Girls   ADOLPH DEHN

"*What* Cliveden Set?"   A. BIRNBAUM

Henri Barbusse

Writing and War

During my series of lectures in this country I often had occasion to evoke the great figure of John Reed—a man who although gone from us is the compelling ever-living rallying ensign for the revolutionary writers and artists throughout America. I was not fortunate enough to know John Reed personally. I could do little more than bow my head before the marble plaque covering his tomb at the foot of the Kremlin wall on Red Square in Moscow. But I know his magnificent work, *Ten Days That Shook the World*: a book which has also shaken public opinion in our old countries of Europe. And I am deeply aware of the final destiny of this work.

John Reed did not come from a revolutionary, but from a bourgeois, background. He was a talented writer and journalist like any number of others. But he became a revolutionary the moment his sincerity and integrity as a human being came into direct contact with events.

This is what happened to several writers, notably to Emile Zola, who always jealously detached himself from things of a political and social nature; but the moment he was drawn into the whirlwind of the Dreyfus affair, the moment he found himself in contact with the baseness and shame of militarism and French anti-Semitism, he openly hurled himself into the path of social action, in fact, into the path of socialist action.

And that is what happened in my own case, if I may for a moment compare myself with such personalities. It is what happened to me as a result of contact with war.

Before World War I I was a bourgeois writer with individualistic tendencies. Unfailingly I wished to avoid taking a position with regard to some particular event or the career of some particular public figure. I was searching for the wheels of events, which were responsible for surface happenings. Through the image of the individual I searched for the immense strands binding each human being to all others. And by virtue of an instinctive Marxist foreknowledge, beneath the contemporary complexities of an emotion such as love I looked for the irrevocable material laws which stir and impel. Moreover, I was moved by a deep current of good will of idealistic pacifism. The application of this viewpoint to the concept of the motherland was expressed in my volume *L'Enfer*—which proved to be rather an audacious book for the period when it appeared. But I had not as yet searched into the proportions and depths of the contemporary social inferno.

The World War completed my education as a man. The war forced me to understand many things; and foremost among these, the terrible, full scope of collective destinies.

Being myself a private soldier and mingling with other privates, I witnessed the first awakenings of conscience stirred in the human beings behind their uniforms. In the midst of the horrors of the battlefields and behind the cinematographic slow motion of that interminable war, I saw how the men around me—men from the so-called "common people", workers, and peasants—were little by little seized by increasing uncertainty, doubt and uneasiness. They began to ask themselves questions, and the first of these ever-recurring questions was: "Why are we fighting?" They did not know why. They had been told it was to save civilization from barbarism, to smash imperialism by smashing German imperialism, so that this war would be the last of all wars! They began to catch a glimpse of the mirages and lies behind those proclamations exploited by the imperialist enemies of Germany. And they began to understand that their superhuman suffering was all in vain; that they were merely the instruments and martyrs of a cause not merely *not* their own, but *against* their own interests.

My book *Under Fire* was the story of that great awakening of consciences. It tried to depict the crowds and files of men opening their eyes as they were half-sinking in mud and blood and half-buried in the trenches as though in their graves.

It was in the very midst of the war that I, a writer, began a social undertaking with ex-soldiers. In the midst of the war, during the early months of 1917, together with several comrades on furlough from the front we established the Republican Association of Ex-Soldiers, a special kind of ex-soldier organization. Its purpose was not merely to defend the interests of ex-soldiers and victims of the war (which was both its right and duty), but also to fight against war so that the coming generations would not have to undergo what we suffered, and so that the false promise made to us: that this World War was the last of all wars, might become by the force of things, which is to say, by the force of men, a final reality.

Both because and in spite of being a literary man, as well as a witness who by his own writing had produced his testimony, I took the initiative of internationalizing this organization. On the morrow of the war, in 1920, at Geneva, we founded the *Internationale* of Ex-Soldiers. All of us met there: ex-soldiers from France, Germany, Austria, England, Italy, Alsace-Lorraine; and we who had tracked each other down the battlefields now held out friendly hands. Not only did we swear never to bear arms against one another, but we resolved that it is not only during war that we must fraternize (however fine that might be), but it is also *before* war that this must be done. We thereupon established a charter stating that in order to be truly effective the campaign against war must enter the social plane against the economic, against the permanent, causes of war–that is, against the regime of capitalist imperialism.

Later, mingling once again in everyday life "behind the front," I came to understand more and more clearly that the fate of soldiers suffering and dying on the battlefields for the profit of a few powerful parasites and a handful of large industrialists and politicians is exactly the same as the fate of the workers toiling and wearing themselves away for interests entirely alien to their own. I at last understood that the ex-soldier bearing the scars of war is nothing other than the bloody symbol of the entire working class.

I undertook to bring into being and to vitalize various organizations with branches everywhere, among which was the Clarté movement, whose aim was the rallying of all intellectuals to the cause of all workers. Another such organization was the movement for definite and final campaigning against war and fascism, which grew out of the Amsterdam Congress–a united front movement to which the National Congress Against War (highly important from every viewpoint) will contribute a new vitality in this country.

To return now to literature properly defined. We are, from the viewpoint of the future, inheritors of a tradition which has never ceased gathering strength in the course of the ages, and which consists in bringing to the art of writing more and more of concrete realism, of exact materialism.

As I said in discussing this matter in one of my last books, there took place at first in the minds of men a kind of absolute cleavage between (1) things of earth and life, and (2) the explanation of these things. There was, so to speak, an earth whereon life unfolded itself, and a heaven where one might find the reasons for things; and an abyss separated the two. One might say that human progress consisted during the course of the centuries in bringing the reasons-for-existence and causes-behind-facts gradually from the supernatural level to the natural, from mysticism to logic, from heaven to earth.

Following science, literature has undergone this same evolution. To go back no further than the last century, we find three important stages: first, romanticism, which despite its insufficiencies, puerilities, and often disorderly lyricism nevertheless succeeded in bringing profound and warm effusions into the cold, narrow formations of classic poetry. Then, the second stage, realism, genially sketched upon romanticism by Balzac, to be subsequently so clearly modeled by Flaubert. And the third stage the naturalism of Zola.

And now realism must go one step beyond: it must have social breadth. First of all, we must give it this amplitude because of professional dignity. As writers our task is to portray our epoch; and if we wish to be truthful we must evoke life not merely in its details, but in its totalities. We must show its gigantic outlines, its vast social currents which are now changing the face of the world. And since we charge ourselves with the task of recording the reflection and echo of a period in history, we must not ignore (nor permit to be ignored) the fact that we have come to the point where mankind has to take steps not merely for the sake of progress, but for the very salvation of humanity!

Today it is not only a matter of restraining oneself from repeating and carefully sifting the eternal tragedy of the human heart: the adventure of love, desire, of old age, and of death (however moving and profound these things may be–they are always material for masterpieces–they always turn in the same circle that ends in nothingness, since the destiny of the individual always ends depressingly: in death). Today we must enter into the collective drama! It is even more stirring than the drama of the individual, and it does not end with death. We must raise on the stage a new protagonist, the most imposing of all: the masses.

Sometime ago I wrote a novel about aviation. Having devoted considerable time to flying, I had been struck with a new vision which this product of mechanistic civilization opens upon life. When one has climbed to a certain height one no longer sees a man isolated, nor a house by itself; one sees a multitude. From that height a city consists of people having a new and unified form. One sees the outline of the world no longer as it is abstractly reproduced on a map, but rather the geographical configuration of countries in flesh and bone, if I may put it that way. Such is a true vision of the world. But it is not enough to give merely the appearance of great sections of the universe. We must add as well their significance.

But there is the possibility of errors in interpretation. I was present in an audience of French schoolchildren at a showing of a moving picture of the war. The intention was pacifist propaganda. The pictures realistically impressed the spectators with the infernal desolation of battlefields and the pitiful, monstrous movements of the dead and the dying. But the display stirred the minds of the young spectators with currents of hate, being placed face-to-face with the "enemy"–with anti-German, chauvinistic sentiments. Doubtless the spirit of a work of art proceeds organically from the work itself without artificially adding to it explicit "propaganda." But, to repeat, it is essential that each and every element of a definitive judgment be gathered together in such a way that the underlying tendencies in the spectacle or in the adventure assume unequivocal shape and permit no possibility of false interpretation.

A writer is a public man. I have often used this formula and I use it once again. He is a public man because his product is not fated to remain inside the walls of his workroom, but to go out from there and to be distributed to as great an extent as possible. The writer has not the right to deceive himself, because in deceiving himself he deceives others. He who, to a certain degree, makes an impress on public opinion must show public opinion, which is still so unsettled and uncertain, precisely where the human species is being led today.

Writers having become aware, freed from the general ignorance and understanding which has too long been the lot of the intellectuals, must join with the renovators and liberators of the social system and league themselves with the proletariat—with the working class, which is alone capable, in these days in which we live, of saving the living generations from the abyss and the deluge into which they are being thrust.

What I am telling you now I recall having said not many years ago to some intellectuals in Russia. I explained to them in substance that the intellectuals must not form a group apart; that it is not up to the proletariat to go to the intellectuals, but it is up to the intellectuals to go to the proletariat.

We all agree, of course, that the artist should remain an artist. Each one to his own trade, in accordance with the exigencies of the law of division of labor. Now, there is no occasion for pinning professions of political faith to the pages of books. But let the writer place himself on the side of the exploited against the exploiters, on the side of the oppressed against the oppressors—openly, clearly, and honestly!

To writers and to young people who aspire to become writers I say: Accept whichever role you wish to take in this mass rising of conscience and efficacious will which we have initiated throughout the world in our united front movement against war and fascism. Literature must become valorous in its militant vanguard as long as conditions remain as they are. Corrective and indicting books must rise out of the world until the time that a logical society will have been established —a world in which war and social reaction will no longer have reason for existence and will be no more than phantoms of the past.

January 9, 1934

Alfred Kerr

Gerhart Hauptmann's Shame

(Not long ago Gerhart Hauptmann wrote a new drama. To establish himself in the good graces of the Nazis, he added a prologue in which he hails the "awakened" Germany. He is known also to have received a group of storm troopers in his villa in Italy and to have greeted them with a Hitler salute. This latter incident so agitated Alfred Kerr, drama critic of the Berliner Tageblatt, *now in exile, that he published the article below. As a consequence the* Voelkischer Beobachter *has demanded that the government confiscate Kerr's property.—The Editors)*

The writer of these lines was a lifelong friend of Hauptmann. Hauptmann is older than I, but we were both young when we first met. We trod together the path of life until today, no, until yesterday. I was the guardian of his prestige in Germany. I marched with him through sun and rain, yes, even through rain. I struck to the right and left if ever he was attacked. I myself lashed him when he weakened. I gave him courage when he was wrangling with his convictions.

I loved, behind all the drama-scribbling, the man, the reticent, rare, and hallowed friend.

From yesterday on we are strangers. I don't know this coward any more. May thorns grow in his footsteps, and may the realization of his disgrace strangle him. Gerhart Hauptmann has lost his honor.

Berlin. A summer evening. Two years ago. We were in the garden of our friend, Professor Johann Plesch, the heart specialist. Einstein was numbered among the guests, as was also the charming young painter, Slevogt, who created the beautiful frescoes in Plesch's veranda. Ten or twelve other men of intellect were there. I stood with Hauptmann on the lawn.

I remarked to him how uncertain he had become in his political opinions.

"You will surely not become a–. You are still the creator of the *Weavers*."

Hauptmann wavered. It was difficult for him to expose himself positively. He never finished a sentence, but rather, charmed his listeners by his Parsifalian remoteness from reality. He always agreed with me. We were like one.

Plesch is now in England because of the ugly situation in Germany. Slevogt is dead (his spirit guards the frescoes), and Hauptmann. . . .

And Hauptmann cringes before the murderers. The man who all his life was the poet of human friendship, caters to mankind's deadly enemies. He found no word of protest to say against the most vicious barbarism. He doesn't want to endanger his income! Before his eyes the most inhuman Bacchanalia took place. His nearest friends were the victims. He was silent. These private matters are not important. With the reputation he commands in the world, he could have struck a blow at the sadists, the liars, who before his own eyes swooped down on his weavers, and on people whose only sin is their birth.

He became friends with Germany's prison wardens. He understood well their tactics of concealing every atrocity committed with the phrase, "Germany." With the last ounce of his ebbing courage he hung out the swastika rag on his house, prompted by fear, desire for further success, or foul weakness.

Hauptmann is worm-eaten to the bottom of his soul. He is far removed from such righteous men as Toscanini and Albert Einstein.

I know, Hauptmann, what you will tell me (with a troubled conscience). A tremendous national awakening, and so on! You lie! There are national movements which are decent, and besides, this is not at all a national movement. You above all know it. It is nothing but a usurpation of power by stupid bandits. A melange of brutality and lies! The rebirth of lawlessness and mercilessness! You didn't have the courage to withstand their overtures, when they tempted you with the promise of staging one of your plays–in order to exalt their name, a name which is spat on by the entire world. You became their servant.

Shame! Shame! Shame!

The crown prince once said to Hauptmann's youngest son, Benvenuto, "Tell your father to be prepared, so that he shouldn't be under the wagon when we come to power!"

Hauptmann told it to us himself, with a smile. Although royalty did not come to power, Hauptmann kept himself in readiness.

Hauptmann's mode of living was the cause of all his perverse actions. For many years it has been impossible for him to be without two bottles of wine a day. He claims that without it he suffers from fever. God gave him this excuse, and I was always indulgent.

No! With the same dose of Radishëimer or Macon one could visualize just the opposite reaction; honest decisions, a courageous step toward truth. Not wine, money influenced his actions. It is terrible to have to say this. Yet it isn't the first time that I have reproached him on this account. Hauptmann's great need of money brought him to a state where he threw on the market unfinished plays and novels in which his genius was barely visible under the heaps of balderdash. His three dwellings; Agnetendorf, in the mountains, Hiddensee, at the sea, and Rapallo, in Italy cost him money. It cost money to support the son who at thirty is married to the third wife. It cost money to maintain the snobbish luxury indulged in by the grandson of a weaver. The world-renowned writer of an anti-capitalistic drama was destroyed by money.

And what was gained by it all? The Nazi press ridiculed Hauptmann's visit to the Hitlerites. They wrote sarcastically that it was a sight for the gods when the socialistic poet stretched out his arm in a Hitler salute. This was at the celebration in honor of Horst Wessel, the procurer—a sight for the gods. But at the Gerhart Hauptmann lyceum his name is extinguished. It is extinguished also in my heart. He died before his death. Despised even by those who are despised. May his gravestone be hidden under weeds, his picture buried in dust.

(Translated by Arnon Ben-Ami.)
January 30, 1934

Michael Gold

A Bourgeois Hamlet of Our Time

Some ten years ago the Theatre Guild produced a most unusual play, *Processional*, by a young author named John Howard Lawson. This play centered about a bloody strike in a southern coal mining camp. It was one of the first serious attempts made on the American stage to portray industrial America. Talent of a high order was obvious in its writing, yet the stark reality of its subject matter was sicklied over with vapor from another world.

For this author, like his contemporary Eugene O'Neill, of the *Hairy Ape*, committed the aesthetic and moral crime of creating a worker in the author's own image. The powerful fighting miner in Lawson's play, like the giant stoker in O'Neill's, was not allowed to fulfill his own destiny. Somewhere in the play the juices of life were let out of both these primitive heroes of a new historic class. They were jerked about like marionettes, spouting the sort of minor poetry popular among disinherited sons of the bourgeoisie living in postwar Greenwich Village.

Futilitarianism was the garment then fashionable in the bourgeois studios and gin mills. Lawson had tackled a strike theme, it is true, but the strike, in his limited vision, was comprehended as it might have been by a cub reporter for a tabloid newspaper. At the end of its superficial yet theatrically effective sensationalism, the miner asks himself, like most of O'Neill's straw men, "Where do I belong in this warring industrial world?" As if a miner chained to a coal camp could ask such a question. And he can find no answer but nebulous poeticism and Greek fate: evasion in another literary masquerade.

In *Processional* the strike relentlessly pursued its violent course only to prove the author's real theme, which he stated rather pompously, in a program note: that America was living to the rhythm of jazz, and jazz was the music of speed, futility and chaos; in other words, a strike meant nothing; it was only another piece of jazz, a brief violent orgasm, a crazy dance between two eternities, etc., etc.

It is true Lawson permitted his defeated miner one consolation at the last curtain. The girl Dynamite Jim had raped a few scenes back told him with jazzing feet and shining eyes, as they paced through a jazz wedding, that she was about to present him with a little baby. "I'm gonna raise my kid," she ecstatically chanted in jazztime. "I'm gonna raise my kid." This is of course an ancient and beautiful cry, but I am sure no victim of the depression today would thank his wife for such a gift. Neither would have Lawson's miner in real life, his eyes gouged out by the Ku Klux Klan, another victim of fascism.

A baby, however, wonderful, is no compensation for a bitter strike that has just been brutally crushed by klansmen and soldiery; or an answer to the industrial problem.

I am dwelling on this early play by John Howard Lawson because its talent aroused great hopes for this author which one is compelled to admit have never been fulfilled. He has written and had produced almost a dozen plays since *Processional,* and all of them have been stultified by the same painful confusion. The world has changed enormously, but this author has learned nothing. He is still lost like Hamlet, in his inner conflict. Through all his plays wander a troop of ghosts disguised in the costumes of living men and women and repeating the same monotonous question: "Where do I belong in this warring world of two classes?"

Now nobody, least of all the Marxians, demanded of the young Lawson of *Processional* that he show the coal strike a victory or that he make the miner a mouthpiece for Communism. The play was greeted with much sympathy in the left-wing press. It was clear that this was the first essay of a gifted fellow traveler, and that a young writer ought not be condemned for not having read Marx. Few American "intellectuals" then had heard of Marx and Lenin. The writers had not even read Tolstoy, or learned to approach a strike with the same serious attempt at understanding its own historic nature that Tolstoy made in writing of Napoleon's battles in *War and Peace.*

But ten years have passed, and it is fair to ask an author,

even one who is a fellow traveler, "What have you learned in these ten years?" In Lawson's case, the answer tragically seems to be, "Nothing. I am still a bewildered wanderer lost between two worlds, indulging myself in the same adolescent self-pity as in my first plays. Hence my lack of maturity and esthetic or moral fusion."

When an ailment of this kind persists so long, any amateur Freudian can tell you that there is concealed a deliberate will-to-sickness. The patient really refuses to surrender his sickness, because it is a comfortable shelter and alibi against responsible action. From the two latest plays of Lawson's presented this season, and his *Success Story* of last year, it seems to me that Lawson, like many other fellow travelers, is hiding from his own fervid desire for bourgeois success, and the difficulty, often, of reconciling this dross with the revolutionary conscience.

In his *Success Story* of last season, Lawson presented a portrait of a poor and clever young New York Jew who comes to work in an office, burning with radicalism and resentment against the capitalist system. In a few years he has pushed aside the decadent New Englander who is his boss, and taken over the business. His radicalism proves to have been only the mask for an overwhelming craving for money and bourgeois success, and leads him to the familiar cry of futility.

In this season, *The Pure In Heart,* a young girl in a little country town yearns to go to the city to become a great, wealthy, famous actress. She does so; and in New York runs into a group of show people burned up with the same crazy need for success, and a young drifter who has become a criminal because he also craves success, and knows no better way of getting it than the gun. The young couple are shot down at the last curtain, making maudlin speeches about futility.

In *Gentlewoman,* which was presented this season by the Group Theatre, the rather boorish hero is purported to be a free-lance radical journalist with a miner-father and a background of migratory I.W.W. struggle and labor. He meets a wealthy upper-class woman, and breaks through her comfortable shell of illusions by his hard "revolutionary" crudeness. Her husband kills himself because he is sexually impotent, and she goes to live with the virile Red. (It is amusing to note that in the few Broadway plays recently in which a Communist has been introduced, he is always a sexual superman!)

Now what happens in the affair of this couple who arrive at each other from such different worlds? They hold the familiar tedious conversations on futility. "Ethical sterility. I'm not a real radical–I'm just on the lunatic fringe. I'm 10 per cent revolutionist, and 90 per cent faker. I used to think I was a Communist, but I'm just a bourgeois slob. I'm one of the flotsam and jetsam boys. We're both adrift on separate rafts. Red! no. I'm nothing! We little people–why do we get so tangled up in our own problems?"

These are bits of the Red hero's conversation. And at the end he decides to give up the luxury she is surrounding him with, the tainted money that comes from exploited cotton mills and mines. He is going to the farmers' strike in Iowa, ostensibly to report it. To do this, he has to surrender everything–the gentlewoman he loves, her swell apartment, and the baby she is about to have, forever!

Now some of us have covered many strikes without giving up our lovely and useful spouses. This is really an uncalled-for sacrifice, that has never yet been demanded by a district organizer of the Communist Party. Tossing away money, too, that could be splendidly used for printing the *Daily Worker,* the *New Masses,* or a mountain of pamphlets, is likewise a false and sinful gesture.

But that's not the point. What counts is, that again Lawson has taken what might have been a revolutionary theme and botched it dreadfully. He has again projected his own confused mind on the screen of history, and tried to convince an audience it was the face of "Revolution."

Audiences are peculiar, however. Even when they like a bad or cheap play, it has to have some grain of truth in it. The plays of Lawson are synthetic concoctions: they begin, often, with some fundamental truth of character, then dissolve back into the solipsist's world of unreality. Worse, still, they make an impression of insincerity, as if the author were writing to a box-office formula.

But Lawson tries to be sincere, I believe; it is no formula with him, but a fixation. Always this single theme of the declassed bourgeois colors every line he writes. Today, however, the declassed bourgeoisie of America are not feeling futile, strangely enough. They are beginning to organize, in one form or another, and are preparing to play a serious political role in American history. They are grim, and completely cured of their Menckenism. The fact that Lawson cannot see this is another of the penalties he pays for a delayed adolescence.

In one of his early plays, *Nirvana*, the confused Lawson hero makes the O'Neillish attempt to escape into a religion that will console him. He wants a modern god, however; he talks about finding some "electro-magnetic Christ." In another play, *The International*, the futile hero and his Communist heroine are involved in the Soviet-British struggle in China, and come out of it singing a musical comedy love duet that consoles them. So it goes. Yes, it is all confusing, and one need not go into details.

Lawson was a man of great potential talent. He had always had large ambitions. He had attempted epics of the historic period, vast canvases worthy of a playwright in our time. He had set himself another great task: to bring poetry back to the drab naturalism of the American stage.

But why have his epics seemed trivial in the theatre, why do they shrink to the narrow Hollywood frame? A bitter strike serves only as background for a love story with a Floyd Dell happy ending, and to offer the sophomore notion that America can be explained by its jazz. The revolution in the Far East becomes a piece of Ziegfeld Orientalism and the background for another unimportant love story.

Lawson's poetry sometimes flashes out a line that has force, but in the main, it is pretentious, dull, inflated, "eternal." It is often on the verge of bathos. It hasn't that real poetry that comes when one is emotional about the humble truths. When this poetizing is placed, as it is in the plays, next to "daring" sex epigrams meant squarely for the lowest type of box-office appeal, the effect is often gruesomely vulgar, like the drunken speeches of a literarious college boy in a cathouse.

But what can anyone do with such a mass of conflicts in one author? It is, of course, his own difficult problem, but one doubts Lawson will ever solve it until he has honestly faced himself, and found out what he actually believes. Yes, to be a "great" artist, one must greatly believe in something.

When a man has achieved a set of principles, when he knows firmly he believes in them, he can, like the Soviet diplomats, make compromises, box office or otherwise. Until then, a man or an author is forever betraying the fundamentals. This is what Lawson and the liberals always do; he has no real base of emotion or philosophy; he has not purified his mind and heart.

Postscript: The Group Theatre is to be congratulated for its fine direction and acting of *Gentlewoman.* But this is its second play of the season with as "box office" an intent as anything ever thrown together by Al Woods. What has become of all those tremendous manifestos with which it promised us to change the American Theatre? Not forgotten so soon?

A personal note to Ed Massey who directed *The Pure in Heart:* Ed, you and your actors died a noble death in a poor cause.

April 10, 1934

John Howard Lawson

"Inner Conflict" and Proletarian Art

(A Reply to Michael Gold)

Mike Gold calls me "a bourgeois Hamlet." Here's a long soliloquy. The fact that his scathing review of my plays in the *New Masses* of April 10 made me angry is of no importance. What I have to say is significant because it relates to many writers whose position in regard to the class struggle is similar to my own. Our problems, and specifically our relation to proletarian criticism, deserve careful consideration.

In the first place, I unhesitatingly admit the truth of 70 per cent of Mike's attack. In fact, it's so true and I am so aware of it, that I am surprised by his calm assumption that I proceed in ignorance of my own faults. I would not be worth my salt as an author if I were not acutely familiar with the problems facing me in breaking away from bourgeois romanticism and being of some genuine literary use to the revolution.

But to tell the truth is one thing. To tell it one-sidedly and with complete disregard of the connection between these facts and other facts, is to give a total impression which is neither fair nor constructive. It's certainly the business of Marxist criticism to view the facts as a whole.

Mike says that I am "lost" in an inner conflict: "Through all his plays wander a troop of ghosts disguised in the costumes of living men and women and repeating the same monotonous question: 'Where do I belong in the warring world of the two classes?'" You're dead right, Mike. I'd be a fool to resent this clear statement of a problem confronting myself and hundreds of other writers. As far as I myself am concerned, I think a glib answer to this question is worse than no answer at all. For a person with my particular equipment, a genuine acceptance of the proletarian revolution is a difficult task. I'm not alone in this: it's a tough job for anyone who faces it with a realistic sense of the implications.

Russian literature and theatre since 1918 offer a record of great achievement; but this record clearly shows the immense difficulties of creating working class art–even in the workers' fatherland. The difficulties in a capitalist country are much greater; prior to 1933 I know of no novels or plays in English which can be called completely successful from a proletarian point of view. A few have recently appeared among which I believe *The Disinherited* is the most important. But the majority of American fellow travelers are struggling with the problem of their own orientation. This is strikingly evident in the work of John Dos Passos, which combines great revolutionary fervor with all sorts of liberal and individualistic tendencies.

Mike Gold deliberately ignores the historical background which is intimately connected with my development as a dramatist. He ignores my repeated statements (with which I assume he is familiar) that my work to date is utterly unsatisfactory in its political orientation, that the left tendency in my plays has been clouded and insufficiently realized, and that the only justification for my existence as a dramatist will lie in my ability to achieve revolutionary clarity.

Mike says I've learned nothing in ten years. If Mike thinks the *realization* of this problem is nothing, I think he vulgarizes and underestimates the nature of the "inner conflict." We all know that many American intellectuals are so confused about the whole issue that they waver idiotically between Communism and various manifestations of social-fascism. Five years ago I had similar tendencies toward confusion, because I was emotionally revolutionary and had not made a disciplined study of the issues. In the intervening period I've kept my eyes open and have not neglected my education. I am a fellow traveler because I have not demonstrated any ability to serve the revolutionary working class either in my writing or in practical activity. I don't think my convictions should be relied on or taken on faith–we've seen far too much of the unreliability of intellectuals. Nevertheless I believe my position has been arrived at by serious processes, and is both definite and disciplined.

I readily admit that my plays have achieved no real clarity. But my work shows an orderly development: after the childish high spirits of *Processional*, I turned to a confused religious escape in *Nirvana*; that was the inevitable next step considering my background and intellectual processes. *The International* was a serious attempt to portray a world revolution, but my lack of theoretical background betrayed me into many inexcusable errors and a general air of anarchistic sentimentality. However, the play does *not* end only with a love duet. It ends with barricades in the streets of New York.

I believe *Gentlewoman*, in spite of faults, shows a considerable ideological advance. It is concerned solely with bourgeois intellectuals. The lines which Mike quotes jeeringly are clearly intended to indicate that the matters which puzzle these people are characteristic of a dying bourgeois class; that these psychological difficulties are completely *outside* the living struggle of the workers. I also endeavor to make clear that the dividing line between Communism and social-fascism is increasingly definite, and that "you can't play both sides against the middle." When Mike speaks of "tossing away money that could be splendidly used for printing the *Daily Worker*, the *New Masses*, or a mountain of pamphlets," he's simply ignoring the actual lines spoken in the play. The only money available in the play, which comes from brutal exploitation of workers, is only available if the people conform to the standards of the old lady who lives by that exploitation. Moreover, the hero is not a Red, and I point it out consistently; he's a confused Bohemian who is trying to orient himself. Now it's perfectly possible to write a play about middle class and "sterile" people on Marxian lines; it seems to me correct to end such a play with the definite statement that the only solution, the only hope for these people, lies in Communism. Unfortunately, *Gentlewoman* is not fully developed in terms of theme and has many faults from a Marxian standpoint.

Nevertheless, I sincerely believe that the unanimous antagonism with which these plays were greeted in the bourgeois press was due to their uncompromising and correct picture of bourgeois decay. If I'm wrong in this, I certainly want to know it. But Mike contents himself with discovering the half-truth that my preoccupation with bourgeois decay shows that I am still involved in it. He's right as far as he goes. He could say the same thing about any of our left-wing writers who go beyond straight reporting and endeavor to reach an aesthetic synthesis. These plays obviously belong to a transition period and show the consequent unsolved contradictions. Instead of doing a real job of analyzing these contradictions, Mike places me in the past tense: "Lawson *was* a man of great potential talent."

I'm still around, Mike, and I'm not asking for any favors. I don't want any pats on the back because I don't deserve any. Whether I turn into a revolutionary dramatist or a "bourgeois Hamlet" is up to my present development, and there's no reason why you or anyone else should take any step of that development for granted.

Marxian criticism is the only criticism with which I am in the least concerned, and I expect it to maintain a consistently high and severe standard, and to give me concrete assistance. It fails to maintain this standard when it goes to unbalanced extremes. Now and then some distinguished writer is welcomed with open arms: Sherwood Anderson and Theodore Dreiser are cases in point. These prima donnas receive a few rounds of radical applause and the next thing you know they're in the camp of the New Deal and fascism.

I'm not a prima donna and I don't mind being kicked around. But I can't help seeing that this sort of unbalanced attack and failure to weigh tendencies might do a great deal of harm to many writers who are sincerely struggling to clear their own minds, and who would feel (with considerable justification) that they were being kicked in the face. I object to blithe acceptance of writers whose left conversion is meaningless and grows out of temporary emotional excitement. I also object to hasty judgments against intellectuals whose progress toward the left has been slow and who are aware that there is no sense in lip service without a lasting comprehension of the issues.

I appreciate Mike's services as a proletarian writer, but I object to his sentimental and mock-heroic attitude toward revolutionary themes. This attitude seems to me to color his otherwise brilliant column in the *Daily Worker*. It gives the impression of self-satisfaction and glibness, as in his review of such a great novel as *The Disinherited*, he condescendingly encouraged the author and spoke reminiscently of his own proletarian childhood.

He dismisses me with condescending assurance. "When a man achieved a set of principles, when he knows firmly he believes in them, he can, like the Soviet diplomats, make compromises, box office and otherwise." This is a smug statement of an essential fact. I don't believe it's easy for anybody to make compromises, whether he's a Soviet diplomat or not. If Mike knows so much about compromises, "box office or otherwise" under capitalism, I wish he'd give me lessons. I don't know how to do it, and nine cases out of ten I don't think it can be done. It takes hard courage and hard thinking to accept a revolutionary line and stick to it.

An intellectual struggles with this problem in terms of his own environment and background. I see no justification for referring to this struggle as "futilitarian." I think it's cheap radical snobbery to refer to me as dead and buried, to call me "irresponsible," "forever betraying the fundamentals," etc., etc. These phrases are deliberately misleading. They would be justified if Mike made out any real case against me as being counterrevolutionary, drifting toward any sort of liberal betrayal of the working class, sympathizing with any reactionary or reformist tendency, or answering confusion in terms of social-fascism. If I'm guilty of any such tendency, either in my plays or in my personal activity, I'd like it thrashed out. But Mike's case simmers down to the fact that I ask a *"monotonous* question": "Where do I belong in the warring world of two classes?" I'm sorry the question bores him, but I intend to make my answer with due consideration, and with as much clarity and vigor as I possess.

April 17, 1934

Robert Forsythe

[1]

Hollywood—and Gorky

When *Little Man, What Now?* appeared as a book, I was reproached for saying that it fell considerably short of greatness by reason of the fact that Hans Pinneberg, the hero, was definitely a moron and in no sense representative of the little men who struggle along in this most beautiful of all possible worlds. The book critics loved Herr Pinneberg's descent into the abyss because it was so perfectly artistic. He started down and he kept going down without a word of protest. When you protest, it is propaganda and J. Donald Adams and Hansen will not be amused.

In the movie which has now been made by Frank Borzage for Universal, with Margaret Sullavan and Douglass Montgomery heading the cast, and made with that studied amalgam of viciousness and reverence which characterizes Hollywood, it is so apparent that Pinneberg is an imbecile that the spectators at Radio City Music Hall were commenting upon it openly. By making Pinneberg a character so helpless that the faintest crisis would overwhelm him, it is easy to create the impression that all men out of work are misfits who deserve treatment as mental incompetents rather than technological victims. In Hollywood's behalf I may say that in this instance they were following Fallada's book faithfully. I stress the point because no later than a month ago Mary Colum in *Forum* was annihilating Marxist fiction by the mere device of setting up *Little Man, What Now?* as a Marxist classic. Any critic who failed to see that the book was a perfect prelude to Hitlerism should have had his commitment papers prepared.

The plot goes like this: Pinneberg, a simple little fellow, marries Lammchen. (In the book, Lammchen's father is a Communist and she is a radical herself, but have no fears about that; it doesn't come out in the picture.) He loses his first job when the boss finds he has married somebody besides the boss' homely daughter. They then go to live with his stepmother, who is a dubious old dame living with a pleasant crook named Jachmann. She is also doing something disgraceful in the way of throwing wild parties, but I was never able to make out from the book or the picture what it was all about. However, it is so bad Hans won't stand for it when he finds it out. They leave. In the meantime he is working for a men's clothing store, making 150 marks a month, which in my crude arithmetic is $37.50 a month. (The dialogue is all in English with the exception of the salary amounts.) He is paying 100 marks a month rent and with his first pay his half-wittedness, which has been lurking in the shadows, becomes almost violently evident. Of his 150 marks pay, he spends 130 marks to buy a dressing table for Lammchen because she happened to admire it in a window.

From then on it gets worse. They go to live in a quaint old loft over a furniture store which can be reached only by a ladder. Hans loses his job at the store, and Lammchen is going to have a baby. But she has a wonderful constitution. No matter how near she approaches the confinement period, Lammchen shows no signs of it. She gallops up and down the ladder; she goes to a dance with Jachmann.

Pinneberg is now a bum. Whenever you see him he is going around in the rain with his coat collar up and water running down his neck. But he is game; he won't complain; and he is pretty much annoyed by a man who talks about "equality." (The film curiously enough says nothing about how you divide everything up equally and the same people get it who had it before and you can't change human nature.) The "equality" gentleman is given no name on the list of characters. He is listed simply as "Communist" and you should see him. He looks exactly like Wallace Beery. The same bulky, threatening figure, the unshaven physiog, the harsh voice. I'm not exaggerating. And they must have looked all over Southern California to find anybody bedraggled enough to play his wife. The inference is plain that if the big bozo would stop talking and go to work, mama wouldn't like that. Ah, these Russians—if they would only drop their propaganda and stick to Art.

Hans is out wandering around in the rain one afternoon

when he gets knocked down by the German replica of one of Mr. La Guardia's cossacks. This is something new for Hans; he doesn't like it so he shows his resentment by coming home with his tail between his legs. He's a failure. He's licked. He's done. And what does he find? Don't anticipate me, but you're right. The baby has been born during his absence. And now everything is different. Are we downhearted? No! This is a new bit of life, we have created it and we must look after it, for Life Goes On. And just to make it complete, up the ladder comes his old friend Snickefritz who used to work with Hans in the store and is here to offer him a job in his new establishment in Amsterdam. The depression is over, God is in his heaven and a little child shall lead them.

But they really don't go about the business properly. A child being born—ridiculous! It should have been quintuplets which could have been sold to the Century of Progress in Chicago. That would silence some of these radical fellows. If they'd stay home and do their duty by their wives, there wouldn't be this talk about depression, and unemployment and all that nonsense.

Comparisons are not only invidious, but they are deadly when *Little Man, What Now?*, Hollywood's pathetic attempt at grappling with life, is placed by the side of Gorky's *Mother*, which is being shown at the Acme. The contest is so unequal that no American could make it without embarrassment. In my admiration for the direction of Pudovkin and the acting of Baranovskaya as the mother and Batalov as the son, I find myself running into such adjectives that I hesitate to use them.

Put very plainly, *Mother* is one of the great Soviet pictures, which means that it belongs with the greatest of all times. In the years when Hollywood was screwing up its courage to produce a chocolate soda like *Little Man*, the New York censors were barring *Mother*, or *1905* as it was originally known. It is the story of the working class mother who fights with her son in the factory strikes which preceded the 1905 revolution in Russia. The father is a scab, a strikebreaker, and is killed in the strike. The mother seeks to protect her son, but he is arrested. He escapes from prison. They are both shot down by tsarist troops in a May Day demonstration.

That is the bare outline and it gives nothing of the vitality and warmth and deep emotional content of the film. Where do the Soviet writers and actors get these qualities which make a picture like this so beautiful and stirring? What is it that these forlorn Artists in Uniform have that can never be duplicated by the great free souls of Beverly Hills and Hollywood Boulevard? It is almost cruel to press the point.

June 12, 1934

[2]

Thomas Wolfe

When I first knew Tom Wolfe he used to come into my office at Scribner's, ducking his head to get through the door and being careful not to rest his hand too heavily against anything in that ramshackle coop, for fear of pushing the whole affair over. He had a way of talking with his chin pushed out and the aggressiveness of that was heightened by the half-hoarse voice and the intense manner he invariably employed in even his casual conversation. When I kidded him, I always did it with an inward fear that this time he wasn't going to get it and I'd end up with my head in a pulp.

But he was a great guy and nobody took that sober manner seriously except when he got in a real rage and showed signs of tearing the building down. He was six feet seven and huge and he always looked as if he was on his way to a fire, having pulled his pants on as he was sliding down the pole. He evidently tugged his trousers up about him before going out, for the lining of the top of his pants always showed over the belt. It strikes me now that I have no idea how he dressed in his later years, because I can only think of him in that old raincoat which he wore winter and summer.

But our real love in common was baseball and we used to eat a hasty lunch on Saturday (I didn't get off till one o'clock) and then barge on up to see the Yanks or Giants, getting there at least an hour ahead of time so as not to miss anything. Tom would sit there and fill me with the latest sports gossip, worrying about Hubbell, debating about Joe McCarthy's talents as a manager. After a time the words would sound familiar to me and I'd recall that I'd read them the day before in the sporting pages, just as Tom had.

Coming down after the game, Tom was always a spectacle

for the crowds because he would be standing, holding on to a strap, and his head would be so close to the roof of the car that everybody was waiting to see him bust right out through it after one of his vigorous speeches. He never hesitated to speak, wherever he was, and he spoke then above the roar of the train, his voice so powerful that people two cars on either side trembled. Part of the time I'd be trying to shush him and the rest of the time I'd be trying to make believe I wasn't with him. The most scandalous moment was when we got on the subject of critics. *Look Homeward, Angel* had been a great success but he kept away from another novel for five years, a great deal of the delay being due to apprehension of what they would do to his next book. At the height of our discussion on this matter, Tom suddenly shouted at the top of his lungs, his face stuck forward and his eyes flashing:

"That goddamn Harry Hansen! He wants to ambush me!"

As a matter of fact, Mr. Hansen did nothing of the kind but Tom was convinced that there was a plot on to ruin him.

By this time you'll have the idea he was a humorless man, which is farthest from the truth. His books disprove it and his conversation utterly annihilated the notion. I've never heard a funnier story than Tom's experience with the lady agent who was going to make him a Hollywood big shot after the appearance of *Look Homeward, Angel*. The negotiations went on for months. There were "feelers" and then "nibbles." Very mysteriously, she was engaged in a "dicker." Would he take this, would he take that? Tom kept getting more excited and finally the agent rushed in with the great news. It was settled—well, practically settled. Tom's eyes bogged out. He had visions: five thousand a week, a private car out and back, probably even a chauffeur and a butler.

"It's all settled," cried the lady. "If you can just hitchhike out there, I've made an appointment for you to talk to a man. . . ."

His next best story, and he had hundreds of them, all told in the most subtle way with no straining for emphasis, concerned Sinclair Lewis. Lewis had just made his speech in Stockholm accepting the Nobel Prize and had mentioned Wolfe among the future greats of America (Hemingway, O'Neill, Mike Gold, and a few others I have forgotten). Tom was in London when Lewis got there and of course they met. They had dinner and talked till about one o'clock when Tom got on a bus and rode an hour and a half across London to his lodgings. He was taking off his clothes when the phone rang. It was Lewis, urging him to come back at once, very important. Tom got into his clothes again, rode another hour and a half back across London, and arrived to find that Red was engaged in conversation with a third man.

"You see!" cried Lewis triumphantly to the third man, as Tom came in. "Didn't I tell you he was a big bastard!"

There are no end to the stories by and about Tom and I mention them now because I loved the big fellow and want others to know what sort of man he was. His death last week hit me harder than anything that has happened to me in years, and the kind words in the press about his accomplishments and about his undeniably great future were, for once, not misplaced. Some of my fiercest arguments have been with good friends who have complained of Wolfe's lack of discipline as a writer, his tendency to overwrite, his lack of form. Such fault-finding about Wolfe has always infuriated me. I know his shortcomings and I still maintain that he was a genius, one of the very few we have. It is true that Maxwell Perkins at Scribner's helped him a great deal, and it is even truer that in late years the guiding genius in his life has been a remarkable girl named Elizabeth Nowell, his agent, but it was Wolfe himself who was the great man. When I think of us other thin, smidgely, anaemic writers, I laugh at the criticism of Wolfe, who was a flood of imagination, truly a big man, a writer in the grand tradition.

He could have been the great radical writer and I think he was trending that way. In his early days he had great contempt for the Jews and many people resented that, but I ask them to recall that scene in *Of Time and the River* when he tells of the Jewish boy who irritated him to desperation and finally followed him home to his hotel to ask him more questions. Tom was an instructor at New York University, and this last appeal was too much for him. He hated the job and he hated this persistent youngster. He turned on him in rage, denouncing him. The boy quietly heard him out and then told Tom how desperately he needed to get an education, the haste in which he had to do if he wanted to finish. It ended with the boy being Tom's best friend. He was losing his prejudices fast, the cheap ones, and gaining the important ones.

He had loved Germany because the Germans made a fuss over him as a writer, but the arrival of Hitler changed all that and his story about the Nazi terror which was published in the *New Republic* was among his best things.

The tales about his verboseness as a writer are true. But almost none of his needless words were worthless words. The hundreds of pages which were eliminated from Wolfe's books were enough to make the reputation of a lesser man.

When the little sectarians in the earlier days were calling Wolfe a reactionary, he used to come to me to talk it over. I told him then what I tell any writer now: the truth is enough for us, that's all the radicalism I want from a writer. It's the material a writer uses and the way he handles it that make him a liberal or a reactionary. We had long arguments about it and I always insisted that he keep writing the way he was and keep learning.

I forget whether it was last year or the year before when he came back from the funeral of his father. There had been a great crowd there, both because the old man was a character and because Tom had made him known for all time in his books.

"You know," said Tom, trying to get it straight in his mind, "the only people I could talk to were the fellows who worked in Papa's shop, the stone cutters. I didn't seem to know the rest of them anymore."

September 27, 1938

Jack Conroy

[1]
Somebody in Boots

If you have a yen for yarns dealing with the "glamor" of hobo life, with picturesque vagabonds sired and conceived by Hollywood ex-tramps of the genus Jim Tully, you are likely to find *Somebody in Boots* (Vanguard) painful and disturbing reading. It is a story of American *bezprizorni*, cheap criminals, bums, whores, perverts, jailbirds, and scum of the earth. There is little of the "gentle satire" of Robert Nathan, for whom love in a Central Park toolshed laughs at locksmiths and the depression. Algren knows how to be gentle and tender, but he cannot forget the sadistic bulls, the crummy jails where sheriffs profitably impound "vagrants" yanked from freight trains and feed them—or less than half-feed them—on rotten grub for which the counties pay the sheriffs at the rate of sixty cents per day for each man.

Commonwealth College, the small Arkansas labor college now under investigation by the state legislature for its activities in trying to organize sharecroppers, publishes a literary magazine, the *Windsor Quarterly*, and in the current issue an excerpt from *Somebody in Boots* was scheduled to appear. This excerpt, entitled "Thundermug," is a sordid and revolting episode of jail life known to almost every hobo who has served time in a Southwestern hoosegow. But Algren, so far as I know, is the first writer to tell baldly about it. Though "Thundermug" appears on the index page of the *Windsor Quarterly*, the pages allotted to it appear blank, and the college officials sorrowfully admit that they dare not print the story because it "violates ancient taboos" and would surely invite further persecution from fundamentalists whose sensibilities would be outraged by the Elizabethan robustness of Algren's speech.

And *Somebody in Boots* does "violate ancient taboos"

throughout. It is a violent and brutal book, and articulates boldly and in plain words about unspeakable things, such as unnatural practices among prisoners. "Lonely" people in jail who manage somehow to gratify their desires cannot be credibly dished up in the delicate manner of Miss Kay Boyle. A fight in stir is not like the clean, manly give-and-take of "action" magazines or even the refined Hearst's *Cosmopolitan*.

"There is nothing quite so terrible to see as a fight in a blue, steel and stone all around, up, down and across. You fight between steel hinges, iron spoonholders, projecting bolts, on a gray stone floor. There is no one to cry "Stop!" no one to shout "Foul!" no one to say, "I guess he's had almost enough."

It's stomp and bite and gouge, and the knee ramming the groin or the vicious kick between the legs. The other prisoners and the jailers howling like wolves and betting on the outcome.

Cass McKay, Algren's protagonist, is the son of a fanatical railroad engine hostler in a small Texas town, and before Cass is dry behind the ears he dreams of escape by the freight train route.

"Ah'd like to git out of this pesthole some day," he mused to himself. "Ah'd go to Laredo or Dallas or Tucson–anywhere ah'd take fancy to go. Ah'd get mah right arm tattooed in New Awlins, ah'd ship out f'om Houston or pr'aps f'om Port Arthur; ah'd git to know all the tough spots as well as the easy ones. Ah'd always know best where to go next. Ah'd always be laughin' and larkin' with folks."

Unendurable as his home life was, Cass found the road no bed of roses. He learns that he must not associate with Negroes, and that it is a lamentable breach of jail etiquette to show any pity for a friendly Mexican boy whom he is forced to beat with a belt at the order of Nubby O'Neill, judge of the kangaroo court. He becomes a petty thief in Chicago. He is weak, boastful–altogether useless as a member of society.

One would judge upon hearing all this that *Somebody in Boots* is a pretty grim performance. And so it is. But there is a surprising leaven of the macaber humor one finds in the best prose of H. H. Lewis, who also writes realistically of the hunted and booted of the great Southwest. Algren does not fail to explore skillfully and effectively all the nuances of his theme, but it is evident that he has not set out to produce a "stark" document or a labored "shocker." He does succeed in mirroring an aspect of American existence that few writers have dealt with, and in doing this with a passionate and convincing awareness. The lewd songs of the boxcar and jailhouse, the bawdy jokes told around jungle campfires fed by creosoted ties, the human cattle shunted from town to town, outraged, beaten, betrayed; the cheap cooch shows of Chicago's South State Street–the story of the raping of a Negro girl who ventured to ride in a boxcar full of men desperately hungry for womanflesh–any womanflesh. All these components and many more as representative make up a design for living that is all too familiar to those who have "one hell of a time getting beat up, shot at, dragged out, thwacked, swinged and belammed from one slop-and-soup line to the other."

Somebody in Boots is an angry book, and nobody can be doubtful as to Algren's political position. However, in the latter portions of the novel he sometimes indulges in direct invectives which seem merely hortatory and add little to the texture of the narrative. The experiences of the various characters, so clearly and powerfully presented, comprise in themselves a terrific indictment of capitalistic society. The only important affirmative character in the book, Dill Doak, a radical Negro performer in the tawdry burlesque for which Cass is a sidewalk barker and roustabout, never quite achieves commanding stature as an individual. But these are only minor flaws in a moving and tremendous canvas, brilliantly and solidly executed. *Somebody in Boots* is a novel which serves to elevate still higher the constantly rising standard of American proletarian literature.

April 16, 1935

[2]

An Anthology of WPA Creative Writing

When the Works Progress Administration set up the Federal Writers' Projects, it was with the professed intention of helping creative writers, who as a class have never fared well and whose situation during the depression, with magazines failing and book publishers curtailing their lists, was a particularly cruel one. Unfortunately, the W.P.A. made no provision for direct publication of creative work, and its aid to poets and novelists was of an oblique kind. These writers were obliged to drudge away at the tiresome compilation of guide books, a slightly glorified job of cataloguing. They were, however, drawing a small salary, and this enabled them to eat—at least sparingly—while they employed their spare time on endeavors closer to their hearts.

From the outset, the projects were eyed with suspicion by chambers of commerce and other vigilant heresy-hunters. A guide to the Ozarks was squelched by the Springfield, Mo., Chamber of Commerce, because it intimated that some Ozarkians do not speak the purest English and some of them live in cabins. In the words of the state W.P.A. director, who thoroughly approved of the chamber's complaint, the primary and paramount object of the guide books should be to attract buyers of farms. Only very recently, a tremendous hullabaloo resounded from cultured Boston where the Massachusetts state guide book was threatened with suppression by the governor, who demanded that the culprits who had "maliciously besmirched" the state be dismissed. What particularly aroused the governor's ire was a reference to Sacco and Vanzetti. The only hope for any vital affirmation in the state guides is in the restoration of complete authority to the Washington office, and this seems at the moment a remote possibility.

American Stuff is intended as a demonstration of what sort of stuff the federal writers have in them, and, since it was not written on project time, and was not published under project auspices, the authors presumably have been allowed a great deal more leeway than is possible in the official publications, which bear sad scars of the emasculating knives of witch hunters. The anthology contains short stories, sketches, excerpts from novels, essays, folk lore, and verse, supplemented by some prints borrowed from the Federal Art Project. Almost without exception, the work of the lesser known contributors is superior to that of the several established authors who are represented. Too often the veterans' offerings exude the odor of mothballs and are marked with the pallor usually induced by long burial in dark corners of trunks. Claude

McKay apostrophizes the "Ho Moon, Sad Moon," while Harry Kemp redeems his conventional conception of "Wind of Change" with a final affirmative stanza. Strangely enough, Harris Dickson, a Dixie wheel horse who habitually portrays the Negro as a cringing Uncle Tom or an amiable, indolent, and imbecile Rastus, and who recently published a thoroughly reactionary book about King Cotton, has contributed an excellent selection of Negro folk sayings.

The most successful material in the book is found in the sketches and short stories. Richard Wright's "The Ethics of Living Jim Crow," an autobiographical sketch, easily surpasses others of its genre. It deals poignantly with the question of just how far a "good nigger" (in the Southern chauvinist's phrase) may go before he earns the fatal stigma of a "bad nigger." J. S. Balch's "Beedlebugs" emerges with more honors than any other short story. A windy, rainy night, and automobile smash-up, cops, whores, and sit-down strikers figure in a tale related with salty, pungent phrase and admirable economy. Jerre Mangione's "Man with the Cracked Derby" and Ivan Sandrof's "Just for Fun" are specimens of the superior variety of proletarian short story the *Anvil, Blast,* and the then flourishing crop of "little" magazines published in 1934. Too few of these have found their way into print since. Only a few of the fiction selections are trivial, derivative, painfully whimsical, or "arty." Eluard Luchell McDaniel's delightfully artless style may be sampled to better advantage in the February 1935 issue of *Story,* but his "Bumming in California" here included has the fine racy flavor of a Negro hobo's unstudied conversation beside a bonfire of railroad ties.

The poetry section is perhaps the weakest in the volume. Edward Bjorkman's "Old Barham on Democracy" becomes inordinately wearisome and didactic, and Robert B. Hutchinsons's "Canzone: So Seeing This Manner" springs seven classic allusions in one sonnet. The Negro work songs and the folk songs offer a welcome contrast to the traditional laments, roundelays, and impressionistic verse.

The jacket announces that this material has been "selected for artistic excellence or simply to represent the range of interests covered." The range of interests is indeed wide, and the anthology as a cross section of American literature and life is more than a little successful. Dr. B. A. Botkin of the

University of Oklahoma edited for several years his vital "regional miscellany" *Folk-Say*, and Scribner's published *Life in the United States* a few years ago. Both of these deal with vital aspects of the American scene with a candor new to contemporary letters, a forthrightness that probed beyond the picturesque and quaint minutiae which ordinarily supply grist for the regionalist's mill and into the troublesome question of man's daily bread—of those who sow but seldom reap. *American Stuff* has been edited with the idea of imparting some conception of the varied talents at work on the Federal Writers' Projects, talents which are as diverse as Eluard Luchell McDaniel's on the one hand and Travis Hoke's on the other. Hoke, a professional writer, enlists the practiced funny man's art in an effort to make his "Sitwell Improved Funnoiser" a hilarious piece, but it falls pretty flat. McDaniel's humor gushes as unaffectedly as a mountain spring, his misspelling even adding to the effect. *Folk-Say* and *Life in the United States* were edited with an explicitness of purpose perhaps impossible for the compilers of *American Stuff*, and the latter volume's very catholicity is responsible for much of its weakness as a collection of social significance. It is only necessary to compare Leon Dorais's timely and assuredly "American stuff" story, "Mama the Man Is Standing There" or Ida Faye Sach's moving "Fair Afternoon" with Dorothy Van Ghent's pedantic essay, "Gertrude Stein and the Solid World." Interest in Miss Stein, shipped up by her vaudeville stunts of two or three years ago, is scarcely enough to warrant this usurpation of a great deal of space that might have been used to much greater advantage.

What *American Stuff* does indubitably demonstrate is that there are numbered among the workers of the Federal Writers' Projects many nimble creative minds that need some other outlet than dust-dry tomes for the guidance of tourists and the delectation and glorification of chambers of commerce.

September 14, 1937

Edward Dahlberg

Waldo Frank and the Left

It becomes increasingly doubtful whether it is possible to have a major school of writers without the aid and lenses of the critics. Both from the Right as well as from the Left there is today a babel of criteria that makes for the interment of works of art rather than for their creation. "The education of a people with a view to culture," said Nietzsche, "is essentially a matter of good models."

The *Saturday Review of Literature* used to be afflicted with that peculiarly Jamesean malady known as gigantism. Every three months it used to discover an enormous genius and every fourth month it bewailed the fact that there were no great novels being published. The progression of this "will to believe" in literary criticism has since then been consistent, linear and downwards. And the true opponents of this gigantism have either vanished or withdrawn. Louis Vernon Parrington, a critic of scope and ample understanding, is dead; Van Wyck Brooks, the most impassioned and despairing man of American letters, has retired from the contemporary field; and Edmund Wilson, highly gifted, and author of that remarkable study in imaginative literature, *Axel's Castle,* has gone into retreat.

In such a period of chaos when graduated distinctions between books seem of marginal importance, Waldo Frank's *The Death and Birth of David Markand* has appeared.

The Death and Birth of David Markand is a swan song of the American bourgeoisie and Waldo Frank's farewell to that class. For a just perspective of the book something of a restatement of its contents is in place here: David Markand, a stockholder in the United Tobacco Industries, is deracinated, twisted, and wishes to escape from the death and mouldering around him. His wife seeks surcease in cloistered Catholicism, but Markand, altogether alien to such fraudulent nostrums, wants to get out into the world of production and labor, among the oppressed farmers and proletariat to learn and to unknow. His relentless peregrinations, industrial, social, erotic, are continental. Markand, tortured, mazed, starves, works as itinerant laborer in the Chicago stockyards, as coal stoker and as bartender in New Orleans. He meets up with Georgia crackers, Negro sharecroppers, chambermaids, Wobblies and Marxists. Each panel of city, street and incident is a torturously heightened experience for him, a "transvaluation of values."

The depiction, all too brief, of John Byrne, a working-class leader, and Jane Priest, who has evolved from a poor white to a class-conscious organizer, and of the knavery and stark wickedness of the coal operators, is one of the most authentic pieces of labor narrative in the American novel. It is doubtless a transcript of the reign of terror in Harlan, Kentucky, where Waldo Frank, a member of a writers' investigation committee, was blackjacked. The prose here has impact and political pungency: "The four men rose. Lowrie, the greatest local operator and the richest man in Howton, was short with a frog-like body and a flushed face in which the little eyes shone green and the mouth set like a trap. Beside him was Judge Freeter, incumbent of the local United States District Court, a huge man with lofty, gray locks, aquiline nose and fierce small eyes. On the other side of Lowrie was County Prosecutor Lincoln, a trim youth with a low brow, who kept twiddling the *Phi Beta Kappa* key on his vest; and on the other side of the judge was a man with a full-moon face, eyes watery blue, a pug-nose and pudgy hands—Governor Garent of the state. They shook hands with the miners, and said over and over: 'Mighty glad, suh, to meet you.' The miners carefully laid their guns under the table. . . . In this instant, the truth between them lived on the table. The governor opened his mouth to dispel it; his voice issuing from the moon visage was a reverberant tenor, velvet to the closest ear, yet audible, one felt, to the farthest Appalachian slope. He said: . . . 'For I'm here, I tell you, as Gov'nor of your state to say to you that if you've a right to what you want, a right as Americans, by God, sirs! you're going to get it.'" And twenty-four hours later, John Byrne and Jane Priest, strike leaders, lie buried underneath a fresh foot-stamped mound of wet earth, murdered by the Governor's deputized thugs. For firm and gainly chronicling, the following is typical of one cross-section of the book:

"He traveled to Minneapolis and marveled at its difference from St. Paul. A smooth, blond town, closer in color to wheat, and yet it had a tidy hardness that made Markand understand the farmers' hate of middlemen. Middleman town it was. Abolish the middleman would mean to abolish Minneapolis—its haughty houses, swanking boulevards. St. Paul was darker and lustier."

The novel is varied in tone and texture; there are passages of erotica which rival those of John Donne, and there are other sexual episodes which discomfit the reader in much the same way that D. H. Lawrence's often do.

For picture, pigment and social insight compressed into violent and fragile imagery the reader should note the following: "The red-clay road gashed into banks, high or low: the young corn and cane racing with the breeze; the already sturdy cotton, and always the red road ... cabins standing on stilts, so sudden rains could sweep under and leave them alone: cabins rhythmic in shape and weather-hued like the reflection of dappled flowers upon water. Sparse farms of white folk, larger, stiffer, with more rubbish in the yards; always the red road. Black folk on foot, faintly emergent from the red earth and the blue-gold sky, like their red duroc hogs; sparse white men, splinters from an alien world of coolness and of angles...."

Compare the above passage with the bass drum profundities of Thomas Wolfe, selected by Burton Rascoe in the *Herald Tribune* as a specimen of profoundly imagined prose: "After all the blind, tormented wondering of youth, that woman would become his heart's center and the target of his life, the image of immortal one-ness ... the immortal governance and unity of life." Thomas Wolfe is the most recent bourgeois hero of gigantism.

One or two critics of the *Death and Birth of David Markand* have assailed Waldo Frank as a mystagogue and have said that his approach here to Communism is special, tinctured with the religiosity of a convert. There is, of course, no one way, or any one hundred ways of perceiving or arriving at a new social and class outlook. In this book the fault is not Frank's. It lies in the electric fusion of images and sensations, in his quickened and, as it were, stratosphere prose-responses and antennae, which have been mistaken for transcendentalism or what Lenin called God creating or God building. Whatever Frank was in the past, he is not a mystic in this novel. The deity, whenever alluded to by the author, is altogether a literary and social device, as, "It is easy to see which of these two classes of men the Lord has smiled upon."

However, Waldo Frank's book raises several very significant aesthetic problems for the American Writers' Congress. Revolutionary novels about the middle class in which the proletariat has no dominant role, or only an incidental part, have received a rather tepid reception. The technic of indirection, strikes, class war, murders, hunger, used as a dramatic cyclorama to heighten the torture and the awareness of the protagonist, the more peripheral and roundabout approaches to Communism in fiction, have been summarily dismissed or ineptly considered. Vacillation, conflict, anguish have been viewed as unrepresentative sick emotions of a sepulchral figure or milieu. This attitude is not without a touch of Babbittry and a not too dim echo of the slogan: nothing succeeds like success. In short, is it essential that a character in a revolutionary novel walk out of the book or off the stage like a Marchbanks? Is it necessary that the David Markands or the Studs Lonigans beset by the present-day Furies know all that the readers know? The poignant dilemma of poor Ernest in *The Way of All Flesh* is a case in point. Ernest, to the very end, jots down abstruse metaphysical insights and axioms; he never emerges triumphant from the clerical haze and aura of the church–but the reader does.

This brings us to another point: the introspective psychical man. Jung, dealing with psychological types, has written that the extroverted person has "an element of caricaturing depreciation" and is more easily describable than the introvert. But the contemporary author, whose novel, torso-ed like its heroes, with realistically drawn legs, arms, bodies but no hearts or intellects, has excised sensibilities and introversions. "Layers and layers of sensation and no heart in it" characterizes the truncated protagonist of modern American fiction, bourgeois or Communist. Parrington has stated the problem in his addenda on Sinclair Lewis: "These brisk pages are filled with astonishing verisimilitude, speaking an amazingly realistic language, professing a surprising lifelikeness–yet nevertheless only shells from which the life has departed."

And it is these "shells" that we have learned to pity, and even despise, not because they are tortured and harried but for the very opposite reasons, because they are so miserably supine. Almost every character in American fiction today, Clyde Griffiths of *The American Tragedy*, the Jeeters in *Tobacco Road*, Conroy's itinerant semi-proletarians, Dos Passos' men and women (who always go from place to place but never evolve), are from the point of view of creative energy and will, horizontal.

What has happened, among other things, is that reporting, a doggerel, slangy prose, has taken the place of a literary vocabulary. As a method of chronicling and as a stenographic record of surface relations and tabloid events, the use of the Americanese is often highly effective. But it imposes definitive limitations upon the writer, so much that a conscientious critic must constantly remind the reader that the prose, and the cerebral processes projected, are not the author's mind. Consequently, insights, nuances, graduated perceptions cannot be gotten even out of a very highly formalized journalese. Nor a whole man. In fact too often when an American novelist who is Left or liberal tries to suggest a mood of sadness or some emotion, he writes that his character felt "kinda goofy or queer." However, it is not entirely surprising that the novelist who has given us the most complete character, the living, vibrating man, David Markand, in the class-conscious American novel, has been given short shrift by some reviewers.

The Death and Birth of David Markand is a major novel of our times. Waldo Frank has been a voice of the middle class, the intelligentsia, the students, the teachers, for a decade or more. The frustrations, the chaos and anguish of Markand are, one might say, *ipso facto*, the representative fluxional emotions and doubts of the social conscience of an entire class and era.

April 23, 1935

Matthew Josephson

For a Literary United Front

At the proposed Congress of American Writers I should like above all to see established the basis for a literary united front. I believe that the political duties of writers in view of the present world crisis can be set forth in a series of minimal demands, broad enough to embrace people of various persuasions, as in the case of other organizations which have arisen recently to defend human rights and combat barbarism. As to the literary duties of writers I believe that here, too, a clear understanding should be reached where there has been much dissension and controversy.

The dissension to which I allude and which I have noticed in the radical press for a year or two, it must be emphasized, has not been over great human and historical principles, but rather on technical literary grounds. It has centered itself not upon the question of whether we should engage in making a revolutionary literature and furthering the aims of the working class, but upon *how* we should do so. In this department there has been, in my opinion, a good deal of "left literary infantilism," which has helped the masses of the people in no conceivable way. In the light of certain formulas, left-wing writers have devoted a surprising amount of time to laboring the supposed technical shortcomings of their colleagues and fellow travelers. They have policed and "corrected" each other; they have indulged in a farrago of what I consider false Marxian literary criticism. And though such tendencies may well be encouraging signs of "growing pains," consequences of a commendable if ill-controlled enthusiasm, I think it is time for some of us to try to discourage excesses, to introduce into this situation a little more order and good sense.

Here are some excesses: Recently a young playwright, who merits all possible encouragement, produced a work of humor and satire which was a picture of the frustration of a lower middle-class family, a picture which pointed clearly to social revolution as the only solvent of this frustration. At once a left-wing critic of the most dogmatic stripe reproached the playwright for his sense of humor, for "wisecracking," for allowing his "flair for language and humor to run out of hand," etc. Perhaps I am overemphasizing what he did. But he certainly left the suggestion that proletarians might never laugh again if he had *his* way; he forgot that humor and mockery is probably the most powerful agent in forming opinion; that the revolutionary movement can scarcely have enough of it. I was glad, therefore, to see this critic well rebuked in the pages of the *New Masses*; for his own good, an example should be made of him.

Under the head of excesses I would also place certain criticisms of our younger novelists, John Dos Passos, Erskine Caldwell, Edward Dahlberg, and others avowedly sympathetic to the major aims of the working class. Dos Passos, it seems, "has not sufficiently emphasized the strength of the working class"; Caldwell "very inadequately suggests the latent power of the Southern proletariat. . . ." and Dahlberg's work, it is said, "might even be cited as demonstrating the helplessness of the American proletariat." I think that such judgments (which are typical of the narrow criticism I object to) do not take into account our stage of social development in America, the need for infinitely patient, destructive labor on the part of such writers as Dos Passos and Caldwell, the need for understanding the actual folk-customs and *moeurs* of our people. Moreover, they are contradicted by the great appreciation shown by the revolutionary Russian audience for the work of a man like Dos Passos.

Another case: A contemporary writer, whose interests lately have been chiefly critical and philosophical, came one day to the pass where he felt himself converted to faith in Communism. He wrote of his convictions in his own way. Immediately upon publication of this moving profession of faith, another young man who was but a slightly less recent convert set to work, night and day, to prove by the most elaborate rationalizations that my friend was actually an "unconscious" fascist! A real bloodhound, a perfect detective, this critic. (There are a few Sherlocks like him, and I think it would be better for the proletariat if they were persuaded to spend two hours raising funds for the Scottsboro boys for every one hour given to hunting down their fellow travelers.)

A critic should be careful before he decides to punish a writer for errors or crimes which are "unconscious"; that is, which have neither declared themselves nor have been committed as yet. A critic possesses a certain official power to create prejudice in the mind of his public, only a small part of which may have occasion to seek out the evidence in the case. No court or jury anywhere would condemn people for their "unconscious"; it is not Marxian and it is not even truly Freudian. Yet it is done a little too freely by certain critics who act at once as detectives, prosecuting attorneys and judges. Honest men may be outraged at finding themselves branded as "enemies" and "fascists"; and those who are not magnanimous enough may be driven to silence and indifference.

Almost as dangerous, it seems to me, is the temptation of Marxian critics, as John Strachey has pointed out, to ignore style and quality. The revolutionary movement will need all the quality and craftsmanship possible in its writers. A novel, arranged according to a formula pre-established, such as certain dogmatic Marxian left-wing critics have offered, may fail completely to enlist the interest of its readers. And Lenin, we must remember, said very simply: "Our workers and peasants have the right to true, great art."

The experience of Soviet Russia offers us lessons of tremendous importance which we must translate into terms of American conditions and possibilities. But I am not at all inclined to accord the same importance to some contemporary Russian belletriste's laborious glossary of Shakespeare's *Hamlet* that I would to Lenin's political action in 1917-1924, or that of Stalin in the decade of strenuous reconstruction and social change that followed.

In Russia the question of a proletarian literature and a proletarian aesthetics seems to me by no means resolved. Certain definite limits have been marked out. Lenin, for instance, indicated that he would not tolerate a literature which opposed the revolutionary program. Under the circumstances existing then and now in Russia, his position is entirely logical. But such exclusions did not justify the excesses of the R.A.P.P's (Proletarian Writers' organization) program of several years ago. These arose from a sincere and very enthusiastic desire on the part of many writers to be among those who "also serve," though only on the literary front. They wished perhaps to be as heroic as the Red Guards in the Civil War. But the Battle of Books is scarcely the same thing! By 1932 the R.A.P.P. must needs dissolve.

When I was in Russia, early last year, it was explained to me that the rigorousness of the proletarian writers' group coincided with the difficult and exciting days of the launching of the first Five Year Plan for heavy industry, a moment of self-sacrifice and danger. But with the passing of the more urgent period, much more liberal criteria of literature and art were introduced.

The philosophy of Marx and Engels has enormously clarified the history of art and culture as well as of economic life. It has exposed completely those "massive interests moving obscurely in the background" of books and paintings, as well as national policy. To Marx, the individual genius of a Raphael was not understandable save as part of his social-economic background. But neither Marx nor Engels suggested any fixed pattern of what proletarian literature should be. There are ideas in the correspondence of Engels from which subsequent scholars have drawn interesting deductions; deductions which are apparently still in the process of evolution. Special attention has been given to the notable passage of Engels' letter to an English woman writer of the 80's, in which he asks her to show not only the sufferings of the poor, as she has done, but also how their united action foreshadows a victorious outcome of their struggle. Yet, at the same time, Engels says with admirable restraint:

"I am far from finding fault with your not having written a purely socialistic novel, a *Tendenzroman,* as we Germans call it, to glorify the social and political views of the author. That is not at all what I mean. The realism I allude to may creep out even in spite of the author's views. Let me refer to an example. Balzac. . . ."

To Engels as to Marx, the realism of Balzac was the best medium thus far developed for conveying social truths. Marx further pays tribute to Balzac's amazing powers of observation and his clairvoyance, though the author of *La Comédie Humaine* was a Catholic royalist. Lenin expresses a similar divided admiration for the magnificent but contradictory Tolstoy. All this is extremely pertinent to us today; but we presume too much when we imagine that upon some theoretical formula based on Balzac and Tolstoy, or some other technical pattern, we can evoke profound observation, clairvoyance, dramatic power, almost automatically. Tolstoys and Balzacs do not appear at command.

The last post-revolutionary decade in Russia has been a period of immense and varied literary activity; many of its works and personalities hold a remarkable interest for us. There has been a promising ferment out of which great literature will come in time. But there has been too little time and perspective, too little repose from the continuous revolutionizing tempo; men have been too close to world-shaking events. In this connection it is significant that the heroic Communist leader, George Dimitrov, at a conference of Soviet Writers, remarked frankly (*New Masses*, April 16, 1935):

"I must admit ... that I have not always the patience to read our revolutionary literature. I cannot read it and I do not understand it; I am not a specialist. But in so far as I know the masses, the workers and their psychology, I must say: no, this will not meet with much approval from the workers. The worker looks at these books and sees that they contain no figures, no examples to emulate. A revolutionary writer is not one who merely repeats: Long live the Revolution!"

Dimitrov is somewhat unjust to numerous excellent works, but his warning is most timely.

The philosophy of Marx dominates literature in a profound, rather than in a superficial or ceremonial sense. In a striking way it now works to stimulate a new generation of writers, not only in America, but in England, and France. I hope, however, that we American writers, while admiring the social achievements of Soviet Russia and seeking as far as possible to defend the peaceful building of socialism from the aggression of fascist powers, should not feel it necessary to adopt the more transient theories or restrictions of Russia's literateurs.

On the other hand, while I may not say to the playwright, novelist, poet, how and what he should write, I would point out to the American writer that he has his duty as a man, as a citizen. It is inconceivable that he should not take sides with the masses of the people in this day of social crisis. And taking sides in the day-to-day struggle must inevitably change the man in the writer so that the revolutionary knowledge and purpose becomes a true part of his understanding and his emotions. The action of the man and citizen, as I have written elsewhere two years ago, takes deep effect upon the creative part of him. It is a long and delicate process, compounded of disciplined observation and clairvoyance whose proportions we cannot estimate or prescribe in advance, out of which, not ready-made slogans and words-of-order, but veritable poetry and high drama is produced.

The relation of the creative man to political ideas has been expressed very well in a recently published essay by the young English poet, C. Day Lewis, *A Hope for Poetry*. The coming proletarian revolution offers the one hope for poetry; indeed, for civilization itself, he maintains. However, the "poetic function" of the man, he says, should not be directly shaped by political ideas, but it is his "humanity" which should be concerned with such ideas.

"In which case they will inevitably come into communication with his poetical function and . . . affect his poetry. . . . If a poet is going to be receptive of political ideas, it is essential for him as a man to feel strongly about them. . . . The man must pass the idea through the medium of his emotion before the poet can get to work on it."

Here the young Oxford poet, who has already taken his stand with Marx and Lenin, is saying in another way what Dimitrov felt and said more simply and bluntly.

April 30, 1935

Two Letters

To the New Masses

A time like the present is one in which almost any man hesitates to imagine anything he is doing (continuously, I mean, from one established point in his life to the end of it) is of the slightest importance. (Yesterday while drinking a cup of coffee, I read that 15,000 human beings have been destroyed in about seven days in the war in China.) A writer's best subject has always been one man, and death to one man has always been a writer's most ultimate and lofty theme, but when 15,000 men are destroyed in less time than it takes the average writer to write one short story, a writer (if he reads the newspapers or listens to the radio) is left with a feeling of despair for people or despair for art, but not for both, unless the writer is inwardly sick and has been for some time. The despair I feel now, as usual, is despair for art, even though I know its true power, its true importance, and the urgency of its continuance, even if it is poor art, as it is today all over the world. Poor, I mean, in the sense that it is never great and unbalanced at the same time.

For this reason, I hesitate to make an issue of some of the comments of Robert M. Coates in his review (issue of August 31) of my latest book, *Little Children*.

At the same time I feel that not to accept and follow through the impulse I feel to say what I have to say would make me guilty of that kind of intellectual and moral inertia which, in significant and articulate human beings, has been partly responsible for the maintenance of needless error, violence, and waste in the behavior of great living masses. Not to speak, I mean, out of an honest impulse, or any theme, however seemingly inconsequential, is, I believe, a kind of passive selfishness essentially criminal, and essentially too characteristic of the artist who is politically unbiased and yet deeply concerned with the fate of human beings. The biased speak often enough, and lately even act, for which I have only the profoundest respect and admiration. The recent performances of André Malraux, Ralph Bates, Ernest Hemingway (and others, several of them now dead), as artists, zealots and human beings, are in the noblest sense performances of heroism. I know no man can be without bias, least of all myself, but some demand the right to remain politically unbiased, on the ground (I speak for myself) that they do not understand thoroughly enough what it is all about. In the midst of universal political bias, absolute faith, and almost vicious sincerity, I should like to admit that, so far as a political method of achieving order is concerned, I am unable to make a decision, for the reason that in making a decision I should become a member of a force whose opponents include too many human beings who are helpless and who are the subject of literature, and whose submission becomes the object of whatever force I join. I do not believe any group, however small, unless it is integrated by a criminal impulse, which is unlikely, deserves to be beaten into submission by any other force, however noble its impulse. These are all people, right or wrong, and they are all the subject of our art. I should not like to contribute in any way to the premature ending of any of their lives. At the same time I insist that I am not, as some would be apt to charge, sitting on a fence, living in an ivory tower, turning my back on reality, or otherwise ignoring the most vital issues of our time. I am simply trying my best to continue honestly to function as a human being of good will and as an artist whose basic desire is to point out error, emphasize truth and dignity, and to assist in the achievement of and maintenance of the most equitable kind of order.

All this is by way of reply to Mr. Coates' belief (brought to expression, most likely, by his present political bias, and because he was doing his review for your magazine) that I need more direction, philosophic and artistic, in my aim. (It does not bring into the issue any of the more classic and universal intentions of art, at any time, war or peace, as for instance the intention to isolate and focus attention on purity, innocence, innate health, natural humor, and that amazing, inevitable, and instinctive capacity for renewal in the spirit of man, which is so fresh and delightful in the infant of our kind—the subject of my latest book—and which so far, has never been destroyed by politics, war, disease, fire, flood, earthquake, the wrath of God, or the very opposite of this capacity in man himself.) That would be an appropriate discussion for a time unlike the present, and I can wait for the arrival of that time.

In my opinion I have had direction in my aim from the outset, and my enemy has been, if the most obvious, certainly the most worthy of attack, and if those who have troubled to read my stuff have failed to appreciate this truth, the fault is not mine. (Which accounts in part for my writing to any writer or editor who mentions my name or work in his newspaper, magazine, or column.)

New York   William Saroyan

Mr. Saroyan misunderstood my intention in the passage he quotes from my review. I believe with him that the artist can function in many ways in revolutionary or other struggles, and active participation in politics or in warfare is only one of them. At least, we all say so, and it's usually very comforting.

What I meant, and what I said (though in the pompous way all us critics have to use) was concerned with all this only as it affects his way of writing. You can't read many of Saroyan's stories without feeling that he picks his subjects too much at random and too sentimentally; fails to "place" them enough with respect to their human and artistic implications; and so, when he writes them, misses a lot of chances.

It's a hell of a subject to make cracks about, but I can't help feeling that he hasn't yet digested either that cup of coffee or the fifteen thousand Chinese.

Gaylordsville, Conn.   Robert M. Coates
September 14, 1937

William Carlos Williams

An American Poet

During the past ten years or so a man named H. H. Lewis, a persistent dirt farmer and dairyman of Cape Girardeau, Missouri, has been thinking for himself about his condition as a "free" American citizen, descendant of some of the most famous of Kentucky pioneers. And he's been thinking of others too, like himself, trying to make sense out of what confronts them today in their enjoyment of life, liberty, and in their pursuit of happiness.

Like the pioneers Lewis hasn't been content merely to think. Nor has he been willing to accept a parochial viewpoint. He has wandered for years up and down the country for a look-see. Then he returned home to work and to become vocal. His medium is, curiously enough, verse. He has published four cheaply printed, paper-covered booklets. They constitute a phenomenon worthy of widespread consideration. They are entitled, *Red Renaissance, Thinking of Russia, Salvation,* and *The Road to Utterly.* It is the beginning of a definitely new sort in American literary history. It is an important beginning. It might lead to extremely important results.

In the first place, the format of these issues is forever right. This is the way poems should be printed. It is closest to word of mouth, next to Homeric singing and a universal stage. It attacks the problem of style at the source: directly in the exigencies of publication. Publication is the weak line in the essential process of conveying undamaged writing from writer to reader today. And that comprehends style. The thought of publication is at the source that beckons most writers to destruction. Because they must write, then, under implied restriction making publication at least possible, a cheap pamphlet is more likely to rest upon some depth of style for its appeal, the truth personal.

A man has to write in a certain way in order to be published in the accepted mode—his book selling for not less than a dollar. That forces his hand; it ruins his style. It transforms truths to lies. Given cheap books—if the purveying of them can be solved also—there will be in fact a renaissance. Woolworth is the logical medium, advertising being definitely out. Woolworth might make money hiring the right sort of literary sales manager. It could be done. Books like these of Lewis' at ten cents—not twenty-five cents—each, widely distributed, would free the intelligence from the tyranny of bought and sold profit printing.

Better than all conventions, all resolutions, all associations: to be published and distributed cheap and fast, voluminously. That, all but the last, I'd say is Lewis' first contribution. Later the *de luxe* editions, on parchment, of Villon, of anyone come with time, savored with time. But today distribution and availability are the pressing needs while there is yet time to know what is thought and said with a direct bearing on the day.

This has been solved in Russia where one can, apparently, read infinitely. Here we are starved, choked—writer and reader both. Our tastes dictated to us by cash, by the power held to limit what we shall know and express. This is no question of obscenity or sedition: there is legitimate news to be handed about. Lewis' cheap editions, though not cheap enough, are the right sort of gesture (before having once looked into them). Already this very shape of the book carries a mark of what should be inside.

Without saying that Lewis is important as a poet, which is a point that will have to be very carefully considered before a proper opinion can be arrived at, I will say that he is tremendously important in the United States as an instigator to thought about what poetry can and cannot do to us today. He speaks in no uncertain terms. He speaks with fervor, a revolutionary singleness and intensity of purpose, a clearly expressed content. He knows what he wants to say; he is convinced of its importance to a fanatical degree. He has been hurt, and he yells the how, why, and wherefore. In all this he resembles the American patriot of our revolutionary tradition. There is a lock, stock, and barrel identity between Lewis today, fighting to free himself from a class enslavement which torments his body with lice and cow dung, and the persecuted colonist of early American tradition. It doesn't matter that Lewis comes out openly, passionately, for Russia. When he speaks of Russia, it is precisely then that he is most American, most solidly in the tradition, not out of it, not borrowing a "foreign" solution. It is the same cry that sent Europeans to a "foreign" America and there set them madly free.

Again and again Lewis comes back to it with that brain-bursting elevation which men believe in, believe that America represents.

That *is* America to the whole world, that cry:

> *Russia, Russia, Russia, Russia*
> *Roaring with each for all....*

That's pure American revolutionary stuff. I should say that is the first important thing to establish about Lewis as a poet in this second quarter of the twentieth century. There is no one that as directly expresses the mind of the United States as Lewis does now.

This isn't Auden or Spender. Nor is it Aragon's *Le Front Rouge* of an essential, if unobserved, French underground. This is a Missouri farm hand, first cousin to a mule, at one dollar a day. On the other hand, all of these have one thing in common—the content of the poems involved is the essential matter; all are united in being definite movements toward political action communistic in nature. Or, to be more specific, action. The content of the poems constitutes the avowed weight of them.

There is a movement in the practice of poetry (avoiding identifications of the *worth*, the content, spoken of above) largely in opposition to the character of the poetic impetus of the first quarter of the century in America (as elsewhere), which constituted a revolt in the form of the poetic matter, a clearing away of the formal impediments—for what! Implied in the work of the best writers of the first quarter of the century was a barrier in the forms themselves. It was necessary to break them down, invent new ones. And it was for an important reason that this had to be done.

Was this work a preparation for Lewis and the second quarter of the century! If so, has he been able to profit by what was offered him? Or has he missed the significance or been unable to seize the reins, going astray into charged doggerel, poetry having been pushed aside?

Taking the familiar clock-face of the statisticians as the whole of poetry, as written in the widely separate ages of its greatness in the world: how much of it will represent the best poetry of this century and how much of it is Lewis?

This brings his strength at once forward. Fervor, intensity comes to a focus by the singleness of his purpose; the clear objective, Communism, as a great desideratum to a fooled and betrayed people. This the first quarter of the century lacked.

Let it be noticed that I am speaking of poetry. It is not necessary to defame the ancient practices of the art to praise Lewis or anybody. It is quite essential that one stick to pure poetry, in fact, when talking of it, whatever its incentive may be. But it is also quite possible that those who, traditionally, might be inclined to slight Lewis—from an eminence of culture—might really be doing so from what is really an eminence of bad practice.

The great segment of all poetry is belief, from which springs the rhythmic nature of the created work, and this belief, when it is at its full, asserts life, with fervor, with confidence (directly or indirectly), not death. Here Lewis excels, and this may be the determining factor of the new quarter of the century and the one after it. Lewis may be the very essence of the innovator, and so, *good*—in spite of a total lack of all other excellence: his work good *poetry*.

It may be that the new of today *must* strip themselves for action, must divest themselves of much that the first quarter of the century poet could afford to carry. They cannot be so burdened and *go* as they must. Perhaps this is the inevitable step. Not that there is an inevitable clash between the two stresses—one complements the other—but because it must be so, for reasons of poetry, to have poetry get ahead, to have it mean its full.

Looking at Lewis' books, in the poems themselves one will find what he uses of the poetic means, what he has carried over from the work immediately preceding him in his own country, because he has the fervor, and by that and whatever else he has will be measured his poetic worth and by that again the importance of his contribution to the cause he loves, the kind of work he does for it.

But whatever *his* interests may be in writing poetry, there can be no doubt about what the critic's attitude toward him should be, solely to determine the worth of his poems as poetry.

Without hesitation I say that there is here no question of high art. Lewis has read from many of the well-known English and American poets and frankly copied their forms, using them as they come readily to his hand. It might be anything from Gray to Whitman, including the books of limericks, nursery rhymes, popular songs, Poe—anything you please, even back to Shakespeare—he'll borrow the form and turn it to his own purpose. Once in a while he makes the form ring with meaning. Sometimes the attempt falls flat. But through it all runs the drive that might catch fire, actually, in a word, a phrase—bringing the mind seriously to the task of realization. At moments the charge is so great that it lifts the commonplace to lyric achievement.

> *Russia, Russia, righting wrong*
> *Russia, Russia, Russia!*
> *That unified one sovereign throng,*
> *That hundred and sixty million strong*
> *Russia!*
> *America's loud Example-Song,*
> *Russia, Russia, Russia!*

The use of the word "Russia" resembles that of Aragon's "S.S.S.R." It goes to his head, as he says repeatedly, it maddens him with hope, with conviction, with certainty, with belief, the belief that sets him singing. His songs are songs, as good as he can make them, of triumph, realization. A poet's vision of a real future.

From the work of the first quarter of the century he has taken one positive thing, his dialect. Once in a while we come upon the inversion of Milton and hymn books. But in general he uses words with the confidence and the natural ease of a native speaking his own language as he hears it spoken in his own place and day. It adds to the impact of his seriousness.

He uses rhyme, but unaffectedly. Therefore, he uses it well. He does not let it take him for a ride for effects. He uses it in songs obviously intended for mass singing in trucks and in marching about "on business." There rhyme marks lines usefully, gives the pace and the measure.

He takes a direct interest in his day. He speaks of the political situations existing at the time he writes. He speaks directly, and so automatically does away with the putrescence of symbolism with which the first quarter of the century was cursed. He might fall into simple allegory, but it is so plain that it goes for fact simply.

He has picked up from Joyce—or out of his own head—the valuable time-saving trick of inventing words, compressing them to give a new twist to the meaning: Joyce Killer, flag-rags, daily-bathism, demockratism, dogmatrix, Rusevelt.

He can write, though, with the effectiveness of the expert man when he does a thing like this:

> Uh needs a pair o' breeches,
> Mirandy needs a skuht.

Then he speaks of the donkey, "used to middles," which is afraid to ruin the rows of growing cotton the farmer is forcing him to plow under, saying at last: "Sumpin' sho' is rotten!" Then the piece goes on:

> I'll say,
> Phew, for Chrissake,
> The brains of the "Brain Trust,"
>   that's it,
> Rrrrrrotten!
> Pity the poor American donkey,
> Pity the poor American farmhand,
> The one nervously zigzagging,
> The other compelled to jerk him back
>   to the row,
> Plowing under cotton!
> Such an "assinine"
> Torturing
> Strain on the sound sense of both!

In our need plowing under "what would be wealth in Russia." To this he comes back to again and again. Here his convictions have forced him to write well.

The four booklets show little or no progress in form that I can discern. If anything, I think the earlier ones are better, more forthright, cruder with a more patently outraged conscience. Lewis has let go, seeming to be repeating himself. Not that there can be too much repetition if his purpose—to bring about the revolution which will be the consummation of his effort—is to be achieved. He may dig up a richer nugget any day, some hot song that may force itself to everybody's lips—the *Marseillaise* of tomorrow. Maybe something he has written already will catch on and be carried to the front.

The influence of Lewis' work on other writers cannot but be good, for whatever his merits as an artist may or may not be, he has the one great strength without which there can be no art at all—the sincerity of belief in his own songs, in their value, and in their power to penetrate to the very bones of the listeners. This is a good thing that must come as a blast of healthy wind among the frailer stuff of the more cultured— no positively *not* more cultured but less cultured—writers.

If Lewis' subject matter should distress some readers, it's about time they learned what makes their fruit and vegetables grow for them, what kind of thoughts their cultivation breeds in a man, and, finally, what the meaning of poetry is.

November 23, 1937

Rafael Alberti

Words for Federico García Lorca

These are the first words I've written about you since your death, Federico, since that crime for which there are no words committed against you in your own Granada. Although these few lines are intended as a prologue to your *Gypsy Ballads (Romancero Gitano)*, they are written for you, sent to you, speaking to you through the hearts of the Spanish people who will read them, and who continue to learn your poems by heart.

I remember now the first day of our friendship, in the little garden of the Student House in Madrid, in October 1924. You had just come back from Granada, from Fuente Vaqueros, and you brought with you the first ballad for your book:

> *Green as I would have you green.*
> *Green wind. Green branches . . .*

I heard you read it for the first time. Your best ballad. Without doubt, the best in present-day Spanish poetry. Your "green wind" struck us all, leaving its echo in our ears. Even now, after thirteen years, it continues to sound through the newest branches of our poetry.

Juan Ramón Jiménez, from whom you learned so much, as all of us have learned, created in his *Arias Tristes* the lyric ballad, strange, musical, unforgettable. You, with your "Romance Sonambulo," invented the dramatic form, full of secret chills and mysterious bloodstreams. *La Tierra de Alvargonzalez* by Antonio Machado is a narrative romance, a terrible Castillian tale put into poetry. It can be told as a story. The happenings in the "Romance Sonambulo" and other poems to be found in your *Romancero Gitano* cannot be recounted. They elude all the efforts of the story-teller. You, on the foundations of the ancient Spanish form of the romance, along with Juan Ramón and Machado, created another style, strange and strong, at once both a support and a crown for the old Castillian tradition.

Then the war came. The people and the poets of our land wrote ballads. In ten months of warfare, nearly a thousand have been collected. You—and you are the greater for it—seem to have influenced almost all of them. Your voice, hidden under other voices, is heard in our struggle. But that which speaks to us the loudest is your blood. It cries out with all its strength, and rises like an immense fist, clenched in accusation and in protest. Nobody wants to believe it. It's impossible. Nobody feels that you are dead. We can't imagine you standing in front of a firing squad. They took you out at dawn. Some say to a cemetery. Others, on a road. The truth is . . . but can anyone speak the truth about this? That's how it is.

> *With their patent leather souls*
> *They come down the road . . .*

Who could have warned you that these same civil guards of your poems would one day kill you at dawn on the deserted outskirts of your own Granada? That's how it was! That death wasn't yours.

I was on the island of Ibiza on that eighteenth of July when the insurrection broke out. The civil guards came to look for me. I fled. For seventeen days I wandered in the mountains. Rainer Maria Rilke says that some people die with the death of others, not with their own death that properly belongs to them. It was your death that should have been mine. You were executed. I escaped. But your blood is still fresh, and will be for a long time.

The editions of your *Romancero Gitano* increase. Your name and your memory take root in Spain, in the very heart of our land. Let no one try to transplant those roots. The earth itself where they penetrate would not consent. It would burst into flames, into shot and shell, and scorch the hands of those who try to uproot you. The Spanish Falangists, your assassins, attempt villainously now to take advantage of your glory, riddled by the bullets of their own guns. They want to make of you, falsely, the poet of imperial Spain—Mussolini's poor imperial Spain! Let them try! In their shamelessness your executioners seem to forget that your name and

265

your poetry continue to march, now and forever, on the lips of the fighting people in the ranks of Spain's anti-fascist forces. Each poem of yours we recite echoes like a powerful accusation against your assassins.

We remember. We shall remember. We can't forget. We recognize the faces of those who would expose you, standing your body on foot again to help them continue the terrible farce of the most stupid and horrible of crimes committed in this war. But we will not consent to it. They will fail. We will keep your hands clean—we who were your friends and fellow poets, Luis Cernuda, Manuel Altolaguirre, Emilio Prados, Vicente Aleixandre, Pablo Neruda, Miguel Hernández, myself. With the same sad and magnificent people of your poems, we will guard your memory, your constant presence, and celebrate your name with the fervor that the poets of old held toward the young Garcilaso de la Vega who rode without a helmet against the ranks of the enemy and died, honored alike for his bravery and his songs.

January 11, 1938

Carl Carmer

Stranglers of the Thunder

Figures born out of the folk imagination people the arts of many European countries. Folklore has inspired many poems, paintings, and statues. Sometimes art creations have been so direct as to be actually folk art itself—as in the case of cathedral gargoyles; more often they have been the results of an artist's conscious laboring with folk materials. The countries of Europe are so small, however, in comparison with the United States, and the centuries have given their folk stories so many years in which to accumulate, that few of their artists, no matter what their medium, could grow to man's estate without being at least aware of the heritage of picturesque legend with which they were surrounded.

In America, however, the vastness of the nation and its short history have combined with circumstance to separate the artist from this stimulating material. Native folklore has had but little time to grow. The American artist, in the past too greatly influenced by classics and contemporaries, has not, as a rule, been of a social class familiar with the naive products of the popular fancy, existing only through word of mouth, passed down through centuries by narrators whose only literature they were.

Despite the country's comparative youth America has a folklore, and that quite aside from the legends already in existence among the Indians before the white men came. Some of it was brought to the new land from countries across the seas and has been preserved much as it was, by people geographically isolated, like the descendants of the Scotch Highlanders of Elizabethan times, who have lived many generations in the Appalachians and still sing of "Bonny Barbara Allen" in a wailing ballad whose origins are lost far back in the dim mists of early English history. In Louisiana the Acadians sing songs and tell stories that were first heard

267

beside the hearth fires of eighteenth-century France, clinging to them with an affection that has out-lasted both a voluntary and an involuntary exile. In the Dakotas the blond Swedish-American is dancing to the tunes to which his fathers jigged in the fields of Scandinavia. And in the central states in many a community of German complexion the fantasies of the fatherland, though translated into English and ever changing in the telling, still attract groups of enchanted children.

To the question of America's rightful claim to this treasury of other lands, it may be answered that once a people adopts a folklore, it makes it completely and peculiarly its own. With no printed page to discipline the itinerant narrator, a story grows and changes while it is told. It is translated not only into the prevailing language but also into familiar and commonly visual terminology. Thus the "Ballad of Lord Randal," an old Scottish song still echoing among the North Carolina mountains, has become, through generations of singers who never saw a nobleman, the simple tragic story of Johnnie Randall who killed his sweetheart. And the Johnnie Randall of that story is an American mountain boy whose lank figure might well be painted or molded, whose fate might be subject for play or opera or poem.

But it is not merely in the borrowed folklores of other lands that America has enriching material to offer her native artists. America has an authentic, autochthonous folklore of her own. Wherever American people have tarried long enough to have the feeling of belonging to the land, the roots of their imaginations have crept down into the soil. And the harvest, as might be expected from a young and sturdy folk, has been strong and hardy. A gusty, exaggerated, sometimes sardonic humor has been the keynote of much of our native folklore, regardless of its place of origin—from Texas to Maine. Perhaps Benjamin Franklin set the pace when, disgusted with the inaccurate accounts of his country contributed to the London papers by Britishers who had been only short-time visitors, he wrote of the American sheep whose tails were so heavy with wool that it was necessary to rest them on little carts trundled behind, and of the American cod fisheries in the Great Lakes, the salt water fish having been driven up the Niagara River into Lake Erie by hungry whales. "But let them know, sir," he continues, "that the grand leap of the whale in the chase up the falls of Niagara is esteemed by all who have seen it as one of the finest spectacles in nature."

While it is doubtful if this early American whopper became so generously known as to give story-tellers a mark to shoot at, it is unquestioned that it is a typical American attitude of mind and that the products of the American communal imagination have for the most part been grotesquely exaggerative. In the days when communication was more difficult and books and journals were less numerous, the good story-teller was a proud figure. There were even contests in the sort of imaginative fiction which, for want of a better term, was called lying. My father has told me with pride in his voice that my great-grandfather was boasted by his relatives to be the "biggest liar in Tompkins County." They cited as proof of the contention his tale of snowdrifts so deep in the vicinity of Ithaca, New York, one winter that they did not melt through the summer. He was cutting hay in a meadow one hot July day, he said, when a big buck jumped the fence and got caught in a snowdrift so inextricably that he was able to kill it by cutting its throat with his scythe. Were the picture which this anecdote conjures up to be painted, I can imagine its being bitterly attacked by conservative academicians as but another example of the undisciplined, inexplicable, and indefensible juxtaposition of unrelated objects with which modernists insult intelligence—rather than recognized as representative of the imaginative quality of the average American farmer before the Civil War.

A few of America's writers in the past have caught the spirit of this folk humor—Josh Billings, Artemus Ward, and especially Mark Twain. But most of the country's creative workers were too politely striving toward European culture to recognize the artistic values that lay in the imagination of the people. They were unable to see any analogy between the figures of the saints, painted by the artists of the Renaissance from the conceptions that people had come to have of them, and the fantastic latter-day miracle-workers of American mythology. In an ancient Jewish folk tale of a lad who killed a giant with his slingshot Michelangelo found the subject of a statue. What sculptor will carve us Strap Buckner, who "rassled with the devil" out in the Dakotas? Who will supplant the Lorelei with the maid of the Pascagonla, whose song from the summit of a hill of waters lured the Biloxi

Indians to their sea-games off the coast of Mississippi? Who will turn from Ruth, the sower, to the sturdy figure of Johnnie Appleseed swinging westward with the ballet of the swirling blossoms springing behind him?

The English nursery tale of Jack and the Beanstalk has already been used as material for an opera by an American composer, an opera in which a cow proves an amusing and important character. But no American stage has yet seen Paul Bunyan and his big blue ox who measured "twenty-eight axe-handles and a plug of chewing tobacco" between the tips of his magnificent horns. While one of America's most distinguished poets, Edna St. Vincent Millay, and one of her best known musicians, Deems Taylor, have collaborated on an opera which turned out to be a conventional affair, its verse based on Anglo-Saxon rhythms, its music far from distinctive, the giant shoulders of John Henry lift his nine-pound hammer high in the air; Negro work-songs give him the beat, and the old tragedy of the battle of man against the machine is reenacted.

The native American artist has been busying himself with creating statues entitled *Civic Virtue, The Christian Student, Goose Girl*, hoping as all artists hope, to speak for the age in which he lives, to allow the imagination of the people to speak through him. While he chips at his stone, the imagination of America is articulate, and he cannot hear it. Pecos Bill is riding a twister down in Texas, his star-spurs bite into the flanks of the whirlwind. Kemp Morgan towers above the Oklahoma hills, driving oil wells single-handed. Railroad Bill, hard pressed by the sheriff, turns from a black Alabamian son of sin into a scuttling red fox (here is a more fascinating problem than ever a Daphne becoming a bay tree). In Cajun Louisiana, the talking bulldog, returning from college, takes the bayou steamer for the old home he is destined never to see. Down the Mississippi Mike Fink, half horse and half alligator and part snapping turtle, guides his keelboat. Along the Atlantic coast Old Stormalong stands on the bridge of his clipper while below his sailors, mounted on horses, ride the long watches. Casey Jones opens the throttle of one of the "two locomotives that are goin' to bump." Willie the Weeper dreams of the generous lady who gave him a pretty Ford automobile "with diamond headlights and a silver steering wheel." Tony Beaver turns the Eel River back on its course through West Virginia. The Gambler, twenty-dollar gold pieces on his eyes, leaves old Joe's barroom for the last time, drawn by sixteen coal-black horses, cheered by the music of a jazz band perched on the top of his hearse, speeded along the cemetery road by a dozen crap-shootin' pallbearers raisin' hell.

There should be an American mythology for study in our schools. I believe this with such sincerity that I have tried to write such a book in *The Hurricane's Children*, which was offered to the public in December 1937. In trying to describe this book when I first talked about doing it, I said it was a group of American fairy stories. When it was done, I found that there are no fairies in it. Instead I find a lot of giants proudly roaring that a hurricane was their father and an earthquake was their mother.

The people of almost every nation in the world except the United States have liked to make up stories about "the little people." Even the American Indians made up some beautiful tales about them. But Americans have been so busy doing big jobs that they have never taken time off to let their minds play with the tiny folks who have magic powers. At the end of a hard day's work the American cowboys or miners or lumberjacks or apple-pickers have had their fun out of making up stories about men who could do jobs that just could not be done, and in an impossibly short time with one hand tied behind them. And so I have discovered that this is not an American fairy-story book at all, but an American giant book.

If these stories had existed hundreds of years ago in another land, we would probably be calling them myths today and reading of Pecos Bill and Tony Beaver and Annis Christmas as we read of Mercury and Mars and Juno, or of Thor and Loki and Freya. The stories in this book are the products of our grandfathers' fancies, our fathers', our own. They are the imagination that Americans inherit, and I hope many Americans are going to be proud of it.

If mythological figures are to be allowed a place in art then, and God forbid that they should be barred, let the American artist remember his own immediate heritage. His background may enable him to give to his work something truer than he would have to Hercules or Persephone. Let him remember, too, that much of the appreciation of any art lies in the aesthetic pleasure derived from recognition. The people of a locality will be happier to see in the art works adorning their public buildings, for instance, figures they know and are fond of rather than works representing abstract virtues or the gods of Greece and Rome. It is time that artists recognize in the figments of the American dream the opportunity for the expression of that beauty which is distinctively a part of the land and its people.

The suggestions I am making here to American artists are not meant as arguments for "literary" art as opposed to representations of "abstract" beauty. The subjects I recommend allow more freedom of individual expression, certainly, than those art products which the "abstractionists" are inclined to scorn as mere illustrations. They permit as many treatments as there are artists to present them. Their essence is imaginative liberty. They are representative not of a single narrator's creativeness but of the free soaring fancy of the workers of America, thousands of them in communal search for release from the monotony of the real. They should be welcomed by the artists of the more liberal persuasions, for, like the manifestations of the subconscious which have found expression in the work of Dadaists and Surrealists, they introduce, as Wilenski expresses it, "the incredible proportions and juxtapositions that occur to us in dreams." Indeed they surpass in mad fancy most of the imaginative work of today.

Even to the conservative academician these figures present a challenge, the oldest known to art. For John Henry is any Negro, and Pecos Bill is any cowboy. Rippling muscles of man and straining horse offer their problems as they have since the days of Hellas. But America's worker-created giants should be most heartily received by that already great group of American artists who believe that art should have social significance. They depict the triumph of the laborer over his environment. They are the daydreams of the worker who sees himself embodied in the champion his mind creates. In them defeatism is wiped out by invincible action.

April 12, 1938

Romain Rolland

Unity

A noble call for the union of French intellectuals has just been issued by thirteen writers belonging to different parties. I add my voice to theirs.

Oh, my colleagues of French thought—writers, artists, men of science—allow one of your elders to make his confession, and yours, at this grave hour for France!

All of us have labored as best we could; and no country can be prouder than ours of the great work and the genius of her children. Steadily and without relaxing we continue the line of the good workers in the intellectual field who have been serving and honoring the French community for centuries. But too often we also continue their dissensions and conflicts.

In untroubled times it is healthy for all the debates of the mind to develop to the full: they widen the field of exploration of art and science; they provoke an abundance of experience and of contradictory and complementary discoveries. Even the passions overexcited by these intellectual jousts are the ransom of these conquests, which become the property of all.

But at times when common property is threatened quarrels must cease, divisions must be wiped out at once, and from all the nation's parties hands must be extended to meet together. Let the union be sealed!

At no time has this imposed itself with such imperious necessity as at the present, when not only the fate of a nation is at stake, but the sacred values of civilization—all the culture of the world, menaced in its most precious conquests of the last few centuries, in its heroic efforts for progress, in its dignity, in its liberty. What none of us had foreseen thirty years ago is here: the civilization of the West sees the barbarians issuing from its own loins; it sees rising against it madmen, such as this gang leader who hurled into the dying face of Unamuno, "Death to intelligence!" A fierce wind of a new Islam has risen against the most civilized older nations; fanatic prophets, bearing a Koran for war against the "infidels," are launching blind and devouring hordes, with their fleets of black planes, upon the world.

This savage inundation, which has already overrun the frontiers, which has just engulfed old Austria, which is covering a part of Spain, piling up at the gates of Czechoslovakia, and flinging its menacing defiance to all the democracies of the world, is encircling France from the North Sea to the Mediterranean, from the Vosges to the Alps and the Pyrenees. In the eyes of the world, France has the doubtful honor of having become the last Continental citadel of liberty–of liberty in all its most vital forms, most essential to any human society, any progress: political and social liberty, intellectual liberty, even religious liberty–since at the present time the barbarian tide threatens to carry away, together with freedom of the mind and the ideal of social justice, of mutual respect, and of the equality of men and of races, the religions that claim the two and three-thousand-year old heritage of the Gospel and the Bible.

All the Old World, and all the New, witness this brutal assault rising against them. And when one thinks of the tremendous material and moral forces which they represent, their debility makes one blush. Their weakness indicts their disunion. Their disunion makes for the arrogance and the might of the adversary. If their alliance were sealed, the invasions would be shattered upon it, as the Arabs were at Poitiers.

Let us achieve unity! My associates of all the branches of intellectual activity, let us give the example, let us realize it! Let us declare a truce to all our discords! All of us desire fruitful peace, the peace of the world, peace for all in labor, and equal justice for all. But in our time–at all times–peace is given only to those who have the courage to want it and to defend it. Our old Victor Hugo said, "Let us declare peace for the world!" We can do it only by being united and strong.

April 26, 1938

Edwin Berry Burgum

Hemingway's Development

The preface which Ernest Hemingway has written for his play about the war in Madrid (*The Fifth Column and the First Forty-nine Stories*, Scribner's) is one of the important literary documents of our time. It is not simply the apology that an honest craftsman might write for a play he has not succeeded in getting produced. The preface is a statement about the broader matter of his intentions and attitudes, such as could only come from an author without a trace of meretricious purpose.

"In going where you have to go, and doing what you have to do, and seeing what you have to see, you dull and blunt the instrument you write with. But I would rather have it bent and dulled and know I had to put it on the grindstone again and hammer it into shape and put a whetstone to it, and know that I had something to write about, than to have it bright and shining and nothing to say, or smooth and well oiled in the closet, but unused."

Obviously, with this preface the notion must disappear that Hemingway is only interested in concealing beneath the glitter of his literary style the antisocial pursuits of the playboy and the gangster. Whatever may have been true of the past, Hemingway's recognition is now serious that art must have its roots in social events. He renounces the easy success of reduplicating past molds in favor of loyalty to the changing shape of things. When a writer who has been sensitive to style and technique of expression chooses the risk of an esthetic failure because he will not allow himself to degenerate into the insignificant and the outmoded, his action becomes an important sign of the times. But it is especially significant for those who have aligned themselves with the Left. They have been warned often enough by the high priests of Culture of the dangers that lurk in the doctrinaire, and now an American writer who is certainly as good as we possess tells his fellow writers it is a danger they must run. In the language of politics, they must "take sides against fascism."

About his own play, Hemingway, I think, has been too modest. The success of his turn to the dramatic form in *The Fifth Column* may have been embarrassed by lack of familiarity with practical stagecraft. We may leave this judgement to the event. But it is otherwise with his turn to an anti-fascist theme, for the play makes good reading. We are taken inside a hotel in Madrid that is periodically shelled from without and harbors fascist spies within. The breakdown of normal service in time of civil war sets the action against a background of ironic humor. The electrician is too drunk with wine and anarchism to repair the damaged wires. The manager is more eager to get food for his family from lodgers who may have smuggled it in from France than to serve them. Chambermaids find it more difficult than usual to close their eyes to the unlocked door and the empty bed. But the American, Philip Rawlings, though he plays the game like the rest, does not talk about his real business in the hotel, which is to ferret out the fascist spies. Before he has succeeded, they have shot in his room a member of the International Brigade whom they have mistaken for him. But, through the aid of a loyalist soldier of German birth, he discovers the center of operations and captures the gang.

If *The Fifth Column* were only another story of violence and intrigue in time of war, it would be of little moment. But its sensational events are the mechanism through which a typical Hemingway character gets a grip on himself. Externally Philip resembles the familiar type. Middle class, wearing his education lightly, and unaccustomed to treating money with veneration, he has lived from one love affair into another, never expecting more than sensuality and never satisfied when he has got it. When the play opens he has just achieved another conquest. After knocking out his rival in a drunken fight, he has won the admiration of an American girl who is writing stories in Spain. The war is exciting but inconvenient, and she proposes that they escape it, go through the familiar motions of travel to some mountain resort where nature will leave them alone or to some watering place where bars and cabarets will furnish a more appealing distraction from love than the terror of war. In the old days Philip would have assented with the old disgust for himself and the woman. But now his disgust has for the first time found its reason, and he contrasts the grace and luxury of the proposed debauch with the struggle that thousands of men and women around them are making to safeguard such elemental needs as life and food and freedom. Philip turns away in preference to an illiterate Spanish courtesan in whose love he recognizes the broader element of a common interest in the fight for the survival of Spanish democracy.

The success of such a story obviously does not lie in the nature of a theme which might easily have been treated with banality or sentiment. Philip's seriousness of purpose grows with his participation in the hunt for spies. It is not the result of any reading of treatises or long theoretical discussions. It is the gradual, quite unintellectual response to his admiration for Spanish friends. In every affair of the heart there must be the nuance of wider interests than the personal: the book that both react to in a similar way; the gesture loved because it implies a common snobbism or democracy; the spontaneous turning away from the immediate interest to the same relaxation, whatever it may be. When there is not agreement, these apparently superfluous trifles collect and undermine the basis of passion. In the play they first break through when Dorothy expects Philip to admire the expensive furs she has secured by a dubious financial transaction. Quite in the Hemingway fashion, Philip does not discuss their difference of attitude, but, when he himself comes to feel it keenly, casts her off in a burst of vulgar quarreling.

The whole of Hemingway's development from the beginning of his career as a writer is implicit in the character of Philip Rawlings. The collection of his short stories appended to the play graphs a course the direction of which the play can now be said to have defined. Their arrangement from stories of Nick's boyhood in the Midwest to his mature experiences in European or American cities suggests the interpretation. Hemingway has always been absorbed by certain elementary concerns of men. Influenced by the revolt against intellectualism and respectability led by Dreiser and Anderson, but for him principally by the early work of Gertrude Stein, he has cherished beyond all else the cultivation of the body. The quality he has consistently admired in men has been physical competence. Indifferent to class lines, he has ignored the ideals that Americans have associated with them: success in business, public esteem, the austerity of the puritan, the effeminacy of the dilettante. He has chosen to write of the boy who admires his father's dexterity as a fisherman, the boxer who can plant a sure blow, young men skilled with the gun or the ski. If the millionaire is a big game hunter or in middle years turns to the vicarious participation of betting at the races, he finds him interesting, but not otherwise. His women have never been domestic, but are the hardy reckless consorts of such men. And as lovers, both his men and women have more than a trace of primitive sadism in them. Whether wealthy or down on their luck, college bred or almost illiterate, his characters have shared a common bond of disdain for stuffy class distinctions.

Hemingway wrote of this world so freshly and frankly as to take his audience unawares. He made them like the direct experience of his stories by furnishing them no excuse for the *arrière pensée* of the moralist. He profited, it is true, from the more tolerant attitude that prevailed in literary circles as a result of the propaganda in the works of Mencken, Dreiser, and Anderson. But he never stimulated criticism, as some of his predecessors had done, by justifying his interpretation. He kept himself out of sight as carefully as Flaubert, never indulging in a phrase of open comment, so that the flavor of irony or disillusionment or whatever it might be, seemed to reside in the very juxtaposition of events. But if he was candid about the intimacies of sex, if he allowed the crude cynicism of popular speech to dominate his style, he did not conceal the redeeming sincerity of ordinary human impulse. The little Indian girl who introduces the boy to sex, while her brother looks on, shyly asks for a kiss and hopes with curiosity for a baby. This fundamental trait in Hemingway, of course, reaches its finest expression in *A Farewell to Arms*. Only those who have not realized that Hemingway's cruelty is of the surface could be surprised that he has made childbirth the tragic climax of this novel and his tragic ending the loss of both the child and the mother.

The death of the nurse symbolized (for Hemingway) the destruction of our aspirations consequent upon the World War. He became the novelist of that restless generation of misfits which followed the demobilization of the troops. The brutality of his characters is their perverse response to the brutality with which life has treated them. Something has given way within, though what it is remains obscure; some orientation toward the use of their talents or the grasp of happiness has been rudely broken. They hide the wound beneath a crust of bravado. They learn to drink it off, and come to feel at home with other misfits who have lost their nerve and their decency. They describe with cynical disgust the bullfighter in "The Undefeated," who refuses to recognize his degeneration and gets gored in the fight he believes will restore his reputation. They visit the prizefighter who knows he has fought too long and is betting his own money on his opponent. They meet the crook who has been lying all day in bed because he knows that those whom he has double-crossed are waiting for him outside. Or they accept into their fraternity, with a touch of pride for their own superior comprehension, those whose narrow range of class interests has blinded them to their callousness, as when, in "An Alpine Idyll," the two young sportsmen order their meal with complete indifference to the gruesome story the sexton has told them.

Then there came the magnificence of *Death in the Afternoon*, one of those rare treatises by men of letters which discloses the gulf between scholarship and insight. It is a veritable encyclopedia of bullfighting, the history of the sport, the style of the great fighters, the decay of the national tradition, until it dawns on the reader that he is dealing with the rise and fall of an art form. For Hemingway finds bullfighting the only sport which follows the course of tragedy upon the stage. It is the stylization of death, more ritualized than ancient gladiatorial combats and more humanized, since the superior skill of the man makes it more likely that the bull will die. But for those who were watching for social connotations in Hemingway's development, disquieting symptoms had appeared. The constant question in our minds, I remember, was whether Hemingway was going aesthetic, was going to follow to its end the road that Gertrude Stein had shown him. His style had been without parallel in American writing for flawless achievement of what he sought. It isolated as only fine prose can do the sentence intonation, the slangy penetrating metaphor, which prove how superficial are the differences in linguistic pattern between the American of the middle class and the proletariat. But now that all this sensitiveness was turned, however, beautifully, into lamentation that bullfighting was becoming a lost art, that economic insecurity and the demands of the poor were responsible for the decay of another old Spanish custom, it seemed to adumbrate the cultural orientation of fascism, which is obtuse to the cruelty and vulgarity of the present because it lives in dreams of feudal perfection. Knowing also as we did that the ethos of the gangster about whom Hemingway had written was only that of the fascist vigilante not yet systematized, we hesitated about his direction.

We had forgotten, as events showed, that Hemingway had always lacked the principal ingredient of fascist culture. This is, I take it, to see persons not of one's class from the outside, to fail to penetrate into understanding of the complexity of their psychology and the real nature of their aims. It should not be ignored that there is a kind of fascist interest in the proletariat. When the rich and idle lady takes a proletarian lover, rather than appreciating him for what he is, she is only projecting upon him the depravity of her own passions and her sympathy is similar to that anyone may have for a fine specimen of animal, the dog in one's house or the deer one proceeds to slaughter. But, though Hemingway's characters have often been callous in this fashion, he has never been similarly callous in his relation to them. Indeed, quite the contrary; if he has continually shocked the respectable reader, it has been precisely by the authenticity of his disclosure of other *mores* than their own. He has not sentimentalized the worker or the sportsman. He has put himself on their level and made them articulate. Nor has he ignored what is often the reckless generosity of their characters.

In fact, he has come more and more to recognize that the underprivileged have a resiliency of resistance to degenerating pressures that is lacking in the coddled rich, though the resistance, as in *To Have and To Have Not*, may in the particular case be partial and end in failure. Hemingway's irony, indeed, proceeds from his recognition that the real kindliness and generosity in human relationships is less likely to be found in the reputable classes; just as his cynicism was in large measure a consequence of his absorption in the *mores* of the dominant class and those it had corrupted. But at bottom he had always taken for granted the democratic tradition of freedom and equality. Life in Europe after the war had this salutary effect upon many of our expatriate writers. Bohemianism in these individuals promoted the rediscovery of neglected human values. The sentimental ideal of equality and fraternity, detached from its mooring in middle-class respectability, became for them a real conviction. Though confused enough at first, this reaction to accepted values became more significant as the accepted values continued to degenerate. After Prohibition, in "Wine of Wyoming," Hemingway feels more at home with the family of poor French farmers in Wyoming who hospitably offer him their friendship and the wine they are periodically arrested for making, than he does with the dominant class. The Spanish war immensely expanded these displacements of class feeling, completed the shift from Bohemianism to democracy, and clarified the enigma that the sophisticated and esoteric artist sometimes has the strongest appreciation of the virtues of the common man. It was so with Elliot Paul, and it has been so with Hemingway. And this collection of his short stories is the record of the road that Hemingway has traveled through the confusions of modern life to a clearer insight into the relation between democracy and art.

November 22, 1938

V. J. Jerome

Laureates of Betrayal

History gives repeated instances of desertion of the people's cause at critical junctures by intellectuals—as it does also of unyielding and courageous adherence. During the political vicissitudes of the first bourgeois revolutions, in England and in France, many exponents of culture wavered and retreated. Their vacillations reflected the half measures and compromises—even in its revolutionary stage—of the bourgeoisie which brought them into being.

However, despite their instability, the intellectuals as a group were protagonists of the bourgeois revolution. For they constituted the first representatives of that mass intelligentsia which growing industrialism was to call forth. The intelligentsia in the seventeenth and eighteenth centuries prepared the ideological ground for the bourgeois revolution in England and in France. A few exceptional intellectuals even manifested a critical attitude toward the young capitalism, voicing ideas of utopian socialism. On the other hand, decayed feudalism was still powerful enough to exert an influence on a considerable group of intellectuals and to engage their services in its behalf.

Upon the death of Cromwell, leader of the bourgeois revolution in seventeenth-century England, the not-yet-recreant John Dryden wrote:

> *His grandeur he derived from heaven alone,*
> *For he was great, ere Fortune made him so....*
> *He made us freemen of the Continent*
> *Whom Nature did like captives treat before....*

Dryden was then serving as secretary to Sir Gilbert Pickering, a chamberlain at Cromwell's court, who had been one of the judges to try Charles I. Dryden wrote in defense of the

Great Rebellion against the feudal oppressors and of Cromwell's thoroughness in executing the king:

> War, our consumption, was their gainful trade;
> We inward bled, whilst they prolonged our pain;
> He fought to end our fighting and assayed
> To stanch the blood by breathing of the vein.

Eighteen months later this selfsame Dryden wrote a poem in praise of the restoration of the Stuarts, and shortly afterward a "Panegyric on the Coronation." The ink was still fresh on the "Heroic Stanzas to the Memory of Oliver Cromwell" when they were followed by a lament on the younger Charles' exile during the republic:

> For his long absence church and state did groan,
> Madness the pulpit, faction seized the throne:
> Experienced age in deep despair was lost,
> To see the rebel thrive, the loyal crost.

Dryden now hailed reactionary royalism:

> This mistrustful fowl no harm suspects,
> So safe are all things which our King protects.

With pro-feudal reactionaries restored to the highest state offices—although the Restoration was not a reversion to feudalism—Catholicism again reached out its tentacles, the king being known to have secret leanings toward it. The poet of revolutionary Puritanism became a convert to the church of Rome.

Fitly, this vicar of Bray was chosen a Fellow of the Royal Society and raised to the rank of poet laureate. As fitly he was accorded by Macaulay the rank of "illustrious renegade."

Against John Dryden stands John Milton—the greater poet, the greater man. When venal or cowardly penmen were deserting the republic to flatter the crown, Milton spoke out for the most advanced and consistent section of the revolutionary bourgeoisie, in the face of fierce repression. With militant voice he assailed the restorationists for "this noxious humor of returning to bondage instilled of late by some deceivers." He stood uncompromisingly for democratic liberty, for separation of church and state, for the republic that would make a full sweep of feudal relations. Milton, not Dryden, spoke for the true and forward-looking intellectuals of the seventeenth century—the unsinecured and unlaureled; the disgraced, the dungeoned, the hanged. Where is the honest intellectual worker, of his day and since, who has not reverenced Milton's steadfastness despite poverty, blindness, and the shafts of royal scorn; his superb courage and self-devotion—the deathless stand to the last of that Samson Agonistes?

The great French Revolution came like a lightning streak across the firmament of the entire world, illuminating a path to freedom for the oppressed in every land. In the Declaration of the Rights of Man all of mankind pitted against feudal autocracy gained in stature. The peasant masses, the town artisans, and the advanced sections of bourgeois democracy everywhere rallied to the revolution. In Britain, as on the Continent and in the New World, ardent sympathy for the revolution swept intellectuals in all spheres. Outstanding scientific and literary figures had been stirred by Voltaire's devastating anti-clericalism, by the philosophic materialism of Helvetius and Holbach, by the Encyclopedists' cult of reason, and by Rousseau's egalitarian democracy.

Typifying certain of these intellectuals was the English poet Robert Southey who early in life became a fervent adherent of the revolution. With his fellow poets, Coleridge and Lovell, he worked out a utopian-socialistic scheme, "Pantisocracy," to be realized in the New World, "where Susquehanna pours his untamed stream." In Southey's revolutionary drama, *Wat Tyler*, the captive John Ball, charged with being a rebel and with stirring up the people, answers his inquisitor:

> *I am John Ball; but I am not a rebel.*
> *Take ye the name, who, arrogant in strength,*
> *Rebel against the people's sovereignty....*
> *If it be guilt*
> *To preach what you are pleased to call strange notions,*
> *That all mankind as brethren must be equal;*
> *That privileged order of society*
> *Are evil and oppressive; that the right*
> *Of property is a juggle to deceive*
> *The poor whom you oppress—I plead me guilty.*

Nonetheless, at this very time a wave of reaction in England swept Southey into condemning the Revolutionary Terror in France. His ill proportioned sensibilities were hurt by the execution of Marie Antoinette, and he openly opposed the revolution.

Two years after writing *Wat Tyler* he declared of the people: "As for pigs, they are too like the multitude." (This contempt for the masses was in like language expressed by the Tories of America in Hamilton's profession of faith: "Your People, Sir, your People is a great beast.") For his swinish conception of the multitude, his Tory masters appointed him poet laureate. Byron aptly rhymed this *laureate* with *Iscariot*.

From his favored position Southey looked back with nostalgia to the *ancien régime*: "Bad as the feudal times were, they were far less injurious than these commercial ones to the kindly and generous feelings of human nature and far, far more favorable to the principles of honor and integrity." The best that can perhaps be said for Southey is, as a noted biographer has charitably put it: "He never had been a thorough Jacobin, and he never became a thorough Tory."

And Coleridge, who had looked enviously across the Channel and pointed to the new France as the paragon for a new England:

> *Shall France alone a Despot spurn?*
> *Shall she alone, O Freedom, boast thy care?*

–and Coleridge, who had hung his head "and wept at Britain's name," now delighted the masters of England with his avowal:

> *There lives no form nor feeling in my soul*
> *Unborrowed from my country.*

The renegacy of a host of Southeys and Coleridges in England, France, Prussia, Austria, the United States of America, and elsewhere came at a turning point in the French Revolution. The masses, both urban and rural, were fully convinced that the big bourgeoisie was forsaking the basic tasks of the revolution In August-September 1792 they swept out the propertied citizens' Constituent Assembly, after abolishing the monarchy and the bourgeois-aristocratic constitution of 1791. The democratic republic based on universal suffrage could never have been established save for the root-and-branch destruction of the monarchy, rallying center for the people's enemies. The king and queen were proved to be negotiating with the heads of foreign powers for a counter-revolutionary invasion of France; in their name the European feudal coalition had attacked the young republic in the spring of 1792; and in their name the restorationists and their Girondist conciliators were conspiring against the revolution.

"The fatherland is in danger!" became the slogan of the revolution against the foe within and without. Victory at the frontiers required victory on the home front. The fall of the monarchy symbolized the ascension of the revolution.

The poets' revulsion from the revolution was Tory prose set to verse. The bards rhymed what the bourgeois reasoned. The British ruling class looked with growing uneasiness at the new republic, viewing the end of feudalism in France as the emergence of a rival bourgeois state. Impelled by the industrial revolution, England aimed to seize from France strategic Channel ports and colonies in the East, in order to check her industrial expansion and eliminate her as a naval power. To this end the British bourgeoisie entered into collusion with French royalists and with the feudal governments of the Continent.

Bourgeois England feared, as did feudal Austria, Prussia, and Russia, the impact of the revolution. Jacobinism was sweeping over England, Scotland, and Ireland. There was mounting resentment at Tory oppression and the government's war drive against France. The ruling class was struck with panic. Prime Minister William Pitt, shedding his liberalism like a loose garment, joined Edmund Burke, now the leading counterrevolutionary ideologue, and turned the full force of his class tyranny upon the people. The Habeas Corpus Act was suspended. Public meetings of sympathizers of revolutionary France were violently broken up. All publications opposed to monarchy and aristocracy were banned. Obsolete anti-sedition laws were revived. Political prisoners congested the jails.

War became imperative. The masses of England had to be bludgeoned with patriotism.

The king's execution served as pretext for rupturing diplomatic relations with France—to the very bourgeoisie which had come to power by rolling a king's head from the block!

This time the milk of human kindness curdled in the veins of the British diplomats. And the humane Southeys shed wells of ink for the last Louis that were rivaled only by the tears of later Southeys for the last Nicholas.

The Southeys and Coleridges, the Mackintoshes and Wordsworths made their peace with reaction and were in due course officially rewarded. James Mackintosh became "Sir James"; William Wordsworth was appointed poet laureate. It was to Wordsworth that Robert Browning referred in his poem, "The Lost Leader," which opens with the lines:

> Just for a handful of silver he left us,
> Just for a riband to stick in his coat....

But the lineage to which self-respecting men of science and letters trace their worth is of intellectual leaders like William Godwin, who answered Burke's Tory agitation with his epoch-indicting *Political Justice*; who bravely and eloquently defended the leaders of the radical republican Corresponding Society tried for treason during the anti-Jacobin hysteria in 1794. It is the lineage of men like Joseph Priestley, who sought truth in life as he sought it in the laboratory; who, that night in '91, looking on while the "Church-and-King" mob of Birmingham burned his home, his scientific instruments, and his valuable papers, must have felt even in his bereavement that those flames would yet light up the ages. He fled finally to the America of Jefferson and Franklin.

In 1848 in France the intellectuals, with the bulk of the petty bourgeoisie, joined the bourgeois-democratic revolution. Utopian Socialists—adherents of Fourier, Saint Simon, and Cabet—demanded an end to the monarchy and to the rule of the banking aristocracy. A red-cravated Baudelaire stood on the barricades with the workers in the June Days. But the liberal bourgeoisie, fearing the proletarian advance, retreated into the octopus grasp of the financial oligarchy. The petty bourgeoisie, dreading working-class power even more than big-bourgeois ascendancy, deserted the June insurrection. Betraying its own interests, it left the Parisian proletariat to be slaughtered by the hordes of Cavaignac. With the victory of Bonapartism—harvest of this treachery—the petty-bourgeois intellectuals grew cynical. Their Baudelaire now hailed "the clergy, the military, and the poets" as the mainstay of society; he now gave his devotion to absolutism and Jesuitism. He who had exulted in "the infinite taste of the republic" now reviled the republican as "the enemy of roses and perfumes." He who had been aflame with the slogan, *Everything by the people, everything for the people,* now, lost in pessimism, lamented:

> *Hurry, let us extinguish the lamp that is alight,*
> *Let us sink in nocturnal darkness.*

But the workers did not extinguish their light. Out of the very debris of their defeat they began to build. They rose from the glowing ashes of the June Days to become the "heaven-stormers" of the Commune.

September 24, 1940

Henry Hart

"You Can't Go Home Again"

The last thirty-six of the 743 pages of what, presumably, is Thomas Wolfe's last book (*You Can't Go Home Again*, Harper), contain the finest writing of his turbulent and unfulfilled life. Indeed, they contain everything essential to an understanding of him and his self-consuming struggles to comprehend himself and the world. They provide evidence that, had death not defeated him, a Thomas Wolfe matured in understanding and disciplined in talent would have helped to defeat that class at the top of life which fabricates and perpetuates the irrational society in which the early Wolfe felt so lost.

These thirty-six pages are an event in American literature, for they lay bare, with a lucidity unattainable in any previous decade, the distinction between literature as a mature writer would have it and literature as the owning class desires and wills it to be. There are no ifs, ands, or buts, no irrelevancies, no ameliorating sighs, diffidences, or regrets, and none of that dreadful rhetorical and grandiloquent drool which disfigured so much of Wolfe's work and disguised so many of his ignorances. The problem is defined in terms of its basic essence and is personalized with a truth and poignancy Wolfe never before achieved.

The thirty-six pages comprise a letter of farewell to the editor to whom George Webber (as Thomas Wolfe calls himself in this book) owed his career, his growth, and his potentiality for fulfillment. The letter was not written because of any presentiment of death, as a most scandalously misplaced final paragraph would suggest to the uninitiated reader. It was written because Wolfe realized at last that it is imperative to change the conditions which blight, frustrate, and destroy millions of creative human beings, and the editor preferred to accept "the order of things as they are because you have no hope of changing them; and if you could change them, you feel that any other order would be just as bad."

I suspect that this letter was not part of one of the many manuscripts Wolfe left, but an actual letter written to an actual editor, who is Wolfe's literary executor. It is largely due to the skill of this unusual personality that the present book has been concocted out of remnants from the earlier novels, rough drafts, unfinished sketches, and half-completed projects. That this man should yield up a private letter which indicts himself, and voluntarily make it part of this book, rather than betray the dead, is a brave and honorable illustration of the confusion of our time. For he felt no compunction about excluding material which rightfully belonged in this book, and which depicted other living people and actual events in a way totally different from the one limned by the material that *has* been included. What is to become of the manuscripts which describe people and events not even mentioned in *You Can't Go Home Again?*

The book itself is disappointing, as a second posthumous book is always likely to be. It contains a great deal of writing which Wolfe would have discarded, or been prevailed upon to discard, and a great deal he would certainly have written in a different way had he lived and continued to grow. When I say this I do not wish to asperse the love's labor of those who have, as well as they were able, made out of the materials which were left a book quite like the work of the early Wolfe.

It begins with George Webber living on Twelfth Street and waiting for the publication of his first novel. He encounters Foxhall Edwards, the editor who was to mean so much to him and his career. He takes a trip back home to Libya Hill, and this stretch of narration and description is an heirloom of a time when Wolfe thought he would write an entire novel about a Pullman car—K 19—which is attached to the afternoon train from New York to Old Catawba. Then there is a description of Esther Jack and her husband, and a party at their house, which has been worked over rather considerably in order to spare the feelings of living persons. It is at this party that George Webber realizes that should he succumb to the amenities, luxuries, and blandishments of the world of privilege he could not remain an honest artist in search of truth.

Then the first novel is published. There is very little about this remarkable time of George Webber's life. The effects of a bank failure in Libya Hill are described at greater length. George goes to live in Brooklyn, and there is a little of the sights, sounds, and encounters of that dark period of his life. But it is neither adequately nor truthfully depicted. Too much has been excluded, too much omitted, and Wolfe was too close to the corresponding experiences in his own life to write them with the same ruthless drive and misjudgment with which in his first two books he traduced the hapless lights of Old Catawba. Moreover, learning about the aristocratic world of Foxhall Edwards enthralled him. But beyond all this, he was maturing and had begun to see things differently, and was not ready to write about these years. He was only becoming ready when he died.

There is a disquisition in this part of *You Can't Go Home Again* on the character and personality of Foxhall Edwards which is compounded of very genuine gratitude, inaccurate observation, and Wolfe's forte for exaggerating into legend something which needed the most scrupulous adherence to fact if the reality were to be accurately discerned and truthfully presented.

Then George Webber goes to London and there meets an American novelist who had praised his first book. There is some disgraceful toadying here, of which Wolfe would be very ashamed were he alive to see it in print. This novelist is likened to Abraham Lincoln. A more grotesque effort to praise has never been dissembled. This section of the book is an illustration of what I mean when I say Wolfe would have rewritten if he had lived.

And then there is a little about George's experiences in Nazi Germany—not much, not all, but a little, and perhaps enough to enable the reader to perceive that Wolfe's experiences among the Nazis rent the last concealing curtain and he saw—what he had been trying to see all his life—that the poor are not vicious because of inherent evil—(as his depiction of them so often intimates and, indeed, as is even explicitly stated in the present work)—but because their lives are debauched by those who wield economic and political power.

And then the letter.

Except for the letter, none of it matters very much. It isn't, I maintain, the way he would have written if he had lived, and since it is the product of the tail end of his adolescence and the very beginning of his maturity, as much truth is buried beneath bombast and beneath rhetorical belaboring of the obvious as in his first three novels. Too many things are "nameless," "wordless," and "shapeless" still.

I must confess that I have no idea how this book seems to one who reads it without any knowledge of the author or of the people with whom he was involved. Most of those who have reviewed it are more infantile than Wolfe ever was. I feel that this book and Wolfe's others have a permanent value, not because they depict America, as has been claimed (for they really don't), but because they are a record of the confusion and waste inflicted upon one human creature who wanted to be creative in the United States in the nineteen twenties and thirties. This is the tale Wolfe was really trying to tell all along, when he was still too immature. Now that he is dead someone else must do it in order that all his striving shall not have been in vain.

October 22, 1940

ART YOUNG

5
Essays and Comment

Karl Marx   **HUGO GELLERT**

Two more notches   JACOB BURCK

Michael Gold

[1]

A Night in the Million Dollar Slums

When this "drama critic" was a boy growing up on the East Side, he usually spent his Friday night in the gallery of one of two disreputable burlesque houses, Miner's or the London Theatre, both on the Bowery.

Other nights, after sweating through a ten, twelve and even fourteen hour day for the Adams Express Company, juggling 1,000 pound crates of machinery and the like, the author's Guardian Angel might have discovered him (had that derby-hatted, slimy-winged, double-crossing, racketeering heeler of a Tammany God ever cared) in the dirty cellar gymnasium of a Catholic church.

With his gang of seventeen-year-old savages, here the future critic boxed, wrestled and otherwise received his "lumps." It was that period of adolescence when a healthy boy is infatuated with his own muscles and body. Your critic, during those formative years, had no higher prayer than to grow up into as good a scrapper as clean little Frankie Burns, later to become a lightweight champion, but who then labored in the same branch of the Adams Express as our hero.

Our author, little knowing the literary fate before him, had also no use for books. He hadn't read one since graduating from the same public school as Gyp the Blood, a gunman of yesteryear. The author laid the foundations of his culture by studying the sporting pages, and as a faithful weekly worshipper of the chorus line in the burlesque houses afore-named.

The admission to the gallery of these theatres was ten cents. There were no seats, only tiers of splintery wooden steps to sit on. One went with one's gang, because there was always sure to be some serious fighting. The squads of gallery bouncers earned their pay; for the roughneck audience always made it a point of honor to see how much one could get away with. They yelled insults at singers and dancers who did not please them ("You stink!" was a favorite critical epithet); they threw beer bottles or took a punch at neighbors who had offended them by daring to exist in the same world.

After the show the boys often drank a great many beers, and some continued their education by visiting one of the numerous Tammany temples of feminine physiology where the admission was fifty cents. Well, it was all sordid, physical, brutalizing, but it was all we knew, and there was some fun and vitality in it, anyway. At least it did not pretend to be anything it wasn't; and no chattering slummers like Gilbert Seldes as yet had come from Harvard, and Santayana, and Matisse and Gertrude Stein, to discover this gutter life, and deepen its degradation by that foulest of all bourgeois degeneracies, the aesthete's delight in the "picturesque" side of mass poverty.

With these introductory remarks I will confess to having attended recently a performance of the Ziegfeld Follies. The intellectual drama critics of New York have surrounded these shows with a great deal of glamor; they write of such Broadway spectacles with high aesthetic seriousness: it is obviously a drama critic's duty to appraise these revues; and for the sake of the *New Masses*, I went to one.

Report: There was an underwater ballet, *à la* poor dead Pavlova, with a sweaty baritone singing a sentimental ballad on a bridge. The fake waves shivered, and there was pseudo-Egyptian music. Then a Broadway imitation of a young man, a hoofer with patent-leather hair, hoofed it with a good-looking chorine and sang a fake love ballad, with a refrain something like this: "I Like the Likes of You." The chorus came on; fifty athletic girls in silver hats and gold pants. They danced and sang something. Another hoofer danced a few variations on the old buck-and-wing that only a Negro boy knows how to dance; all others are bleached and tasteless imitations of the real thing. A satire on the country "tryout" theatres so numerous last summer; the chief humor being about the fact that the farmer sells both tickets and eggs; also some cracks about a nudist colony, and the key to the outhouse.

One good line: "This is a society play, no belching here, just rape and adultery."

Climax: "I want you to meet my husband"; and the heroine lifts a window and reveals the rear end of a horse.

Song: A tall drugstore blonde in white rayon decorated with a large gold cross sings a sob song about "suddenly" being a stranger to the man she loves, and fifty good-looking broads in gold and silver and platinum dresses suddenly dance on and sing and dance the same song, "Suddenly."

Another sappy love duet by another patent-leather hair hoofer and girl; then another big blonde beauty with a hard face comes on and struts around exhibiting *her* rear end. A brisk young Englishman delivers a monologue in the old stammer style; a few good lines: "America as a nation is too laxative"; "While one is keeping the wolf from the door, the stork flies in"; "Yes, you are a great nation, you have built yourself up from nothing to a state of extreme poverty"; and there was a Barber College Glee Club, which sang a really funny oratorio, pretentious and solemn, on the theme of "Who's Afraid of the Big Bad Wolf." During this, the chief comedian kept looking down into the beefy breasts of one of the lady singers, weighing them with his hands, etc. (Laughter, applause.)

The chorus appears, dressed in another variation of gold and silver; some humor about homosexuals in a Greenwich Village scene; five more repetitions of the stale young love and hoofing duet; a skit about George Washington and the cherry tree; the reviewing stand of a New York parade, with a trace of satire: "It was seven lawyers who covered Wiggin"; then that good old clown Fanny Brice as the Countess Olga sings sadly about her lost grandeur in Russia, and how now she has been reduced to doing a nude fan dance in Minsky's burlesque show; then a false sentimental pacifist song, "You got sunshine, you got life, why must you fight and die?" etc; and a male dancer in a gold trench helmet and gold tights waving a gold flag at the climax; more chorus girls in tinsel, silver and gold, again and again, trotting on and off.

"You're so lovable, you're so kissable, your beauty is so unbeatable, to me it's unbelievable," they sang, and a chorus boy dressed in gold satin and lace of a priest married them in front of Franklin Simon's upper-class department store, and there was a Maxfield Parrish art tableau to follow, and the tall, mean, slouchy blonde truthfully sang to the audience:

> *You're still seduced*
> *By marcel waves*
> *And not by*
> *Marcel Proust.*

In the audience one sees all the big sellers and buyers of New York and the Tammany lawyers and Yale-Harvard boys and their enameled sweethearts; and business Napoleons with severe horse-faced wives from the suburbs; *Saturday Evening Post* writers (in the chips), stockbrokers, politicians, clothing bosses, heywood brouns, hotel owners, sheriffs, on visits from Georgia and Montana; race track bookies; high powered steel salesmen and shoelace promoters; white shirt fronts, evening gowns; cold, beautiful, empty faces, vivacious dumb faces; hard empty male faces, senile old rounder faces; young sleek worthless faces; the faces of those who "succeed" in New York—New York, to which all the successful exploiters and parasites of America come once a year to see the Follies.

This is the peak of their art and culture. The show I saw was no better or worse than all the other shows of its kind. In fact, it was the same show with a few variations. It was the same show, more or less, that I once saw as a boy for ten cents on the Bowery; and many of the jokes had not even been changed for this audience, though some of them paid $6.60 for their seats.

On the Bowery we had access to nothing better; but these people had every door to life open and could have made a deliberate choice. And this was their choice, this brainless, soulless parade of sterility. This was what they wanted, and it was given them. It was beautiful in its overlavishness, its vulgar parvenu attempt at gold and silver luxury. In this glittering temple a smelly corpse was being worshipped. The audience did not believe in its own laughter; the actors in their own performance. It all meant nothing. It did not amuse. It was inhuman as any robot. Its satire was that of the coward avoiding any politically dangerous theme; its sensuality that of the courtesan; false love, false music, false golden glamor.

This bourgeois form of art for art's sake is no longer

worthy of one's comment or attack. It has only one useful purpose that I can still see: it numbs the minds of the exploiters. Let them continue to support it and be stultified. But I hope they raise the pay of the chorus girls, who, poor kids, are as skillful, disciplined, and overworked as the men on Ford's conveyor belt.

April 3, 1934

[2]

John Reed: He Loved the People

During his brief life span John Reed had already become a legendary figure. It began at Harvard, where he distinguished himself by various imaginative pranks, helped edit the *Monthly* and the *Lampoon*, and attended the meetings of the Socialist Club. When he was graduated, entering life and New York journalism under the tutelage of the wise and fatherly Lincoln Steffens, the legend acquired an all-American magnitude.

That giant gusto, that rash young western strength, all that deep-hearted poetry, exuberant humor, thirst for adventure, and flair for life, composed a character that could not avoid fame. John Reed was among the most famous and highest paid reporters of his day. He covered the Mexican Revolution, he interviewed Presidents, and handled other ace assignments for the biggest magazines.

Yes, he established himself in a golden career which he could have pursued to its end. Why John Reed gave up this "splendor" was always a mystery to many of his early friends. They can be divided into two groups—the opportunists and the aesthetes.

Of the opportunists let Walter Lippmann, Reed's classmate at Harvard, serve as representative. In his early twenties, the precocious author of a brilliant book on politics, his circle of intimate women admirers naming him "Buddha," and bubbling with prophecies that he would be in a Cabinet before he was thirty, Walter Lippmann always had the fishy art and wisdom of a born careerist. Walter Lippmann inevitably felt superior to John Reed. Some twenty-five years ago, in the *New Republic*, Lippmann's sketch of John Reed, half-affectionate, half-patronizing, demonstrated this. Reed had begun to stand out as a Socialist. Lippmann, already a subtle renegade and enemy to socialism, must have felt challenged. His article, the "Legendary John Reed," was the semi-humorous portrait of a romantic playboy, and thus a sly flank attack to destroy the Socialist. Here is God's own reporter, said Lippmann, a poet drunk with life, a high-hearted adventurer and vagabond, but certainly no Socialist. John Reed may believe socialism is another wild poetic adventure. But has he ever read a book on socialism? Has he ever evolved his own philosophy?

John Reed had discovered Marx and the working class, and Walter Lippmann from the heights of Bergsonism patronized John Reed as if he were an illiterate.

This was, of course, merely the intellectual alibi of a renegade. Even then the two Harvard friends had already set their feet on different paths. The eyes of John Reed already previsioned the future of the working class, his destiny; while in the rapt gaze of Walter Lippmann, staring into his own future, there must have already loomed the mystic, shining, beckoning figure of some millionaire Republican master.

To such as Walter Lippmann, to all careerists, go-getters, and renegades, John Reed, from the time he became a working Communist, seemed a pitiful failure.

But then, these same people consider the Soviet Revolution a pitiful failure. But the First World War, and now this second one, appeal to them as brilliant and beautiful examples of capitalist idealism and success!

Few men really choose the career of a Bolshevik. They were born into a certain kind of world, and could not help seeing its crimes and follies. Certain truths about it emerged from their experience. When these truths placed themselves into a synthesis and offered hope for a better world, such men could not escape the logic. Which is to say that a Communist is not any special psychological species of man; he is merely a very honest man.

John Reed had this gift of honesty, a rare thing in a social system where dishonesty offers the best chances for personal survival. The eyes of John Reed were the distinguishing beauty in his face. Reed's eyes were unusually large and clear. They were honest eyes.

No, the opportunists were wrong when they said John

Reed regretted the path his feet had found, the path he trod as America's first literary Bolshevik, the path that led him to a legendary grave beneath the wall of the Soviet Kremlin.

There were always rumors circulated that John Reed was full of mercenary regrets. Later, the hyper-aesthetic lilies like Max Eastman whispered that John Reed regretted his political preoccupations and wanted to get back to "pure" poetry. Still later, hyper-renegades like Max Eastman and other Trotskyites circulated slanders that just before John Reed died he was completely disillusioned with Lenin and the Soviet Revolution.

Whoever prefers the worm's eye view of history will believe such stories. Many good folk once liked to believe that Robert Ingersoll called for a priest on his deathbed. Later Lenin was rumored to be a sadist, who according to the *New York Times* and other such fountains of fact, enjoyed going down to the prison cellars each morning and watching the beautiful countesses massacred.

What gives the general lie to all the mess of rumor that John Reed spent most of his crowded revolutionary life in wishful regret is the fact that he could always have stepped out of the ranks. The return to a well paid job and its brass check was easy and open. All he had to do was to write something like the many "Confessions of an Ex-Communist" that appear nowadays in the *Nation* and *New Republic*, in which contemporary authors purge the Communist movement of their unstable and treacherous persons.

John Reed lived through the First World War, and there were the same pressures and the same renegadism as now. That war affected American intellectuals much like the present one. Some were caught in ivory towers contemplating their navels. They rushed forth at the first gunfire, and set to with an astonishing new-found fervor to paint the war for oil, iron, coal, and mandates with all the ethereal hues of a mystic crusade. George Creel's bureau for inventing inflammatory lies was manned almost entirely by Socialists; one of them once confided to me in an excited whisper the inwardness of this strange contradiction: they were really boring from within, and they were bringing America to socialism.

Greenwich Village broke out in a rash of spies, young literary men were turning in their former pals. The *New Republic* boasted in a famous editorial that the intellectuals had willed the war, though these same intellectuals, after the war (when it was safe and even popular) proved that it had been Wall Street that had willed the war (and what did this make the war intellectuals?).

A host of liberals, progressives, anarchists, art-for-art's sakers, changed overnight, became indistinguishable from the most vulgar and ignorant hoodlum who ever wrecked a German delicatessen shop. Prominent theorists and leaders of socialism, like William English Walling and John Spargo, turned into the lowest of public stool pigeons and Red-baiters. There was no Stalin, nor yet a Lenin, to blame and to curse; but they needed no Dies committee through which to tell the police that the Socialist Party, of which they had been leaders until yesterday, was suddenly receiving gold from Berlin, and was a secret agency of the kaiser.

It was a disgusting time of treason to the merest minimums of human honesty and rationalism; a mass of American intellectuals disgraced themselves, and their profession, in the last war. Only one minority among them could one respect; that which consistently opposed the war and suffered prison, persecution, and the rest of the "democratic" procedure.

John Reed remained an outstanding leader in this opposition. That is the simple fact; he stuck to his guns. It cost him much. The big magazines shut their doors on their "greatest reporter," one after the other. He saw his income and comforts go. He saw the friends of his "playboy" and "Bohemian" period boycott him. His jovial Harvard *Bierbruder* snubbed him. John Reed could have crumpled under all this social and economic pressure; could have done what hundreds of others were doing. But the fact is he didn't. I think that is enough of an answer to the school of whisperers. I think it is even an example to some of the crumplers of our time.

John Reed opposed the war because he understood it better than all the Lippmanns and John Deweys. The Versailles Treaty and the world after the war proved him right, and the Lippmanns and Deweys wrong. But they never choose to remember such little errors, and they never apologize. They never learn.

Every year or so I re-read the classic *Ten Days That Shook the World*, and marvel at its brilliance. The Bolshevik Revolution was met with a great wave of understanding and solidarity by the majority of worker Socialists in America. Nevertheless, few were prepared to disentangle the unfamiliar parties, men, issues and leaders involved in the revolution. John Reed came to the scene without knowing Russian, and without much Russian political orientation. But he had sound revolutionary instincts.

Lenin read his book carefully and wrote a foreword for the American edition. This means that Lenin considered John Reed more than the romantic "playboy" of the Lippmann legend. When I was in Moscow in 1930, I interviewed Madame Krupskaya, the widow of Lenin. She told me, in her charming English, that Lenin was very fond of John Reed. He had great confidence in his revolutionary loyalty and skill.

Reed was the first Soviet consul appointed to New York. This was at a time when Russia was invaded by all, unrecognized as a legal nation. Reed had an enormous task—to break down in some manner this wall of bayonets and hate.

The appointment was withdrawn. John Reed told me it was a person named Alex Gumberg, translator for the Red Cross, who spread slanders in Petrograd about his integrity. This Gumberg, who was friendly with Edgar Sisson, author of the notorious Sisson documents, and a spy operating in Russia for George Creel's Public Information Committee, later came to America as a Soviet representative, switched to a much more "respectable" job as Russian adviser to the Chase National Bank, and was, I believe, a pioneer Trotskyite.

Maybe it was he who helped spread the slanders here that John Reed recanted on his deathbed in the alleged manner of Bob Ingersoll.

Whoever spread it, it never caught on. John Reed's character did not fit such a story. It was, of course, the rankest of lies. In Moscow that same year, 1930, I met an old Bolshevik who had lived for years in New York. He had been on the train with John Reed as a delegate to the congress of oriental nations at Baku. This was the last meeting Reed ever attended. He made a beautiful speech, linking the problem of the Negro people and the oppressed people of Latin America with that of the oppressed Eastern peoples. Coming back from the Baku congress, said the old New York Bolshevik, their train was suddenly halted in a desert valley between two ridges. From one of the hills shots were being fired at the train by White Guards. The Red Army escort leaped out of the armored car, mounted horses, unlimbered some machine guns, and was about to gallop forth, when John Reed asked to go along. He insisted, and finally got the commanders to take him. The Red Army men scoured the hills for half an hour, knocked off a few bandits, and scared the rest. And John Reed galloped back with them, said my informant, full of his familiar glow.

If he had been harboring any secret regrets, he surely would not have been anxious for such an adventure. It was hardly the act of a man with regrets. And this was the last bit of revolutionary action of John Reed. A few days later he died of typhus.

I was a reporter on the old Socialist *Call* when John Reed returned from his first visit to the Russian Revolution, and the city editor assigned me to meet him.

With Louise Bryant I waited at the pier for hours, while a swarm of Department of Justice men stripped him, went over every inch of his clothes and baggage, and put him through the usual inquisition.

Reed had been sick with ptomaine on the boat. The inquisition had also been painful. But I like to remember how he kissed his girl again and again as our old-fashioned open carriage rolled through the New York streets, and how hungrily he stared at the houses, the people on the sidewalk, the New York sky, with his large, honest eyes.

He was always homesick for this country after a stay abroad; and even those Department of Justice greeters did not spoil the delight he felt in being home.

We went to the Brevoort. The dining room was then a *rendez-vous* for the Greenwich Village intellectuals. As we entered, some of his scores of friends greeted Reed in the casual New York manner. I remember the beautiful, red-haired girl, an actress with dreamy white face and moonstruck eyes, who hailed him as we passed.

"Hello, Jack," she drawled.

"Hello, Helen," he said.

"It seems to me you've been away, Jack," she said.

"Yes, I've been away."

"Where?" she asked.

"Russia," he said.

"Russia?" she repeated dreamily. "Why Russia, Jack?"

"There was a revolution," he answered.

"A revolution? Oh! Was it interesting?" she drawled.

His face flushed. He had just been through something that split families, sapped one's last energy, took a cruel price from everyone. He had seen famine, war, disease, mental suffering, chaos—everything that the sick and dying past demanded before it would yield to the new. Yes, it was something too big to describe—the workers in revolution; something that would shake and change the world. And Helen wanted to know if it was interesting—as interesting, let's say, as a batik print, or the new edition of Krafft-Ebbing.

"Interesting," Jack sneered. "You wouldn't know."

Well, I think this sneer at a beautiful girl who was too aesthetic to read the papers, sufficiently answers the Max Eastmans who went around forever whispering that John Reed regretted his revolutionary past.

The Russian Revolution was the forcing-bed of John Reed's maturity. Great art is produced only out of great experience. John Reed wrote his *Ten Days That Shook the World* after returning from the experience of a workers' revolution. It is not only a great essay in living history, but a piece of great art.

Certainly it is destined to last. And John Reed, if he had lived, surely might have returned to other forms of art than reportage—to the theater perhaps, or to poetry. But who can doubt that he would have quarreled with most of the theories of art that prevailed in the Village of his youth—with the insipid *Yellow Book pastiche* of the Eastmans, the inflated mysticism of the Waldo Franks, the flashy, sterile verbalism of the Ben Hechts, the Menckenites, James Joyceans, Sigmund Freudians, and other forms of literary evasion, despair, confusion, and reaction that then dominated the intellectual schools?

For the workers' revolution was not a passing intellectual fashion with John Reed, as it was for others in his time, and it has been with some today.

Let me name that quality I believe was present in Reed which made him an effective Bolshevik. Krupskaya, at the grave of her great companion, believed it the highest quality she could praise in Lenin, the mightiest political genius of our century.

His widow said of Lenin, "Vladimir Ilyich deeply loved the people."

John Reed always loved the people. It is revealed at the beginning of his career, before he was a Communist, when he was reporting the Mexican Revolution of 1910. In the midst of the romantic ecstasy that the Mexican landscape and the wild, outdoor war aroused in the Harvard youth, one finds passages of brooding love for the peon—for the illiterate, gentle, oppressed, poetic, heroic Mexican peon.

The peons stirred this boy reporter as romantically as the events of the war, or the glory of the mountains and Mexican sky. He was adventurous, yes; but he was capable of loving the common folk. And this held him along the correct political path.

I have known few intellectual renegades to the working class who were not inordinately vain of their book knowledge, or who had ever felt this love. If you will look down the dock at the current treason trials in the *Nation*, you will find few who have been close enough to the American people to see life through their eyes. But the whole activity of Communists must be based on the daily needs and problems of the masses. Otherwise, Communism would forever remain in the libraries.

When Krupskaya said that Lenin "deeply loved the people" she did not mean it in the mystic sense of our Walt Whitman. The love of Lenin was more humble, human, and exact. It concerned itself with the amount of taxes the people paid, with their unemployment, their daily conflicts in the factory, the price of bread and milk and clothing. Lenin studied their organizations, he planned in minute detail an organization that could free them from wage slavery.

John Reed's love had begun in the clouds of Whitmanism. It is a fine enough beginning for an American poet who wishes to serve his people; yet the danger of such abstract and Olympian love lies in the fact that its vague, large rhetoric is easily used by demagogues. An Archibald MacLeish has begun to talk in such Whitman strophes, about democracy and the American people. But it is flattery designed for the purpose of using us in another imperialist war. You cannot interest the mystic MacLeishes in such lowly subjects as unemployment, rising food prices, and the segregation of the Negro Americans. But in John Reed the adolescent love that Walt Whitman had aroused, matured into the more human, more real, and effective love that Lenin taught.

Let us remember that the "romantic" Harvard poet, John Reed, was an active participant in many strikes; that for several years he helped edit and write, in the midst of the post-war terror in America, a Party journal of Communist agitation and politics; that he served on dozens of committees in the anti-war campaign; that he made hundreds of speeches in defense of the U.S.S.R.; that he was an organizer and a common soldier of the cause.

It is necessary to insist on this side of Reed's character. He had not merely read a few books and signed a petition or two. He had been active in the midst of the class struggle; nobody could ever tell him it wasn't there. And nothing could ever shake him out of knowing which side he was on.

John Reed was not a fellow traveler. He was a Communist Party man. He had seen the Communist movement in the darkest hours of war and revolution. It worked. It was right about the World War. It was right about the Russian Revolution. It was right about American labor.

This year the anniversary* of John Reed takes on a special poignancy. The second round of war and revolution is upon us in this great century that is to see the end of capitalism. We are confronted with the same tests of personal manhood and social faith that Reed faced. He passed his examinations with a magnificence that some of us may not begin to understand. It is not the cowards, capitulators, and Philistines who carry on his tradition. The bourgeois world can have those prodigal sons; as Kropotkin once said of other renegades, "Let them go—we have had their best, anyway."

Let the fatted calf be killed in the *Nation* office, and the joy bells ring in Wall Street when another weak and repentant sister returns with her sniveling tale of how a bewhiskered man named Marx seduced her.

But John Reed still lives. He still marches in the faithful ranks of the American intellectuals—thousands of them—organized in teachers' unions, youth congresses, newspaper guilds. . . . Let the renegades receive all the publicity. But the

* The twentieth anniversary of John Reed's death.

main army marches forward, heedless of persecution, bearing high and untarnished the great flag of human freedom—the flag of Shelley, Heine, Marx, Lenin, Stalin, Liebknecht, Henri Barbusse, Tom Paine, Abe Lincoln, James Connolly, Randolph Bourne, Gene Debs, and John Reed.

He belongs to us more deeply, significantly, fraternally than ever before, in this vast dangerous hour of stormy change. John Reed belongs to those who can never surrender their faith in the working class and its future.

October 22, 1940

Theodore Dreiser

What Has the Great War Taught Me?

I could limit my reply to one slang American word–plenty.
It made changelessly clear that the entire social order that
preceded that war was decayed, and worse, rotten to the
core. The organized religion of that day and since, what a
farce it proved to be. The boasted democracy of England!
What a trashy material for bolstering up and maintaining a
decadent and disgraceful leisure class at the expense of the
masses! They fought and died, and the remainder were given
a dole.

And then the antiquated King and Emperor business of the
rest of Europe: The Kaiser, for instance, with his cracked
notions of a place in the sun for the Imperial Hohenzollern
family. But who else? The Tsar, neurotic and mentally defective, yet dominating Russia through a neurotic and defective court and leisure class! And in Austro-Hungary, the
Hapsburgs, a collection of defectives out of an asylum, yet
masquerading as Dukes and Princes and Princesses and supported by a brutal, shameless and disgraceful church. And
Spain with its frayed and defective King and a religious
hierarchy so antiquated and mentally threadbare as not to be
able to recognize its own unbelievable lunacies which were
destroying the very body of the people on which it depended
for its existence.

Italy the same.

Rumania the same.

Loafers, wasters, sybarites, enthroned as Lords and Kings
and all bolstered by armies and navies and statecraft and
priestcraft, maintained by the almost unrewarded labor of
the masses, who at the same time were taught that their
masters were divinely ordained!

And then America! Wilson shouting about making the
world safe for democracy and believing that by wasting forty

billions of American money, he had done so. And yet as they said of Mary's little lamb after it arrived in Pittsburgh, "Now look at the Goddam' thing!"

And afterwards, here in America—its democracy made "safe"—for what? Only consider our Trusts and Holding Companies, the Standard Oil Company, Telephone Trust, the Power Trust, the Railroad Trust, the Steel Trust, the Aluminium Trust, the Food and Textile Trusts, holding everything that they had and exacting, as might any tyrant in any part of the world, all that the traffic will bear, all that the man with fifty cents an hour can pay and more. Yet shouting of Democracy, of maintaining American standards—doing things in an American way. And worse, while borrowing a few ideas from Russia—the only decent ones they have—the minimum wage and the thirty-hour week, denouncing Russia as an unbelievable tyranny. And you ask me what has the Great War taught me?

Well it has taught me this—that fifty cents an hour and thirty hours a week for labor won't make up for unmeasured privileges and monopolies bestowed upon our entrenched money aristocracy whose one dream is not the advancement of the mass—nor even the superior mental development of a class, but aimless, meaningless, social leisure and show. And until these monopolies are broken, the masses properly rewarded and the so-called "classes" aligned with the masses as workers and nothing else, I will not believe that, except for Russia and the hope that it still holds out to the world, the Great War accomplished anything. And that is what the Great War has taught me.

P.S.—Not that I believe that human beings are going to be made angels by law, but that by law, for a time at least, they are going to be prevented from being downright devils.

August 7, 1934

Robert Forsythe

Mae West: A Treatise on Decay

When you consider Madame Du Barry and Nell Gwynne, it is evident that Mae West has made a mistake in confining her immorality to stage and screen. Granted that a woman of her intelligence could be prevailed upon to favor a Congressman or a Secretary of War, the spectacle of Miss West affecting state policy as well as private temperatures is something which no future historian could afford to overlook. It is plain that on any basis of comparison she belongs to the great line.

There are so many indications of the breakdown of capitalist civilization that we are inclined to become tender and sympathetic in the midst of the debacle, much in the manner of "don't cheer, boys; the poor devils are dying," but it is obvious that Miss West, more than any of her associates, symbolizes the end of an epoch. Her stage plays, *Sex* and *The Drag*, uncovered such a horrifying picture of homosexuals, lesbians and ordinary degenerates that Miss West was sentenced to the workhouse for ten days as a way of restoring the faith of the populace in the great city. Her motives in presenting the plays were undoubtedly mercenary, but her attorneys overlooked a great opportunity of establishing her as a sociologist and humanitarian, moved solely by her concern for reform.

The movies were more astute in their management of her films. They retained the spiciness, the lustiness and bawdiness, but they carefully confined them to the past. In a sense it may be said that the golden era of Chuck Conners and the Bowery was bourgeois vigor at its peak. With all its dirt and squalor the Bowery managed to maintain an Elizabethan rowdiness and crudity which could pass as strength. The Puritan was at last defeated; men were again honest animals. They killed, they whored and they flaunted the broken bits of Methodist morality in the faces of the nice people who came down to look with fascinated horror at these mad barbarians.

The Christian fathers are quite correct in worrying about Miss West. Whether the success of her bawdiness is a sign that we have conquered Puritanism and are a mature people at last or whether it represents a complete collapse of morality, it is evident that it reveals the lack of authority of religion. The Catholic campaign for clean films succeeded in changing the title of the latest West film from *It Ain't No Sin* to *Belle of the Nineties*, but it is still Mae West in *It Ain't No Sin*.

But it is in her stage plays that her significance lies. If we judged alone from her screen comedies we should be tempted to say that she represented sexual honesty in a world given over much too completely to the antics of the fairy. I refer to the world of the theater and to the race of people known as perverts. Without seeking to alarm you with a sensational exposé of vice conditions in the green room, I may say merely that the condition within the profession is notorious. The facts of the matter are plain enough, but I may not be able to convince you that they have historical importance, and I am not even going to attempt to prove that the bitterly reactionary character of the stage, with the few exceptions you recognize so well, are the result in some small part of this disease. We know quite well that the reasons for reaction are class reactions and if I make any point at all in this respect it would be to indicate that introversion is essentially a class ailment and the direct result of a sybaritic life which finally results in profound boredom for lack of any further possible stimulation or titillation. It is invariably associated with those twin elements of perversion, sadism and masochism, and generally reveals itself among the thinned-out representatives of a decaying class. The sadistic cruelty of Hitlerism is no accident. It is the unmistakable symptom of an incurable malady.

I am not a psychologist and what I have to say about the coincidences of history in this regard are not to be taken as gospel from the scientific archangels, but three widely separated incidents prior to the World War have always struck me as being significant. There was first the Oscar Wilde case in England. The divorce suit of Sir Charles Dilke with its resultant exposure of the hypocrisy and moral laxness of the aristocracy had been the first break in the dike of British class superiority. It showed that not only were the nobles human but they were something less than admirably human. Even this, however, was outshadowed by the revelations of the Wilde affair. The wave of indignation swept Wilde to jail, but it also revealed the fact that sexual debauchery was so common among the nobility that Frank Harris could report, without legal action being taken against him, that seventy-five members of the House of Lords were notorious perverts.

Not long after Germany was stirred by the revelations that Prince Philipp Eulenburg, intimate friend of the Kaiser, had been accused by Maximilian Harden of indulging in unnatural vice. Harden had attacked Eulenburg publicly in his paper *Zukunft*, trying to force a charge of libel. Eulenburg refused and was disgraced. Evidence later produced in another trial at Munich proved conclusively that he was guilty. What was even more damning was the knowledge that others besides Eulenburg of the Imperial court were involved and that conditions were generally bad in high circles. The war came along several years later to place the world's attention on other forms of perversion such as mass slaughter and it was only with the advent of the *Fuehrer* that homosexuality was raised to the rank of statesmanship.

There was a third case in Russia which practically coincided with the outbreak of the war. By a coincidence France at the same time was so stirred by the sensational trial arising out of the killing of Calmette, editor of *Figaro*, by Madame Caillaux that the death of the Archduke at Sarajevo was almost overlooked by the smartly gowned crowds who gathered in court each day for the details. In the same way the nobility of Russia could scarcely take their fascinated gazes away from the St. Petersburg scandal long enough to watch the troops marching to the front.

What Mae West did in the plays I have mentioned and what she does in her motion pictures is to show in her frank cynical way the depths to which capitalistic morality has come. There is an honesty in her playing which is even more devastating. It is not the bouncing lechery of Ben Jonson but the mean piddling lewdness of the middle classes getting their little hour of sin before the end. Miss West has a marvelous capacity for the theater and she acts in what might be termed the grand manner, but I can never hear her "C'm up and see me some time" without thinking of Ruth Snyder carrying on her cheap pathetic romance with Judd Gray. Because she epitomizes so completely the middle-class matron in her hour of license I feel that Miss West has never been properly appreciated as the First Artist of the Republic. It is palpable nonsense to be concerned about such children as Katherine Hepburn, who will be as forgotten as Mary Miles Minter in a few years' time, when we possess a lady who could assume her position now as the Statue of Liberty and who so obviously represents bourgeois culture at its apex that she will enter history as a complete treatise on decay.

October 9, 1934

[2]
Redder than the Rose

When I reached that portion of Isidor Schneider's interview with Gertrude Stein in which she referred to herself as more Communist than the Communists, I put my hand to my head and uttered a cry which bystanders have since told me sounded like "peep" and slid fainting into the waste basket. From this you might assume either that I was fatally stricken by the brilliance of Miss Stein or merely irritated by her presumption, but you would be entirely wrong. It was purely a physical matter. Twice previously on the same day I had heard the same words from other lips and I very much suspected that I was being made the object of a plot.

Mr. Edmund Wilson once indicated his desire to take Communism away from the Communists but that may have been youthful zeal and it is hardly likely that he entertains such hopes at the moment. If he feels, however, that he is more Left than the Left, he is entirely in style. Just where this new rallying cry for ex-Democrats, ex-Humanists and ex-Communists arose is not clear but it is in full swing and a revolution happening within the week would be a terrible thing with such wild people around to lead it.

Naturally it is not merely a matter of force; it is a problem of dialectics and philosophy and the philosophy is so marvelous that the historians of the future will bow in wonder before such logic and discernment. I know an interesting fellow who is a writer, a playwright, a philosophical anarchist and a supporter of Herbert Hoover. I have never had the courage to question him about his Hoover affiliation, but he could probably sustain it on the ground that only by fostering tyranny can we have freedom. His long stay in Hollywood at a fat figure has been explained as his way of bankrupting the industry and thus bringing about its downfall. He is now said to be at work on a play which proves that Tom Mooney framed the State of California.

I have another friend who is eighteen miles east of Lenin going rapidly further Left. He is a broker and a Trotskyite and I am no longer able to face his scorn. The last time I saw him he was coming out of the Waldorf-Astoria and although I tried to hurry by, he caught me and said some very harsh things about the timidity of the Communist Party in this country. He might still have had me there, backed against a window containing the treasures of the late Tsar, if his chauffeur had not interrupted to say that the car was waiting. When I say that my friend is a Trotskyite, I must explain that he is also a Technocrat and in addition has been reading Malaparte. His theory is that Trotsky and four good engineers could put New York City at the mercy of the revolutionists by turning off the lights and overpowering Fiorello while he was scurrying about in his nightshirt hunting a candle. My friend explained this to me as the theory of permanent revolution; all you do when you want a new revolution is turn off the lights.

Unless something is done I am afraid we are going to face indignation from people who are expecting a great deal from us. Intellectually it seems that we are not as daring as we had thought. I know of a lady who has been successively a Suffragette, a Catholic and a Socialist. For some time she has been requesting the services of the more agile and younger male comrades in educating her in the intricacies of Communism but they have evidently failed at the job. The last report of her was as chairman of an Utopian meeting, which I am informed is much more Communist than Communism as well as much more Rosicrucian than Rosa Bonheur.

It is, however, around the tea table that the true essence of radicalism is attained. I must report a wave of indignation in such circles at the delay in the revolution. One lady only recently was remarking that her brother, a major in the army, is an excellent man to approach on the matter of revolt. She indicates that she would speak to him. But beyond that she was not pleased with the conduct of the Party. She said that although she had just been won over to Communism, she felt that she was far more advanced than many of the Party members and she was at a loss to account for the lag. She said she had been speaking to the servants on her estate and whereas they had all been ardent Republicans when she spoke to them in the past, they were now all ardent Communists, answering her questions of were they Communists with the reply that they were Communists indeed. She felt that if her people were of that opinion, the servants on other estates must have like views and she couldn't understand what was holding things up.

On the cultural front I have recently had contact with a Hearst reporter who rather frightens me with his enthusiasm. He has not joined the Communist Party but he tells me he is far more Communist than the Communists. In covering a strike about a month ago, he wrote of the hoodlums who crawled up from the gutters like insects coming out from under a rock after a rain. I ventured to suggest that although the strikers were workers, they might not like to be called insects and besides it played into the hands of the owners, but he answered me in a manner which quite overcame my fears. If you talk about these people scornfully enough, said my friend, they will eventually become angry and revolt. In the meantime you fool Mr. Hearst by seeming to be on his side. He said that when the time came—and he had ideas on how slow the Party was about bringing it to pass—we would know what side he was on. He would stay with Hearst stirring up the workers by telling lies about them until the victory was won; after that he would bring us the technical newspaper skill a proletarian paper needed.

There is a possibility that many individuals who are more Communistic than the Communists will go completely berserk and end as Theosophists or Seventh Day Adventists but there is little that can be done about it. I had thought of offering myself as a sacrifice to the bloodthirsty by appearing at the *New Masses* Ball and allowing hand grenades to be hurled at me as I stood on the platform near the bass viol but that was before I read Isidor Schneider on Gertrude Stein and before I met Mr. Cartwright. Mr. Cartwright said almost immediately that he was more Communist than the Communists, and that he had great admiration for Adolf Hitler. But I thought you said you were a Communist, I observed meekly. Certainly I'm a Communist said Mr. Cartwright sternly. I'm an anti-Jewish Communist. It seems to me that this is carrying specialization and sectarianism so far that my death in Webster Hall could have little weight. I am afraid that even the passing of a noble fellow such as myself will not win over the groups which, when they feel the need of a name, will undoubtedly be known as the anti-proletarian Communists. Only prayer, I am sure, will be of avail with such fine folk.

December 4, 1934

Harry Thornton Moore

Red Nettles

*(Those familiar with The Red Network, in which Mrs. Eliza-
beth Dilling, Patriot and Puritan of Kenilworth, Illinois,
publishes a list of contemporary "menaces," will perhaps be
glad to have this list extended back into history. The present
list does not pretend to be exhaustive.)*

Aristophanes: Ancient Athenian writer of immoral comedies recommending Pacifism.

François Marie Arouet, alias *Voltaire:* Radical philos-
opher and freethinker of eighteenth century; wrote immoral
novel *Candide,* which ridicules optimism. Much of his life
spent in exile; probably helped prepare the French mind for
revolution. Prison record.

George Gordon, Lord Byron: Immoral nineteenth-century
poet, exploiter of free love; wrote *Childe Harold, Don Juan,*
and other notorious poems celebrating licentiousness. Also
wrote revolutionary poetry; died while aiding Greek revolt.

Heinrich Heine: Infamous advocate of free love; lured
from his native Germany to Paris by success of revolution of
1830; was supported for a dozen or so years by secret fund
for "political refugees"; died an outcast in a Paris garret. His
works were ordered banned in 1835 by the German Bund;
a hundred years later the present German government also
finds him unfit. Jew.

Victor Hugo: Nineteenth-century French "liberal" and
"Humanitarian"; exiled by Louis Napoleon, forced out of
his native land for eighteen years. Wrote books audaciously
defending the poor; lent moral support to Commune of 1871.

Thomas Jefferson: Revolutionary American agitator of
eighteenth century; author of notorious pamphlet, *A Sum-
mary View of the Rights of America,* from which was later
drafted the insidious Declaration of Independence, that "all

men are created equal," and, a document declaring that "it is the Right of the people to alter or abolish" any existing "Form of Government" which becomes destructive of the "unalienable Rights" of "Life, Liberty and the pursuit of Happiness."

Jesus of Nazareth, alias the *Christ*: Vagrant ex-carpenter; Jew; anarchist; vituperated the rich; put to death by honest citizens of Judea. Organized the unemployed, etc. Teacher of notorious propagandist Saul (alias Paul) of Tarsus, who was beheaded by Nero.

John Milton: Wrote licentious Garden of Eden scenes in *Paradise Lost*, an epic secretly glorifying the revolutionary activities of Satan. Wrote pamphlets defending divorce and freedom of the press; was Latin Secretary and friend of Oliver Cromwell, the revolutionist who overthrew the British aristocracy in seventeenth century.

William Shakespeare: Profligate drunkard of time of Queen Elizabeth; frequenter of taverns and advocate of free love; wrote immoral plays which have to be bowdlerized before they can be studied by high school students. Author of infamous play *Richard II*, concerning the overthrow of a sovereign, a play which the sympathizers with the Earl of Essex caused to be performed at the time of the Essex Rebellion as an inciter of the populace, which performance resulted in a court reprimand for the Globe players. Also wrote *Coriolanus*, which nearly caused civil war and revolution when presented in Paris in 1933.

Henry David Thoreau: Dangerous American anarchist who opposed war with Mexico; jailed for refusing to pay taxes. Wrote seditious essay *On the Duty of Civil Disobedience* which, among treasonous utterances, states that "under a government which imprisons any unjustly, the true place for a just man is also a prison."

George Washington: Revolutionary general in American war of independence; traitor to land of allegiance, England; consorted with such vicious agitators as John Jay, Thomas Jefferson (q.v.), Patrick Henry, *et al.* First "president" of presumptuous Republic founded upon ideals of freedom.

December 17, 1935

S. J. Perelman

"Thunder over Alma Mater"

"It's up to us to crush this Red menace, fellows!"

The speaker was none other than our friend Tom Rover, and as he looked into the intent faces of his classmates, his eyes flashed fire. For once the Rover Boys, fun-loving Dick and serious-minded Tom, were united in a common purpose. Not in years had the hoary walls and storied elms of old Effluvia College been threatened with such a crisis. But let us hear it from Tom Rover's own lips as he awakened his fellow students to the danger facing them:

"I found out just in the nick of time," vouchsafed Tom in manly tones, producing several newspaper clippings. "These sneaking Reds have been plotting a revolution right here in old Effluvia! Certain weak-minded members of the faculty, goaded on by insidious alien doctrines and abetted by unscrupulous students, are preparing to seize power, set up a soviet in the Administration Building, and nationalize the girls of Sweetbread Hall!" The collegians exchanged startled glances, but Tom's charges were irrefutable, for everything he said was supported by the clippings from the Hearst papers he held in his hand.

"This is an unexpected turn of affairs," frowned Dick gravely. "Who is responsible for this disloyalty to our ideals and institutions?" Tom's sense of sportsmanship would have prevented him from replying, but at this juncture the culprit revealed himself unwittingly. Muttering a coarse oath, skulking Dan Baxter, followed by several of his toadies, slunk from the hall. Seizing the opportunity, Tom followed up his advantage.

"As you know, men," he continued, "one worm in an apple is often enough to spoil a whole barrel." His epigram was not lost on his hearers, as several appreciative chuckles testified. "This hulking bully whom you all know as Dan Baxter is really Dan Baxtrovitch, a notorious single-taxer, anarchist, and firebrand who has been sent here by Moscow to foment discord in the ranks of American youth." At his mention of Moscow, his audience recognized the name of a poorly ventilated city in Russia which the unsuccessful revolutionaries were using as a base. Fortunately its downfall was imminent, as the gentle but firm armies of several nations were on their way to deliver its cowed inhabitants from a reign of terror.

"These ruffians will stick at nothing," declared Tom, compressing his lips. "Hourly they are widening the rift between capital and labor and swaying the freshman. They use specious arguments such as our twelve million unemployed, when everybody knows that there are more than enough jobs to go around if the lazy scum would only work. But their real designs are even more loathsome. They are scheming to divide up our allowances evenly, convert our football team into shock troops, and force us to subsist on beet soup!" A great roar of protest welled up from his listeners as they realized how the subversive forces had been boring from within.

"Is there still time to outwit these destructive elements?" demanded Tom's cronies in determined accents.

"If we hurry," returned Tom, alive to his responsibility. "Come closer, fellows."

With all will his friends gathered in a resolute little knot around him and in hurried whispers prepared a plan of battle to combat the impending menace to dear old Effluvia.

The college librarian blinked in surprise as the door of the reading room swung open and a group of earnest students entered. In a trice he was courteously trussed up like a fowl by several juniors while the rest of the unit searched the shelves for incendiary literature and carried it outside to the waiting bonfire. Soon the works of a number of inflammatory and un-American writers of the crazy so-called "modern" school such as Sherwood Anderson, John Dos Passos, and Carl Sandberg were swelling the blaze amid the vociferous applause of the student body. Alert and clear-eyed volunteers joined enthusiastically in the hunt and gave vent to righteous wrath as volumes of "Dry-as-dust" economics and sociology by firebrands like Veblen and Babbitt advocating the overthrow of democracy crackled into ashes.

Meanwhile another band of stalwart athletes led by Dick Rover had cornered several of the younger professors in the

English department, who had openly been inciting under-classmen to revolt by sponsoring collective bargaining. The pitiable wretches were given an opportunity to recant by their gentlemanly captors but countered with stubborn refusals. Only when a copy of the *Nation* was found secreted under a pillow did the vigilantes' patience come to an end, and after some innocent horseplay involving castor oil and a rubber hose, the cowardly "intelligentsia" admitted their mistake. Some of the more exuberant youngsters were for riding the offenders out of town on a rail, but under the restraining hand of Dick Rover, the chop-fallen radicals were allowed to take the oath of allegiance and remove their coats of tar and feathers.

Fifteen miles out of town Tom Rover, bending low over the wheel of his speedy rocket car, glanced hurriedly at his wrist watch and raced forward through the darkness. Would he be in time? One of Dan Baxtrovitch's minions had confessed that beautiful Eunice Haverstraw, head of the Sweet-bread soccer team, had been abducted to a low roadhouse by his leader. Tom uttered a silent prayer and pressed the throttle to the floor.

Baxtrovitch, his coarse features suffused with vodka, had pinned Eunice in his non-Aryan embrace and was attempting to rain kisses on her averted face. Plucky albeit she was, Eunice's cries echoed in vain in the soundproofed room. She was almost losing consciousness when the door crashed inward under Tom Rover's powerful shoulders. Crossing the floor at a bound, he drove several telling blows into Baxtrovitch's kidneys. Flaccid from years of easy living, Baxtrovitch realized he was through preying on young American womanhood and sank to the floor, shamming a dead faint. But close on Tom's heels a party of his fellow clansmen entered briskly, wearing conical soldier hats improvised from copies of the *American Weekly* and *Time*. The radical leader, who had hoped to escape by simulating unconsciousness, was securely bound and removed to face charges of syndicalism in California which had been pending for some time.

"Oh, Tom!" breathed Eunice, as she nestled in the protection of his brawny young arms, "I–I was afraid you might be too late!"

"Not Tom," came an unexpected voice. Turning, the pair

descried the lineaments of elderly Job Haverstraw, head of the Haverstraw Woolen Mills, field officer of the Key Men of America, and Eunice's father. "I knew he'd be on the spot. Thank you, son," he added, his eyes suspiciously moist. Then a twinkle invaded them. "And after you're married, I'll need you as general manager of my plant. Some of the workmen have been grumbling about our fourteen-hour day, and I know you can set them an example of Americanism and fair play."

And there, face to face with success and their new destiny, let us leave them until the next episode, "The Rover Boys and Their Young Finks."

December 17, 1935

Vincent Sheean

Furtwangler versus Toscanini

Dr. Wilhelm Furtwangler's letter to the *Neue Freie Presse* of Vienna, published on September 7, states the classic view that "the artist must be as much above the political controversies of the day as the art which he serves." This opinion, no matter how illogical and inhumane it may seem to us, and no matter how stale it has grown by parrot-like repetition, is worth examining again when it is stated by an artist of Dr. Furtwangler's quality. Dr. Furtwangler says:

"Seeing that the press, to my great regret, has taken possession of the contents of a conversation which recently took place between me and Toscanini at Salzburg, I am constrained, against my will, to express myself on the subject."

We may be allowed to remark here that we do not see what constraint was put upon him to write to the press. If an artist is above controversy, why does he argue the point? No matter. He goes on:

"Initially, however, I should like to remark that the relations between Toscanini and myself have always been of the best and that the conversation in question was also carried on in the friendliest of terms. Nevertheless, I cannot concur with the view of my much esteemed colleague when he contends that a conductor may not, on political grounds, pursue his professional activities simultaneously at Bayreuth and at Salzburg."

We have Dr. Furtwangler's word that this is Toscanini's view. Perhaps it is, but so far we have not seen a letter from Toscanini to the press stating it. The learned doctor from Berlin is, in fact, repeating something said in a private conversation. He continues:

"According to my view—I have at all times spoken frankly on the subject—the artist must be quite as much above the political controversies of the day as the art which he serves.

The great masters Wagner and Beethoven addressed themselves in their works not to their own nation alone, but to the whole world; when, therefore, I conduct at Bayreuth today and at Salzburg tomorrow, this has nothing to do with politics. The blame for the reproach that art is being turned to political account in my view rests rather upon those who seem to assume that Bayreuth and Salzburg exist for other ends than for art. Where would we get to if we artists also lost sight of the supernational significance of our great masters? The world must remain open for the artist; and today, perhaps even more than ever before, the free exchange of cultural interests can help to facilitate the mutual understanding so much desired by all nations."

The last sentence, which is worthy of Mr. Anthony Eden, need not worry us unduly at this late day. The rest of the letter is a more exact statement and is worth reading with care. Dr. Furtwangler is no Nazi, or at any rate no ordinary Nazi. So far as I have ever heard, he takes no part in politics. He certainly fought to the end to keep his Jewish musicians in the Berlin Philharmonic Orchestra, and suffered a year's exile for that reason. He is a German, a great conductor, a scholar, and an austere and devoted servant of music. In all these capacities it is perhaps his duty, and certainly his right, to continue to conduct his orchestra at Berlin or Bayreuth or wherever he is called. But when he broadens his position so as to state it in general terms, and thus to imply a criticism of those who do not agree with him, above all those who, like Toscanini, do not share with him the blessings of subjection to the Nazi regime, he is passing far beyond his competence, and it becomes the privilege of any newspaper reader to judge him on his words.

Let us list, as briefly as possible, a few of the comments that suggest themselves on the latter part of this remarkable letter.

First, Dr. Furtwangler has not "at all times spoken frankly on the subject." If he had, there are at least five members of his orchestra who would not have been changed two and a half years ago. If he had, he would not be conductor of the Berlin Philharmonic, and would not be welcome at Bayreuth. What is safe to write to the *Neue Freie Presse*—and even, until examined closely, rather noble—is not safe to write to the *Voelkischer Beobachter*.

Second, if "the artist must be quite as much above the political controversies of the day as the art which he serves," and the opinion can be defended, it was singularly inapposite to name Wagner and Beethoven as examples. Neither was above political controversy; both were men of deep human passions, closely connected with the collective life of their times; neither would have kept his mouth shut for all the Hitlers in Europe.

Third, if the two masters named addressed themselves "not to their own nation alone, but to the whole world," Dr. Furtwangler should say so in Germany where another view of their significance prevails.

Fourth, Bayreuth and Salzburg should have nothing to do with politics, it is true; but since when has that principle been accepted at Bayreuth? Does Dr. Furtwangler think that the playing and singing of the Nazi party song at a festival performance in Bayreuth constitutes being "above controversy?" Does he think that the weeding out of Marxian or Jewish or simply democratic liberal men and women among the musicians constitutes freedom from political bias?

Fifth, "those who assume that Bayreuth and Salzburg exist for other ends than for art" refer only to Dr. Furtwangler's superior officers, Herr Hitler and Dr. Goebbels. Nobody else has tried to make a political partisan show out of a music festival. Certainly there are no national or party hymns, no political cheering, no parades, or manifestations of any kind at Salzburg.

Sixth, the next sentence ("Where would we get to," etc.) contains one little word, one all-revealing word, which Dr. Furtwangler would not dare to use in Germany. The word is *also*. "If we artists *also* lost sight of the supernational significance of our great masters"—and Dr. Furtwangler knows as well as we that the persons excluded by the *also*, the persons who do openly and deliberately obscure the supernational significance not only of Beethoven and Wagner, but of Goethe himself (a miracle of distortion), are the fascist gangsters who are at present his employers.

These are detailed comments. But the ideas Dr. Furtwangler treats with such plausibility in this letter are bigger than the disingenuous phrases that clothe them. What he says, in effect, is that it is none of his business how many Jewish fiddlers are out of jobs, or how many men get thrown out of work in the opera houses and orchestras of Germany because they used to belong to the Socialist or the Communist Party, or how many singers are driven into exile; it is even none of his business what effect this has on the musical value of the performances of German masterpieces for the German people. All this is none of his business. His business is simply to conduct, as well as he can, wherever he is called upon to do so.

Well, perhaps he can convince himself that this is the case. Obviously he has convinced himself, or he would not be the prime dictator (under Hitler and Goebbels) of musical Germany. He has persuaded himself that he, a great artist—and it is simply foolish to contend that he is not a great artist; he is one of the greatest now living—can be the hireling of a gang of thugs, *should* be their hireling because it is his duty to music, and music must be served.

In this persuasion or conviction, it seems to me, we have the true measure of Dr. Furtwangler's mind. He is a musician, scholar, and artist of the first rank, but he has a dry and pettifogging mind. Many things now become clear to us. We see why it is that, for all the structural beauty and magnificence of Dr. Furtwangler's work at its best, there are still things in his own chosen masters, Beethoven and Wagner, which he never seems to recreate for us. Now we know why the torment of Beethoven's soul does not reach us through Dr. Furtwangler's superb performances, except now and then through sheer formal suggestion. It is because Dr. Furtwangler is above all that. The torment of Beethoven's soul was, in fact, as much political as personal. What else is the *Eroica* about, except all men? Are the *Third* and *Seventh* symphonies of Beethoven merely individual and formal compositions to Dr. Furtwangler? So it would seem; the rest of what they mean is beneath him. An artist should be above caring about the fate of all men; he should "make music"—out of what?

Well, we could make a suggestion to Dr. Furtwangler, if he were open to suggestion. He might buy himself a pressing of the records issued last year of Beethoven's *Seventh Symphony* as recorded by the New York Philharmonic Orchestra under Toscanini. If it is too much trouble to him to play the whole thing through—he is very busy, of course, and we all know now that he is "above" a great many things—he can surely spare the time to listen to the Second Movement alone.

When he has listened to these three records, he will have received the proper answer to his letter published in the *Neue Freie Presse* on September 7. The content of that music could never have been fully absorbed and recreated by a musician who was, as Dr. Furtwangler claims to be, "above" life. When Dr. Furtwangler can conduct the *Seventh Symphony* of Beethoven, or even its Second Movement, with not only his own superb musicianship, but with the extra fire and fury of a spirit that has fully comprehended the depths from which this music comes, that has suffered it as the composer suffered it, for himself and for all men—then, perhaps, he can write another letter to the press.

Except that then he wouldn't feel the necessity, he wouldn't be in Germany at all; he would not be Dr. Furtwangler.

October 19, 1937

John E. Kennedy

If This Be Heresy

This is a personal affirmation of faith. I declare my allegiance to the Catholic Church, my church as it was the church of my fathers. And I declare my allegiance to the cause of the faithful Catholics in republican Spain who defended themselves against the anti-Christ of Spanish and foreign fascism. There is no conflict between these two allegiances. Not in spite of my Catholicism, but precisely because of it, do I support with all my heart the cause of Spanish democracy.

By what right do I call myself a Catholic? I am a Catholic first by the fortunate accident of birth. More important, I am a Catholic by conscious choice. The precepts of the Nazarene were honored in my home. As a child I learned to love Him, as naturally as I learned to love my own devout parents. Inevitably, the Jesuit fathers continued the religious education my parents began. I went first to a Catholic grade school, later to a Catholic preparatory school, a Jesuit institution of learning. And finally I attended a Catholic college. Through these school years I found myself always in full harmony with the doctrines and the dogma of the church.

I still find myself in full accord with the religious doctrines of the church.

Obedience to the church was for me always an easy, because a congenial, discipline. The dictates of the church were at one with the dictates of my own conscience, which all my life had been molded by Catholics and Catholicism. It is so today. I am still a practicing Catholic. I hope to remain one until I receive the Last Sacrament of my church. To those who now accuse me of heresy, I can only reply: I am faithful to Him who was the Prince of Peace—*you* are the heretics.

What is the truth about Spain? No one will deny that in that unhappy land Catholics take up arms against Catholics. On the one side, General Franco, the Catholic soldiers of his unsurgent army, and the Spanish hierarchy of priests and bishops. These Catholics have strange allies–Moorish infidels; the Hitler who persecutes the Catholic faithful and the Catholic priesthood of Nazi Germany; the Mussolini who murdered the Catholic people of the Basque country and who boasts of his slaughter, the same Mussolini whose son says, "War is beautiful!" On the other side, the people of Spain; the workers and peasants whose abiding faith cannot be questioned; the village priests; the church fathers who have died with their flock. There are Catholics on both sides. A Catholic must choose. I remember another struggle, between Pilate and the son of a poor carpenter, who lived and died for the least of His Father's children. I choose to stand with the people of Spain.

There are Catholics on both sides. This has always been true of Spain, a predominantly Catholic country. Since the sixteenth century there have been *two* churches in Spain, *two* kinds of Catholicism. One in name, but two in fact. One was the true church of Jesus of Nazareth, concerned only with its evangelical mission. Faithful to this church were scores and hundreds of simple village priests, scores and hundreds of Augustinian and Franciscan fathers. These humble servants of the Lord were deeply beloved by the Spanish people for their gentle teaching and good works.

But, unfortunately, since the sixteenth century, there has flourished another church in Spain, a church poisoned by worldly ambition, a church fundamentally political rather than spiritual, a church which made moneychangers of its priests and turned the House of God into a counting house. This church and its hierarchy held forty per cent of the Spanish land. It was, and all history shows this to be true, a cruel and a greedy landlord which kept the tillers of the soil in peonage and in poverty.

It was *this* church of Spain, this landlord-capitalist church, this church of political reaction and oppression, which earned and received only the hatred of the faithful poor.

It is said that the Communists teach the people to hate the church. Did the Communists teach the peasants and workers of Spain to hate the Spanish clericals who had perverted the teachings of Christ? In Spain, anticlericalism predates the birth of Karl Marx by many years and the Russian revolution by more than a century. In 1834 there was a tragic killing of friars in Madrid and other parts of Spain. Was this the work of Moscow? In 1909 the convents of Barcelona were burned. Was this by orders of the Communist International, speaking from the womb of history? I do not condone these terrible events, which darken all of Spain's long history, nor do I condone the burning of churches today. But these things have happened; they are historical facts. And it is a fact that anticlerical violence is no new phenomenon in Spain, no Soviet-Marxist importation. Anticlericalism is a crime native to Spanish soil, and its seeds were sown and its growth quickened by a corrupt clericalism which seized upon the things that were Caesar's and betrayed the things which were God's.

In the brief space of this article there is not opportunity to review the long history of clerical abuse in Spain. I refer the doubters to the history books. The well-known Spanish scholar, Salvador de Madariaga (who has remained neutral in the present conflict) says in his book, *Spain*, that of all the clericalisms of the world, Spanish clericalism was the worst.

If, in the past, the Spanish people had reason to regard that part of the church which served Mammon and was served by Mammon as their enemy—how much more reason they have for enmity today!

Let me list a few of the reasons. In the years of struggle for a republic and a better life, the Catholic people of Spain found the hierarchy of the church ever implacable against them. Yet they had churchly authority for their right to struggle by democratic means. They had the authority of His Holiness, Pope Leo XIII:

"A few men have placed on the shoulders of innumerable proletarians a yoke that differs from that worn by slaves" (*Rerum Novarum*).

And again:

"Let the distribution of property be more in accordance with equity" (ibid.).

But the Spanish hierarchy did all in its power to block the democratic way to a more equitable distribution of wealth. During the elections of 1936, convents and monasteries for centuries closed against the outside world were opened, and bus-loads of monks and nuns carried to the polls to vote against the Republic.

The hierarchy used its most powerful weapon against the peaceful desire of the people for a better life on earth. It even threatened them with hellfire hereafter. Many priests substituted the Ripalda catechism for the usual Roman catechism, using these important lines:

"*Question*: What sin is usually committed by those who vote liberal?

"*Answer*: Usually mortal sin."

I do not hold with this doctrine. I have voted liberal all of my life. I intend to continue to do so. I am happy that it is not a fact within my church that to vote liberal is to commit mortal sin. If that were true, literally millions of Catholics would have fallen from the state of grace at the last election. These lines should be eliminated from the Ripalda catechism. It is a cruel attempt to dictate political conviction by those who should concern themselves with spiritual matters.

In tampering with the catechism, the hierarchy departed from the wise precepts of Leo XIII, who clearly denounced such practice in these words:

"We must avoid the mistaken opinion held by those who identify religion with a political party going so far as to separate those who belong to another party little less than apart from Catholicism. This, in truth, is tantamount to bringing parties into the august field of religion, to attempt to destroy fraternal harmony and to open the door to a host of difficulties."

The Spanish hierarchy *did* bring political parties into the august field of religion, for the purpose of defeating the democratic progress of the Republic. But it failed of its purpose. By democratic process, progress and the Republic won at the polls.

Then the hierarchy was indeed guilty of great heresy:

"He who resists authority resists God's commandments, and brings condemnation upon himself. Consequently, to disobey and resort to rebellion ... is a crime of *lese majeste* not only human but divine" (Leo XIII, *Immortale*).

Of this crime of rebellion against legal authority, of the crimes of sedition and violence, the Spanish hierarchy today stands convicted. Its partners in crime are infidels, Nazi pagans, confessed anti-Christians, and professors of Christian faith who shame the name of Christ.

How can the Spanish people, the devout women, the simple Catholic men of that stricken land, today not hate the bishops who justify Franco's murderous adventure? How can they forget the destruction of the holy city of Guernica, or forgive the "holy" men who condone it? How can they, who have had their babies torn from their arms by fascist bombs, believe the priest who tells them those bombs defend his Christian faith? A home in flames, a dead child, a crucifix torn from the wall by flying shrapnel. By their fruits ye shall know them. These are the fruits of the church's alliance with Franco and fascism in Spain.

Catholics in America who would uphold Franco justify their position on the false premise that the choice rests between Franco and Communism. I know this is not true and the record bears me out. I am not a Communist, but I am bitterly opposed to fascism. I do not feel that the Catholic Church should force the Spanish people to accept it, because by spirit, by character, and by heritage they were not made for it. As a liberal American Catholic I feel that a victory for the loyalist government will preserve the Republic and the right of the Spanish people to determine by election and by democratic means the form and the spirit of their government.

My heart is with the people of Spain. With the Catholic people whose heroism places them among the great martyrs of history. With the loyal priests, who having baptized and confessed and shriven these people, know that theirs is *not* the mortal sin. My conscience and my religion alike condemn the fascist murderers of these Catholic people. Those who murder in the name of the church are a greater menace to that church than any infidel or Communist. They are priests, and I but a layman. But in Christ's name I denounce their sin. If this be heresy—make the most of it.

March 8, 1938

Lawrence Clark Powell

Who Is B. Traven?

It is four years since that mysterious American novelist who calls himself B. Traven allowed his first book to be published in his own country, in the language in which it was originally written. That was *The Death Ship*. It first appeared in Germany in 1926, in a version written by Traven in German. In 1934 a translation by Eric Sutton from this edition was published in England. The following year *The Treasure of the Sierra Madre* came out simultaneously in London and New York; the former a translation from Traven's German, the latter as written originally by him in English. Add to these puzzlers the fact that all Traven's thirteen books were first published in German from the author's own manuscripts in that language (although written by him originally in English) and we understood why the libraries of the world have classified him as a German writer. Our own Library of Congress, with its customary zeal for full names, expanded B. into Bruno; whereupon, reproved by Traven, it contracted Bruno back to B. and so revised all of its printed cards!

Traven has been called variously an Englishman, a Russian, a Yugoslav, a Czechoslovak, a German, and a Mexican. His agent in London even says that his real name is not Traven. In a recent letter to an American bookseller Traven settled the question of his nationality, if not his name. "May I just mention," he wrote, "that my first name is not Bruno, of course not; neither is it Ben, nor Benno. These names, like the many nationalities I have, among them the German, are inventions of critics who want to be smart and well informed. Several times I have protested in European publications that I am not even of German race or blood. The publishers of the German editions of my books knew from the first day of our relations that I am an American born in the U.S.A. Why my books were published in Europe and not in this country first is another story."

The curious thing is that Traven's German and English styles are both a bit foreign. Speculating on evidence in his books, I hazard that he is a Wisconsin-born Scandinavian. But it really doesn't matter; his books are all we need to have of him, and all that he wants to give us. Like Jack London and Upton Sinclair he is a true international proletarian writer; that he is an American is incidental. His books have been published in fourteen languages.

Like its predecessors, Traven's latest book to be published in this country (*The Bridge in the Jungle*, Knopf), has a blurbless jacket. His publisher is still enjoined from advertising his books, except in certain liberal periodicals, and is sworn to secrecy as far as any personal publicity is concerned. Other American writers, notably Jeffers and Steinbeck, have sought to avoid personal publicity, but I believe Traven is unique in the way he lays down the conditions under which his books are published and binds his publisher to absolute silence. When his Swiss publisher requested a photograph for publicity purposes, Traven promptly responded—with a group picture of several hundred men, explaining that he was among them!

It appears that Traven is a plain, simple man who thinks himself no more important than the plain, simple men who set, print, bind, pack, and ship his books. These men he holds to be quite as necessary as he in the production of a book. He feels that he has enlisted and is living in a new sort of association that embraces the world, in which a man who creates something great creates not for himself or for his personal interests or notoriety, but with the object of serving mankind to the utmost of his strength and ability. This service to mankind is the duty of every man, and as Traven considers writing to be his duty, he recoils from lionizing and flattery. He does not look upon himself as an artist or writer, but as a worker. His American publisher sends him no clippings about his books.

Traven has, of course, been banned by the Nazis. Since 1933, his sole German outlet has been his Swiss publisher, the Buchergilde Gutenberg, in Zurich. In spite of the contempt expressed in his work for what he regards as bureaucratic bolshevism, his books are being published by the Soviets in huge editions. In the U.S.S.R. *The Death Ship* has sold two million copies; in the U.S.A. 2,500.

Of all Traven's books *The Death Ship* is the only one which is not about Mexico. That "Moby Dick of the stokehold" is a masterpiece of which I believe Americans will be increasingly proud. When the movies tried to buy the rights to it, Traven's reply was characteristic—"I write to propagate ideas, not for reasons of profit." And in the book itself is a passage which tells what he thinks of the movies and sea-writers, including Conrad, O'Neill, and McFee:

All the romance of the sea that you still find in magazine stories died long, long ago. You would look in vain for it even in the China Sea and south of it. I don't believe it ever existed save in sea stories —never on the high seas or in sea-going ships. There are many fine youngsters who fell for those stories and believed them true, and off they went to a life that destroyed their bodies and their souls. Because everything was so very different from what they had read in those alluring stories. Life on the sea is not like they make it out to be and it never was. There is a chance, one in a hundred, maybe, for skippers, for mates, for engineers. You still may see them singing in operas and making beebaboo in the movies. You may find them also in best-sellers and in old ballads. Anyway, the fact is that the song of the real and genuine hero of the sea has never yet been sung. Why? Because the true song would be too cruel and too strange for the people who like ballads. Opera audiences, moviegoers, and magazine readers are like that. They want to have everything pleasant, with a happy ending. The true story of the sea is anything but pleasant or romantic in the accepted sense. The life of the real heroes has always been cruel, made up of hard work, of treatment worse than the animals of the cargo get, and often of the most noble sacrifices, but without medals and plaques, and without mention in stories, operas, and movies. Even the hairy apes are opera singers looking for a piece of lingerie.

The rest of Traven's books form an epic of Mexico's common people. All phases of the industrial and agricultural life are treated in turn, always from the proletarian viewpoint. These books, all published since 1926, include *The Cotton Pickers, The Treasure of the Sierra Madre* (gold prospecting), *Land of Springtime* (a general study of Mexico, particularly the state of Chiapas), *The Bush, The Bridge in the Jungle, The White Rose* (petroleum), *The Carreta* (transportation), *Government* (a satire on the effects of bureaucracy on the Indians), *The March into the Mahogany Jungle* and *The Troza* (both on the lumber industry), and his latest book, *The Rebellion of the Hanged*. All but one are novels.

Only four of them are available in English, and only two—
The Treasure of the Sierra Madre and *The Bridge in the Jungle*—in Traven's own English version.

Most of our recent books on Mexico have been written by traveling novelists and sociologists, such as D. H. Lawrence, Thames Williamson, Stuart Chase, Carleton Beals, Joseph Henry Jackson, and Max Miller. These men have gone to Mexico, as writers, expressly to gather material for their books. Traven is a different sort of writer. For the past dozen years he has lived the life of a Mexican worker. "I can't shake anything out of my sleeve," he says. "Others can do it, perhaps, but not I. I have to know the humans I tell about. They must have been my friends or companions or adversaries or my neighbors or my fellow citizens, if I am to describe them. I must have seen the things, landscapes and persons, myself, before I can bring them to life in my works. So I must travel. In jungles and primal forests, to Indian villages, distant ranchos, and to unknown, mysterious secret lakes and streams. It is necessary for me to have been afraid almost to madness before I can describe terror; I must myself suffer all sadness and heartache before I can visit suffering on the figures which I have called into life."

Like Upton Sinclair, Traven has been called a better sociologist than novelist. This criticism is perhaps true of some of his books, but it does not fit *The Bridge in the Jungle*. Here is a laconic work of art which focuses on a single tragic incident in the life of an Indian village, remote in the southern Mexican jungle. There are relatively few of Traven's customary salty soliloquies on the stupidities of capitalism and bureaucracy. An Indian boy falls off a bridge at an evening fiesta; his body is hunted in vain until the old man of the village floats a candle on a little raft, which is drawn mysteriously to a point directly over the drowned corpse. Then follows a minute account of the funeral ceremony, told with mingled irony, pity, realism, and humor. The climax is the march through the jungle to the wretched cemetery, the little corpse already stinking, the mourners guzzling, stumbling, and howling, pigs and buzzards following, to where the drunken schoolmaster in attempting a eulogy topples into the open grave. This is a great scene, worthy of Rabelais, Cervantes, Breughel, or Hogarth.

Throughout the book Traven's gentle love of the Indians

and their ways is contrasted with his disgust at the evidences of encroaching American civilization with its Hooveresque, philosophy of materialistic gadgetism. As Herbert Klein has pointed out, all of Traven's Mexican novels are a sympathetic, almost sentimental, symphony on the theme: "The capitalist class, wherever it has come into power, has destroyed all feudal, patriarchal, idyllic relationships" (*The Communist Manifesto*). Equally detestable to Traven is the record of the Catholic Church in Mexico; he writes:

When I had first come here, I had seen in these people the simple Indian peasants with ordinary courtesy such as one might find all over Spanish America in places where American tourists had never come to ruin the landscapes and try to make natives understand how glorious civilization is and tell them ten times a day how dirty and filthy they are and how badly organized their country is. It seemed that an occasion such as the one I had witnessed was necessary if one wanted to see those people as they really were, to see not only their dirt and their rags, but, what was more, their hearts and souls, the only things in man which count. Radios, Fords, and speed records do not count at all; they are but garbage when it comes to the final balance sheet. It is religion that makes men love their neighbors and that dries the tears of a mother who has lost her baby and that makes you who have two shirts give one to the poor who has nothing with which to cover his nakedness. Is it religion? Death is usually an occasion for lip religion to show off in all its splendor. And here, where death marched silently into a gay party all set for a merry weekend of dancing, I could not see a glimpse of the white man's great religion. I had heard no prayers so far. Nobody had fingered a rosary. The singing of hymns by the communist *agrarista* was only very superficially connected with the Catholic religion because his singing had the eternal worldly meaning of good will to all men, and the Holy Virgin was called upon merely to inform her of what was happening, not to come down and help a poor Indian mother out of her sorrows. And it was because religion as we understand it had not entered either the hearts or the inner minds of these people that they could preserve hearts and souls overflowing with kindness and love.

In his love for the common people, his insistence on their essential dignity and goodness and his desire to lighten their burdens, and in his rejection of the bourgeois standards of a civilization built on material comforts, exploitation, and mass murder, B. Traven is in the great Whitman-Thoreau tradition. He is a natural storyteller who embroiders his tales with philosophy. He writes—or rather, as a German critic observed, he talks–novels that show what a strong and truly romantic proletarian literature can be by being it.

It is to be hoped that he will permit his American publisher to issue the rest of his books about Mexico without too much delay. Our neighboring people have never had a more sympathetic and compelling spokesman. "I consider the Mexican-Indian," Traven writes, "and the members of the Mexican proletariat, which is 95 per cent Indian, as my heart's brother, a brother who is nearer to me than any brother of the body. For I know with what courage, with what resignation, with what self-sacrifice–a self-sacrifice unknown and unheard of in Europe and the United States–the proletarian Indian in Mexico is striving to win his freedom and emerge into the light of the sun." It is Traven's love of justice and sympathy toward the burdened and ragged that have made him a great revolutionary writer. Here in his own words is his writer's credo:

Every man has the duty to serve mankind with his best strength and ability, to lighten the burdens of life for other men, to bring them joy, and to direct their thoughts toward great ends. I fulfill my duty toward mankind as I have always done, whether as worker, seaman, explorer, private tutor in out of the way farms, and now as a writer. I do not feel myself to be a person who wants to stand in the limelight. I feel myself a worker among mankind, nameless and fameless, like every worker who does his part to bring mankind a step forward.

This credo and the way in which his writing exemplifies it very nearly places Traven in a category by himself among his contemporaries. The best thing we can do to honor him is to read his books. Certainly a good example has been set us by European readers.

In the summer of 1936 I spent an afternoon with Lincoln Steffens, just three days before he died. We talked long of Traven. "That man," Steffen said, remembering his own experiences south of the Rio Grande, "is expressing the very heart and soul of Mexico. I am too tired to write to him, but if you can send him a message, tell him I 'get' what he's doing and that I am very grateful."

August 2, 1938

Ernest Hemingway

On the American Dead in Spain

The dead sleep cold in Spain tonight. Snow blows through the olive groves, sifting against the tree roots. Snow drifts over the mounds with the small headboards. (When there was time for headboards.) The olive trees are thin in the cold wind because their lower branches were once cut to cover tanks, and the dead sleep cold in the small hills above the Jarama River. It was cold that February when they died there and since then the dead have not noticed the changes of the seasons.

It is two years now since the Lincoln Battalion held for four and a half months along the heights of the Jarama, and the first American dead have been a part of the earth of Spain for a long time now.

The dead sleep cold in Spain tonight and they will sleep cold all this winter as the earth sleeps with them. But in the spring the rain will come to make the earth kind again. The wind will blow soft over the hills from the south. The black trees will come to life with small green leaves, and there will be blossoms on the apple trees along the Jarama River. This spring the dead will feel the earth beginning to live again.

For our dead are a part of the earth of Spain now and the earth of Spain can never die. Each winter it will seem to die and each spring it will come alive again. Our dead will live with it forever.

Just as the earth can never die, neither will those who have ever been free return to slavery. The peasants who work the earth where our dead lie know what these dead died for. There was time during the war for them to learn these things, and there is forever for them to remember them in.

Our dead live in the hearts and the minds of the Spanish peasants, of the Spanish workers, of all the good simple honest people who believed in and fought for the Spanish

Republic. And as long as all our dead live in the Spanish earth, and they will live as long as the earth lives, no system of tyranny ever will prevail in Spain.

The fascists may spread over the land, blasting their way with weight of metal brought from other countries. They may advance aided by traitors and by cowards. They may destroy cities and villages and try to hold the people in slavery. But you cannot hold any people in slavery.

The Spanish people will rise again as they have always risen before against tyranny.

The dead do not need to rise. They are a part of the earth now and the earth can never be conquered. For the earth endureth forever. It will outlive all systems of tyranny.

Those who have entered it honorably, and no men ever entered earth more honorably than those who died in Spain, already have achieved immortality.

February 14, 1939

(Editor's note: *"Here is the piece," Hemingway wrote me from his home in Key West where he is at work between wars. "I've worked on it for five days ... this comes down from three thousand words." It has been translated into almost all major languages of the world; it can be heard on records in many of those languages.)*

Ruth McKenney

New Masses Is Home

A slight, earnest Negro stood at the speakers' stand.

Twenty-five hundred people, jampacked into every corner of Webster Hall, subsided into a soft rustle.

"*New Masses* is home," George Murphy said. "It can never die."

He spoke, suddenly, into a profound silence. The weary men, fresh from subway ticket booths, from file-clerk cubbyholes in big insurance firms, froze motionless. The girls, frail and pretty, their faces tired from the endless typing jobs; the women, heavy with worry over their husbands' jobs and the rent and how to feed the family on so little—all these people turned now to George Murphy, looked deeply into his face.

"No one can know what *New Masses* means," George Murphy said quietly, "who has never—"

And then he told a few simple stories. Not the stories he could have told, of blood, and agony and despair, not stories of lynching and hunger. Hardly raising his voice, with only a brief gesture, with perfect economy of word, he told about the ordinary, everyday things that happen to a Negro in the United States of America, in 1940.

"But here," he said finally, "but here, I am at home."

In the hushed audience women brushed away tears, men looked suddenly at their scuffed shoes.

"*New Masses,*" George Murphy said, "carries on the traditions of the Abolitionists, of Frederick Douglass. If *New Masses* dies, my people, already the most oppressed in America, are doubly, freshly oppressed. *New Masses* cannot die. *We will not let it die!*"

He walked away from the speakers' stand. The 2,500 people jumped to their feet. Bound together by an electric current more powerful than anything that ever went over high-tension wires, they exploded into a great, inarticulate sound.

The word in the dictionary for it is "cheering," but a better word must be invented. It was a sort of promise, a pledge, a communion with the man who had just finished speaking: *"We will not let it die!"*

This was the "Defend *New Masses*" meeting, held Monday, Feb. 26, 1940. I write the date exactly, because I know it was a meeting to make history.

The editors of the magazine came a little after eight o'clock. They were afraid to come before. The meeting had hardly been advertised at all. Hastily arranged, perhaps it was hopeless to expect more than, say, five hundred people. Five hundred would be fine. The valiant five hundred.

And when we fought our way into the hall, there were 2,500. Hundreds went away because there was literally no longer any standing room.

This was the answer of *New Masses* readers to the FBI and Attorney General Jackson and President Roosevelt. They want to suppress our magazine because we tell the truth about the war (and, incidentally, about many other things in this country). They have harried our editors, calling them to appear on all sorts of ridiculous legalistic charges in Washington. They have threatened indictments.

Our readers gave them the answer: *We will not let* New Masses *die.*

Here was no spiritless crowd, assembled to mourn a beloved corpse. Here was a fighting audience, full of good humor, ready to roar at the jokes and cheer the manifestoes.

The platform was crowded with *New Masses* friends, editors, writers, cartoonists. The names of those who appeared on Monday, Feb. 26, 1940, to defend *New Masses* will some day be written down on a special honor roll. For there were men conspicuous by their absence, "liberals" who hauled down the flag when the enemy guns hove into view. Nobody mourned their absence, for caution is not a lovely thing, even to the man who practices it, and a coward can't have a very entertaining home life.

Maurice Becker, who has drawn for *New Masses* since it was founded in 1911, remarked on the well known locomotive of history and its interesting casualties. The crowd laughed back, scoffing with him at the gentlemen who have found it convenient to turn tail and run.

Joe North set the tone for the meeting as he outlined *New*

Masses' plan to fight–fight–fight against suppression, but John Spivak really revealed the temper and quality of the "Defend *New Masses*" meeting when he stood up to take the collection. For John Spivak raised $740 in about fifteen minutes—$740 from a working-class and white-collar crowd. Hoover can get his millions from Rockefeller, but who except *New Masses* could ask $740 from people to whom every dollar meant a sacrifice?

After that collection the people on the platform felt dwarfed and humbled. Dear reader. It's an old expression, but it's the only one. Dear reader. If the magazine means that much to you, then we don't work hard enough at it, we've got to make it better, we can't let it go down, we simply can't. Dear reader.

George Seldes spoke. To friends of his, that's the best description of the kind of meeting it was. George Seldes broke a steadfast rule—he never speaks from a platform, anywhere. But as the evening went along, George couldn't resist the spirit, the mood of the crowd. Finally he stood up, to an immense ovation, a tribute to his skill and courage and integrity, an ovation to the spirit of the man who has turned his back on money and fame and the plaudits of the newspapers to tell the truth. It may be that George Seldes is no speaker—he says so—but Monday night he made a great speech, carrying the audience with him in cheers and laughter and a final great burst of applause.

"Save *New Masses*," he said. "It is one of the few places left in our country where a writer can tell the truth."

When Arthur Kober was introduced, you could feel the crowd almost talking to him; the whole audience took a sort of proprietary interest in Arthur Kober—their Arthur Kober, the man who has defended them and fought for them and worked for them.

"I pace the floor with the *New Republic*," Kober said, sketching in a fine picture of himself wearing out the carpet, a *New Republic* in one hand, a dictionary in the other. "Every time I read a good piece in it, the editorial disavows it. They must have a special fence down there, about twenty feet wide, with plenty of room for the whole staff to sit on. I read *New Masses* because I know what they're talking about. It gives me peace!"

The meeting ended late but nobody noticed it. The chairman had to say what time it was before the crowd came out of their mood and reached for their hats. All evening long we sat there, laughing and crying a little and feeling warm and good and belligerent. We cheered the messages from Theodore Dreiser–he sent a wonderful one–and Rockwell Kent and a dozen others.

In a way, I think everybody will remember those messages longest. And George Murphy, who said, "*New Masses* is home. It can never die."

March 12, 1940

SORIANO caught these speakers at the *New Masses* meeting in Webster Hall. *Top*: Georges Seldes, Arthur Kober and Ruth McKenney. *Center*: Isidor Schneider, John Spivak and George Murphy. *Bottom*: Maurice Becker, Joseph North and Edwin Berry Burgum.

JOSEPH HIRSCH

Miner's Funeral   ANTON REFREGIER

1.

American Writers' Congress

The New Masses *welcomes the call for an American Writer's Congress sponsored by those writers whose names appear below. It fully endorses the purposes as set forth in the call. This Congress, we believe, can effectively counteract the new wave of race hatred, the organized anti-Communist campaign and the growth of Fascism, all of which can only be understood as part of the Administration's program. Unlike the Anti-War Congress in Chicago, and the National Congress for Unemployment Insurance just concluded in Washington, the American Writers' Congress will not be a delegated body. Each writer will represent his own personal allegiance. With hundreds of writers attending from all sections however, and united in a basic program, the Congress will be the voice of many thousands of intellectuals, and middle class people allied with the working class. In the coming weeks,* The New Masses *will publish from time to time articles by well known writers, outlining the basic discussion to be proposed at the Congress. Of those invited to sign the call a few—whose support of its program is unquestioned—were at too great a distance to be heard from in time for this publication.*—The Editors

Call for an American Writers' Congress

The capitalist system crumbles so rapidly before our eyes that, whereas ten years ago scarcely more than a handful of writers were sufficiently far-sighted and courageous to take a stand for proletarian revolution, today hundreds of poets, novelists, dramatists, critics, short story writers and journalists recognize the necessity of personally helping to accelerate the destruction of capitalism and the establishment of a workers' government.

We are faced by two kinds of problems. First, the problems of effective political action. The dangers of war and fascism are everywhere apparent; we all can see the steady march of the nations toward war and the transformation of sporadic violence into organized fascist terror.

The question is: How can we function most successfully against these twin menaces?

In the second place, there are the problems peculiar to us writers, the problems of presenting in our work the fresh understanding of the American scene that has come from our enrollment in the revolutionary cause. A new Renaissance is upon the world; for each writer there is the opportunity to proclaim both the new way of life and the revolutionary way to attain it. Indeed, in the historical perspective, it will be seen that only these two things matter. The revolutionary spirit is penetrating the ranks of the creative writers.

Many revolutionary writers live virtually in isolation, lacking opportunities to discuss vital problems with their fellows. Others are so absorbed in the revolutionary cause that they have few opportunities for thorough examination and analysis. Never have the writers of the nation come together for fundamental discussion.

We propose, therefore, that a Congress of American revolutionary writers be held in New York City on May 1, 1935; that to this Congress be invited all writers who have achieved some standing in their respective fields; who have clearly indicated their sympathy to the revolutionary cause; who do not need to be convinced of the decay of capitalism, of the inevitability of revolution. Subsequently, we will seek to influence and win to our side those writers not yet convinced.

This Congress will be devoted to exposition of all phases of a writer's participation in the struggle against war, the preservation of civil liberties, and the destruction of fascist tendencies everywhere. It will develop the possibilities for wide distribution of revolutionary books and the improvement of the revolutionary press, as well as the relations between revolutionary writers and bourgeois publishers and editors. It will provide technical discussion of the literary applications of Marxist philosophy and of the relations between critic and creator. It will solidify our ranks.

We believe that such a Congress should create the League of American Writers, affiliated with the International Union of Revolutionary Writers. In European countries the I.U.R.W. is the vanguard of literature and political action. In France, for example, led by such men as Henri Barbusse, Romain Rolland, André Malraux, André Gide, and Louis Aragon, it has been in the forefront of the magnificent fight of the united militant working class against fascism.

The program for the League of American Writers would be evolved at the Congress, basing itself on the following: fight against imperialist war and fascism; defend the Soviet Union against capitalist aggression; for the development and strengthening of the revolutionary labor movement; against white chauvinism (against all forms of Negro discrimination or persecution) and against persecution of minority groups and of the foreign-born; solidarity with colonial people in their struggles for freedom; against the influence of bourgeois ideas in American liberalism; against the imprisonment of revolutionary writers and artists, as well as other class-war prisoners throughout the world.

By its very nature our organization would not occupy the time and energy of its members in administrative tasks; instead, it will reveal, through collective discussion, the most effective ways in which writers, as *writers*, can function in the rapidly developing crisis.

The undersigned are among those who have thus far signed the call to the Congress.

Nelson Algren
Arnold B. Armstrong
Nathan Asch
Maxwell Bodenheim
Thomas Boyd
Earl Browder
Bob Brown
Fielding Burke
Kenneth Burke
Erskine Caldwell
Alan Calmer
Robert Cantwell
Lester Cohen
Jack Conroy
Malcolm Cowley
Edward Dahlberg
Theodore Dreiser
Guy Endore
James T. Farrell
Ben Field
Waldo Frank
Joseph Freeman

Michael Gold
Eugene Gordon
Horace Gregory
Henry Hart
Clarence Hathaway
Josephine Herbst
Granville Hicks
Langston Hughes
Orrick Johns
Arthur Kallet
Herbert Kline
Joshua Kunitz
John Howard Lawson
Tillie Lerner
Meridel LeSueur
Melvin Levy
Louis Lozowick
Grace Lumpkin
Edward Newhouse
Joseph North
Moissaye Olgin

Samuel Ornitz
Myra Page
Paul Peters
Harold Preece
William Rollins
Paul Romaine
Isidor Schneider
Edwin Seaver
Claire Sifton
Paul Sifton
George Sklar
John L. Spivak
Lincoln Steffens
Philip Stevenson
Bernhard J. Stern
Genevieve Taggard
Alexander Trachtenberg
Nathaniel West
Ella Winters
Richard Wright

January 22, 1935

2
American Artists' Congress

The effort of American artists to create a more searching and vital cultural movement is taking on deeper significance. American artists, whose works have ever been distinguished by high creative integrity, have been considerably more hampered than their fellow workers, the writers, by the nature of their economic base. Where the writer had a vast potential audience, the artist was generally limited to creating individual objects destined to pass (if they passed at all!) into the hands of private collectors for private delectation.

It is not surprising, therefore, that writers began before artists to identify their aims with the interests of the broad masses of American people. But during the crisis years, influential artists have also embarked upon a sweeping revaluation of their background and their current direction. Ideological realignments have been powerfully stimulated by struggles for economic security and younger artists especially have been leading the way in effective mass action for government support through the militant Artists' Union.

The interaction of all these forces and the sharp conflicts that have developed as a result of reactionary efforts to stifle progressive artistic expression have thrown the entire American art world into ferment. This complex situation, intensified by the imminence of a new world war threatening universal extinction of art and artists, sets the stage for the forthcoming American Artists' Congress announced in the call printed below.

The Congress can achieve results not merely parallel to those of the Writers' Congress held in New York this past spring. It is not only possible, but imperative that the artists build up and consolidate their ranks into an even wider front as an unwavering bulwark against the destructive forces of war and fascism. A glance at the list of signatories gives ground for believing this aim will be achieved.–The Editors

Call for an American Artists' Congress

This is a Call to all artists, of recognized standing in their profession, who are aware of the critical conditions existing in world culture in general and in the field of the Arts in particular. This Call is to those artists who, conscious of the need of action, realize the necessity of collective discussion and planning, with the objective of the preservation and development of our cultural heritage. It is for those artists who realize that the cultural crisis is not an isolated phenomenon.

The artists are among those most affected by the world economic crisis. Their income has dwindled dangerously close to zero.

Dealers, museums and private patrons have long ceased to supply the meager support they once gave.

Government, state and municipally sponsored Art Projects are giving only temporary employment and to a small fraction of the artists.

The wage scale on these projects has been consistently below the standard set by the House Painters' Union. Present government policy on the Works Program will drive it below subsistence level.

All these attempts have failed conspicuously to provide that economic base on which creative work can be accomplished.

In addition to his economic plight, the artist must face a constant attack against his freedom of expression.

Rockefeller Center, the Museum of Modern Art, the Old Court House in St. Louis, the Coit Memorial Tower in San Francisco, the Abraham Lincoln High School, Rikers Island Penitentiary—in these and other important public and semi-public institutions suppression, censorship or actual destruction of art works has occurred.

Oaths of allegiance for teachers, investigations of colleges for radicalism, sedition bills aimed at the suppression of civil liberties, discrimination against the foreign born, against Negroes, the reactionary Liberty League and similar organizations, Hearst journalism, etc. are daily reminders of fascist growth in the United States.

A picture of what fascism has done to living standards, to civil liberties, to workers' organizations, to science and art, the threat against the peace and security of the world, as shown in Italy and Germany, should arouse every sincere artist to action.

We artists must act. Individually we are powerless. Through collective action we can defend our interests. We must ally ourselves with all groups engaged in the common struggle against war and fascism.

There is need for an artists' organization on a nationwide scale, which will deal with our cultural problems. The creation of such a permanent organization, which will be affiliated with kindred organizations throughout the world, is our task.

The Artists' Congress, to be held in New York City in early December, will have as its objective the formation of such an organization. Discussion at the Congress will include the following:

Fascism and War; Racial Discrimination; Preservation of Civil Liberties; Imprisonment of Revolutionary Artists and Writers; Federal, State and Municipal Art Projects; Municipal Art Gallery and Center; Federal Art Bill; Rental of Pictures; the Art Schools during the Crisis; Museum Policy in the Depression; Subject Matter in Art; Aesthetic Directions; Relations of Media and Material to Art Content; Art Criticism.

We, the undersigned artists, representing all sections of the United States, ask you to show your solidarity with us by signing this Call and by participating in the Congress.

Ivan Le Loraine
   Albright
George Ault
Peggy Bacon
Herman Baron
A. S. Baylinson
Maurice Becker
Ahron Ben-Shmuel
Theresa Bernstein
Joseph Biel
Henry Billings
Jolan Gross Bittilheim
Lucile Blanch
Arnold Blanch
Lou Block
Peter Blume
Aaron Bohrod
Cameron Booth
Margaret
   Bourke-White
Ernest Brace
Edith Bronson
Alexander Brook
Sonia Gordon Brown
Jacob Burck
Paul Burlin
Paul Cadmus
Nicolai Cikovsky
John Cunningham
Lew E. Davis
Stuart Davis
Adolf Dehn
Julio de Diego
Thomas Donnelly
Aaron Douglas
Ed Dreis
Mabel Dwight

Dorothy Eisner
Charles Ellis
Ernest Fiene
Todros Geller
Hugo Gellert
Lydia Gibson
C. Adolph Glassgold
H. Glintenkamp
Aaron Goodelman
Harry Gottlieb
Waylande Gregory
William Gropper
John Groth
Minna Harkavy
Bertram Hartman
Emil Holzauer
Eitaro Ishigaki
Joe Jones
Jacob Kainen
Morris Kantor
Jerome Klein
Karl Knaths
Frederic Knight
Benjamin Kopman
Eve Kottgen
Doris Lee
Russell Limbach
Erle Loran
Louis Lozowick
Eugene Ludins
Jack Markow
William Meyerowitz
Edward Millman
Lewis Mumford
Elizabeth Olds
Peter Paul Ott

George Picken
Walter Quirt
Anton Refregier
Boardman Robinson
Gilbert Rocke
Andree Ruellan
Saul Schary
Katherine Schmidt
Georges Schreiber
Alfred A. Sessler
Ben Shahn
William Siegel
Mitchell Siporin
David Smith
Moses Soyer
Raphael Soyer
Niles Spencer
Benton Spruance
Harry Sternberg
Jack W. Taylor
Morris Topchevsky
LeRoy Turner
Abraham Walkowitz
Lynd Ward
Louis Weiner
Charles S. Wells
Charmion
   von Wiegand
Gilbert Wilson
Arnold Wiltz
Caleb Winholtz
Jan Wittenber
Ann Wolfe
Art Young
Santos Zingale
Nick Ziroli

October 1, 1935